James Swisher

How I Know, Or Sixteen Years' Eventful Experience

James Swisher

How I Know, Or Sixteen Years' Eventful Experience

ISBN/EAN: 9783337219413

Printed in Europe, USA, Canada, Australia, Japan

Cover: Foto ©ninafisch / pixelio.de

More available books at **www.hansebooks.com**

HOW I KNOW,

OR

SIXTEEN YEARS' EVENTFUL EXPERIENCE.

AN

AUTHENTIC NARRATIVE,

EMBRACING

A BRIEF RECORD OF SERIOUS AND SEVERE SERVICE ON THE BATTLE-FIELDS OF THE SOUTH; A DETAILED ACCOUNT OF HAZARDOUS ENTERPRISES, THRILLING ADVENTURES, NARROW ESCAPES, AND DIRE DISASTERS ON THE WESTERN FRONTIER AND IN THE WILDS OF THE WEST; LIFE AMONG THE MORMONS, THE MINERS, AND THE INDIANS; THE PAST, THE PRESENT, AND THE FUTURE OF THE GREAT WEST; THE WONDERFUL GRANDEUR AND BEAUTY OF ITS SCENERY AND ITS LANDSCAPES; ITS GREAT MINERAL AND AGRICULTURAL RESOURCES; A GLANCE AT THE MORE IMPORTANT EVENTS IN ITS HISTORY AND DEVELOPMENT, ETC., ETC.

By JAMES SWISHER,

Illustrated.

PUBLISHED BY THE AUTHOR:
CINCINNATI, OHIO.
1880.

PREFACE

I HAVE written this book, not because I make any pretensions as an author or writer, but at the earnest request of many of my friends in different parts of the country, who have urged me to prepare and publish an account of my travels and experiences.

I have thought it unnecessary to speak, except in the briefest manner possible, of my experiences in the Civil War. I have said enough on this subject, however, to vividly recall to the minds of my comrades-in-arms the thrilling incidents of those dark days, and to awaken the memory of the keen interest and the trembling apprehension with which the dire conflict was viewed from the thousands of homes and firesides, by mother, wife and sister.

I have been vain enough to hope that my book may not be entirely devoid of interest to those who love such grandly magnificent and beautiful works of Nature as are to be seen in so many places in the West. Of these I have given such glimpses and descriptions as the limits of the book and my ability as a writer would allow.

Of the Mormons, Indians, miners, and other classes of people of which I speak, I say only such things as I have learned by personal association and observation.

Although in some cases my account may not be complete and exhaustive, yet I think it will be always interesting and valuable from the fact that it is reliable.

In what I have said of the mining and agricultural resources and the commercial interests of the West, I have been guided by an extensive and varied experience, and a wide opportunity for observation. I have been laborer, lumberman, explorer, guide, traveler, prospector, miner, hunter, Indian-fighter, government surveyor and civil engineer, freighter, herder, stockbroker, and transient sojourner. In one or another of these capacities I have visited nearly every portion of the West, and consequently know whereof I speak.

I do not expect to escape criticism. I am well aware that I am in great need of it. Still I hope that those who read this book will belong to that class of true critics who endeavor, as far as possible, to seek out that which is commendable and praiseworthy, and to overlook that which is imperfect and incomplete. I can but express the hope that each one who reads the book may derive some little benefit from what I have written.

In conclusion, it is but proper that I should here express my sincere thanks to Messrs. Jones Brothers & Co., Cincinnati, for the generous kindness with which they have afforded me every needed assistance and facility for the proper printing, binding and illustration of my book. Their friendly favors shall ever be held in most grateful remembrance.

J. S.

January, 1880.

CHAPTER I.—WITH THE TWENTIETH ARMY CORPS.

Birth-place—Joins the Army—Sketch of the Twentieth Corps—Battles of Lookout Mountain, Rocky Face Ridge and Resaca—Capture of Pine Knob—Kenesaw Mountain—Peach Tree Creek—Siege of Atlanta—The "March to the Sea"—Savannah occupied—Devastation of the "Mother of Secession"—Pursuit of Johnston's flying Forces—The Surrender at Raleigh—Homeward—The grand Review at Washington—Home and Friends. . . . 11-25

CHAPTER II.—UTAH AND THE MORMONS.

The "Western Fever"—In a Utah mining Camp—Situation of Utah—The Mormons—Mountain Meadow Massacre—Bishop S——'s "Revelations"—A horrible Outrage—Murder of D. P. Smith—Another Instance of Mormon Atrocity—Nationality of the Mormons—Adobe Houses—Practical Polygamy—Scenery in Utah—Hot and cold Springs—Irrigation—Mountains and Deserts—Grass, Cattle and Timber—Mining—Early Mining Experiences—Sinks a Shaft, and some Money—The Webster Lode—General Reflections. . 26-44

CHAPTER III.—NEVADA.

Nevada for a Change—Carson City—Lake Tahoe—Mining Fever again—Stock-speculator—The Comstock Mines—The Narrow Guage Railroad—The long Flume—Heat and Water in the Mines—Ventilation—The Sutro Tunnel—Climate of Nevada—Stock and Farming—Hot Springs—Alkali—The brackish Water. 45-53

CHAPTER IV.—CALIFORNIA.

From Carson City to San Francisco—The Enchanting Scenery—Donner Lake—Pulpit Rock—Sad Story of the Donner Family—Indian Tradition—In the old Mining District—Virgin Gold—Geological History—Theories—Placer Mining—Some big Nuggets—Northward—The Yosemite Valley—The "Garden of the Gods"—Nevada Fall—The Giant Trees—California Vegetables—The Golden City—Its Splendor and Magnificence—Fertile Valleys and Immense Crops—The Seasons—Stock-raising—Grape Culture—Drawbacks—Something of a Shake—Volcanic and Desert Regions—The Earthquake of 1872. . 54-74

CHAPTER V.—THE CHINESE.

The Chinese—Their Appearance—Their Dress—Their Numbers—Most of Them in Servitude—The Six Companies—Low Wages—Idol Worship—A Law unto Themselves—The Chinese Quarter—Coolies—Legislation—General Review of California Resources—Wealth *per capita*—Commercial Enterprises—Agricultural Resources—Remarkably Healthy Climate—Colonizing—Government Lands—Area and Population—Internal Improvements. . 75-82

CHAPTER VI.—OREGON AND WASHINGTON.

Portland—The Varied Climate—The Fertile Tracts—Population—The Columbia River—The Cascade Range—The Lava Beds—Fine Stock—Willamette Valley—Agricultural Products of the State—Grains and Fruits—

v

Washington Territory—Lumbering—The Cold Weather—Fish and Game—The Indians—The grand Scenery of the North-west. . . . 83-90

CHAPTER VII.—MEXICO.

Eleven Months in Mexico—The Mexicans—The Climate—Mexican Character—Mining—Primitive Processes Employed—The Dwellings—General Decay—A Stranger's Impressions—Amusements—Gambling—Mexican Horsemanship—Corraling Wild Stock—Lassoing—Riding a Wild Horse—Cheap Horses—The Beauty of the Country—The Delightful Climate—Chihuahua—The Casas Grandes Ruins—Explorations—Relics of the Inhabitants of the Ancient Cities—Other Ancient Ruins—The Moqui Indians of Arizona—The Cliff-dwellers—A Legend—Character of the Moqui. . . . 91-103

CHAPTER VIII.—ARIZONA.

Heat and Sand—Other Disagreeable Features—Mr. Janin's Great Scheme—Prospector's Outfit—*Burros*—Packs and Pack-saddles—Perils of Prospecting—Ancient Mines—The Inhabitants—Drinking and Gambling—Indians—Cock-fighting—Is Civilization a Failure? . . . 104-112

CHAPTER IX.—NAVAJOES.

A Long Trip on Horseback—Chosen Leader—The Outfit—Grand and Beautiful Scenery—First Camp—A Dreary Night—Wet, Worn and Weary—Following a Mountain Trail—Night in the Forest—Indian Signs—An Unexpected Visitor—Sketch of Bennett—" Injuns! Injuns!"—A Fierce Fight—The Indians Retreat—The Killed and Wounded—Burying the Dead—Forward!—An Indian Ambush—But Five Escape—Closely Pursued—Fishing for Food—Worn out—Sad Reflections—A Dreadful Night—Friends Discovered—Names of Those Killed. . . . 113-132

CHAPTER X.—THROUGH THE COLORADO CAÑONS.

The Colorado Cañon—A large Prospecting Party—The Start—No Road—Traveling by Night—No Water—A Mutiny—A Bad Situation—Plain Talk—Another Mutiny—A Separation—Off Again—Deserters Return—Cornered by a Grizzly—Habits of the Grizzly—Hunting the Grizzly—The Grizzly Killed—A Lofty Outlook—Standing Guard—Pleasant Dreams—A Gloomy Ride—Creeping down the Mountain Side—Meets a Panther—A Frightful Situation—The Last Chance—A Lucky Shot—Safe in the Valley—Daylight—The Dead Panther—Trout-fishing—Dreadful Dreams—" Raising the Color." . . . 133-152

CHAPTER XI.—THROUGH THE COLORADO CAÑONS.—[CONTINUED.]

A Mighty Precipice—The Grand Cañon—Buckskin Mountains—"Heads or Tails"—Up the River—Rough Traveling—Down the Gulch—An Impressive Situation—The Head of the Cañon—Ancient Ruins—An Oasis—A Dangerous Swim—Safely Over—Eastern Side of the River—Apache Visitors—" Heap Bad Injun"—Prospecting—An Undesirable Location—Callville—John D. Lee—Murderous Mormons. . . . 153-164

CHAPTER XII.—MONTANA AND IDAHO.

First Settlers—Rich Resources—The Gallatin Valley—Other Valleys—Occupations—Advantages of the Railroads—Staging and Freighting—Corrinne—Warehouses—A Bad Road—High Prices—" Self-risers," " Pilgrims," " Tenderfoots." . . . 165-168

CHAPTER XIII.—LAKES AND SPRINGS OF THE FAR WEST.

Waters of the West—Great Salt Lake—Its Outlet—The Lake Rising—Bathing—Lake Tahoe—Good Place for Captain Boyton—Crystal Lake—Varieties of Waters—Hot Springs—Phenomena in Connection with Hot Springs

—A Large Spring—The Yellowstone—A Tide Spring—A Mud Spring—
The Steamboat Spring—Alkaline Streams—Causes of Hot Springs, Earthquakes, and Volcanoes. 169-177

CHAPTER XIV.—LA PAZ.

Surveying in Arizona—Two Days' Ride in a "Jerkey"—Stage-coach Ex-
periences—The Factotum Expressman—La Paz—A Dilapidated Town—Rough
Customers—The Hotel—The Landlord—A Bad Lot—Street Scenes—Riot Let
Loose—A Rush for "Hash"—The Barroom—The Landlord's Stories—Greas-
ers—A Night in Bedlam—Another Lodging-place—A Drunken Texan—
Pleasant Anticipations—Taking a Tumble—Complimentary Comments—A
Big Dinner—Night Scenes—Routed by Bed-bugs—Another Tumble—Family
History—Impressions of La Paz—Back to Fort McDowell—Does "Roughing
It" Pay? 178-192

CHAPTER XV.—STOCK-RAISING.

Successful Men—Life of a Stock-raiser—The Cow-boys—Branding Stock
—County Inspectors—A Stock Range—Changing Ranges—A "Round-up"
—Description of the "Cow-boys"—Dangers of a Herder's Life—Indian
Raids. 193-201

CHAPTER XVI.—STOCK-BROKER AND FREIGHTER.

San Francisco—"Bulls" and "Bears"—A Good Run of Luck—A Bad
Run—Two-thirds of Capital Lost—Off for Salt Lake City—Meeting Old
Friends—Outfit of Wagons Bought—Instance of Mormon Atrocity—The
Gilson Brothers—Buying Oxen at Manti—Loading up with Flour—Learning
to Drive Oxen—Handling the Whip—Yoking the Cattle—Stuck in the Mud
—Doubling Up—The Second of March—Completely Disgusted—The Final
Start from Manti—Names of the Party—Salina—A Herder's Camp—Snow—
Five Weary Weeks—Advice—Thirteen Miles in Six Weeks—Desolate Coun-
try. 202-218

CHAPTER XVII.—IN GREEN RIVER VALLEY.

Streams in Castle Valley—Description of the Valley—Rock Wells—Bad
Water—Wretched Traveling—Green River Valley—High Water—A Long
Ride for a Boat—A Pleasant Camp—Trip to the Canon—Grand Mountain
View—Mountain Sheep—Back to Camp—Beaver and Otter—Snakes—A Rat-
tlesnake Den—Wolves—An Exciting Chase—Habits of the Wolves—Wait-
ing. 219-232

CHAPTER XVIII.—VEXATIOUS DELAYS.

The Boat Arrives—Ferrying the Wagons and Loads Across—Swimming
the Cattle—A Wearisome Effort—The Virtue of Patience—Cattle Stampeded
by a Grizzly—Back Across the River Again—A Dangerous Situation—A
little out of Humor—A Strange Discovery—A Remarkable Trail—What
Could the Cloven-footed "Varmint" Be?—No Cattle—A Hazardous Undertaking—The Cattle Found—Driven Over the River Again—The Green
Brothers Murdered—Something of their History—The "Saints" and their
Principles—Persecution of the Gentiles—The Green Brothers' Ranch—Their
Horrible Death—Trail of the Murderers—A Clue to the Mystery—A Warning
to Hasten—A Fatiguing Journey—Grand River Valley—The Paradise of Colorado—Ancient Ruins—Two Miles a Day—Serious Reflections. . 233-252

CHAPTER XIX.—MORAL AND DESCRIPTIVE.

Colorado as a Health Resort—Lack of Society—Two Years' Isolation—
A Test of Character—The Lazy Man—The Cheerful Man—Wealth and Rank
—Worth and Character—The Use of Tobacco—Lonesomeness—Money-mak-

ing and Mining—Duped—Carrying Weapons—Game on Green River—A Hunter's Requisites—Methods of Hunting—Mountain Sheep—Deer—Face of the Country—Mirages—Gold—Scenery—A Beautiful Prospect—Civilization Once More—Chief Ouray—The Ute Indians—Their Farming (?)—Los Pinos Agency—Selling Out. 253–271

CHAPTER XX.—SHALL THE YOUNG MAN GO WEST?

A Mining Region—Mining Enterprises—Great Corporations—Their Immense Power—Prosperity—The Real Sovereigns—Advisability of Mining Ventures—Chances of the Investor and Prospector—The San Juan Region—Disappointment and Dissipation—Immigration—Leadville—Mr. W. H. Stevens—Soft Carbonates—Bonanzas—Roughing It—A Mining Excitement—Idlers—Unpoetic Poverty—Overplus of Population—Condition of San Francisco—Let the Young Man Stay at Home—The Puzzled Englishman—Deceptive Appearances—"Cloud-bursts.". 272–288

CHAPTER XXI.—A SPANISH BULL-FIGHT.

Ojo Calienta—The Early Comers—A Front Seat at the Corral—The Spectators—The *Matadore*—The Bull—The First Rush—A Prolonged Encounter—The Bull Vanquished—Another Bull Brought in—The *Matadore* Tossed—Severely Injured—A Panic—Scaffolding Gives Way—A Firm Resolution. 289–295

CHAPTER XXII.—THE INDIANS.

Their Wigwams—Bedding—Hunting and Amusements—Trading—Disposal of the Dead—Instance of Cruelty—Medicine Men—Exorcising Evil Spirits—Religious Belief. 296–301

CHAPTER XXIII.—THE CUSTER MASSACRE.

The Tragedy of June 25, 1876—Sorrow of the Nation—Sketch of Custer's Life—Hancock's Campaign—Hancock Outwitted—Custer's First Indian Fight—"Circling"—Massacre of Lieutenant Kidder and Party—Horrid Scenes—General Sully's Campaign—Custer's Washita Campaign—Yellowstone Expedition—Murder of Honzinger and Baliran—Arrest of Rain-in-the-Face—He Escapes and Swears Vengeance against Custer—Black Hills Expedition—Gold in the Hills—Events of 1875—Campaign against Sitting Bull and Crazy Horse—Custer in Disgrace at Headquarters—The Miserable Belknap Affair—Three Columns Converge upon the Hostile Camp—The Bloody Ending—Close of the Campaign—Sitting Bull Goes to Canada, and Crazy Horse to the Happy Hunting-grounds—Perhaps. 302–348

CHAPTER XXIV.—WHERE SHALL WE SETTLE?

Go West!—Southern Minnesota—Iowa—Southern Dakota—Nebraska—Kansas—The Indian Territory—No!—Texas—Don't Believe All You Hear!—The Indian Border—California: Land Monopoly—Oregon—Climate and Soil—"The Great American Desert"—Probable Population in 1900—Whither is the Surplus Population to Go?—Good Land Pretty Well Occupied—What will be the Result?—Western Wilds will Continue Wild for a Century to Come. 349–381

CHAPTER XXV.—CONCLUSION.

Homeward Bound—Old Memories Aroused—A Surprise—A Pleasant Meeting—Time's Changes—Contrasts—Preparing for a Little Trip—Detained—Another Surprise—A Happy Birthday—Concluding Reflections. 382–384

LIST OF ILLUSTRATIONS.

PAGE.

Frontispiece.

Abraham Lincoln,	13
Jefferson Davis,	16
Gen. W. T. Sherman,	18
Sherman's March to the Sea,	21
Gen. Robt. E. Lee,	22
Gen. U. S. Grant,	24
Mountain Meadow Massacre,	28
Mormon Persecution,	31
Brigham Young,	34
Mormon Tabernacle,	37
New Mining Town,	40
View near Lake Tahoe,	46
Blue Canon, Sierra Nevada,	48
Humboldt Palisades,	52
Donner Lake,	54
Pulpit Rock, Echo Canon,	55
Scene near Eagle Lake, California,	59
The Two Guardsmen,	61
The Yosemite Falls,	63
Bridal Veil Fall, Yosemite Valley,	65
A California Stump,	67
Northern California Scenery,	70
Cape Horn, Central Pacific R. R.,	72
Chinese Quarter, San Francisco,	79
Rapids of the Upper Columbia,	84
View in the Modoc Country,	86
View on the Oregon Coast,	88
Border Mexicans,	91
Mexican Border Town,	94
Mexican Border Invasion,	97
Arizona Sand Plains,	101
A Train of Burros,	107
Perils of Prospecting,	108
Civilization in Arizona,	110
An Arizona Scrimmage,	111
Scene in the Sierra Del Cariso Range,	114
Following a Mountain Trail,	118
Attacked by Navajo Indians,	123
An Indian Ambuscade,	127
The Grand Canon of the Colorado,	134
The Search for Water,	137
Cornered by Grizzlies,	141
In the Colorado Canons,	150
Sunset in the Colorado Canons,	156

	PAGE
Prospecting in the Colorado Canons,	160
Execution of John D. Lee,	163
Great Salt Lake,	170
Vernal Falls, California,	173
"Giantess," Big Geyser of the Yellowstone,	175
A Western Frontiersman,	195
Ready for a Raid,	199
Salt Lake City, 1857,	203
Sevier River, Wasatch Mountains,	213
Herders' Camping House,	215
Shoshonee Indians in the Sevier Valley,	217
Camp in Green River Valley,	223
Night Scene in Green River Canon,	225
Peak in Green River Valley,	230
Orson Pratt, Mormon Prophet,	241
Former Residences of Brigham Young,	243
George A. Smith, Mormon Apostle,	245
"The Swift Dashing Water,"	248
Lonely—Three Thousand Miles from Home,	251
"Oh, Solitude, Where are thy Charms?"	254
Scalp-Dance of the Ute Indians,	260
Hunting Buffalo in the Olden Time,	265
He Paid a Big Price,	276
These Did Not Grow in a Mining Region,	279
An Old '49er Not Yet Rich,	282
Dead Broke,	284
Mexican Outlaws,	290
Mexican Maiden, Lower Class,	291
Pueblo Cacique, New Mexico,	293
Mexican Indians,	294
Indian Wigwam,	297
Black Hawk,	299
Un Indio Bravo, Texas,	300
"Go West,"	305
"Busted,"	307
Custer's First Indian Fight,	310
Western Scout,—Wild Bill,	313
Rude Surgery of the Plains,	319
Scene of the Sioux War,	326
Getting the First Shot,	333
Fighting Hand to Hand,	339
Winter in the Minnesota Pineries,	351
Droughty Kansas,	355
Texas and Coahuila in 1830,	359
Skirmish with Indians,	365
Fort Massachusetts, New Mexico, 1855,	367
A California Big Tree,	371
Nevada Falls, Yosemite Valley,	375

HOW I KNOW.

CHAPTER I.

WITH THE TWENTIETH ARMY CORPS.

THE author of this work was born in Champaign County, Ohio, in June, 1849, and, at the age of thirteen years, nine months and twenty-three days, joined the army. He was assigned to Company E, of the Fifth Ohio Infantry, twentieth army corps, and sent to the field. "What fun I shall have," thought he to himself, as he took his position in the ranks. Little does a boy know, at that age, about the life of a soldier.

Since every one has read and re-read the history of the war, I will condense what I saw into a few words, merely giving a little history of the different battles in which the twentieth corps took part. No body of troops in the Northern army made for itself a prouder history than the twentieth army corps. Its life was crowded with events not one of which brings dishonor to its proudest member, although it was formed from the most daring, cultivated, and resolute men of the North. "The best fruit trees are clubbed the most," and, in the army, detraction often follows the exhibition of superior merit in discipline, appearance, or achievements. From the rigid tests of Manchester, Port Republic, Antietam, Dumfries, Chancellorsville, and Gettysburg, Gen. Hooker brought his men to the Army of the Cumberland at a perilous hour.

The troops of Gen. Bragg, full sixty thousand strong, nerved with an earnest devotion to their cause, and encouraged by the doubtful result at Chickamauga, occupied an almost impregnable position near Chattanooga, while in front of them Rosecrans held an uncertain footing. His soldiers had seen the hopes of an early peace quickly disappear. They were almost appalled at the gigantic proportions the rebellion had assumed. They were disheartened by the absence, without leave, of thousands of their comrades. Their line of supplies was in imminent danger, and the country was at that time enshrouded in such gloom that the growing glory of President Lincoln could scarcely be discerned. It was at this crisis that the men whose badges imaged the lights that rule the night came and kindled a lustre in Wauhatchie Valley, that rose and spread until it bathed in matchless splendor old Lookout Mountain's rugged peak. Rosecrans was saved! Tennessee was saved! A portion of the corps then hurried away to Knoxville, with others from the fifteenth corps, and soon broke the bands in which Longstreet had kept Burnside hampered, almost to the point of starvation. The remainder of the corps went into winter quarters.

It was on the 4th of April, 1864, that the twentieth corps was formed, the beloved Joe Hooker being placed at its head. The corps retained the star of the twelfth corps as its insignia. Its real history began with the campaign that soon opened. On the 8th of May, the enemy was found occupying a strong position on Rocky Face Ridge. A severely contested fight followed. It had been said that if Johnston could not hold that place he could not hold any in Georgia, and the firmest determination characterized the contest until nightfall, when both armies retired; Johnston to his works at Resaca, and our troops to pass through Snake Creek Gap and then attack them again.

Constant skirmishing was kept up until, on the 14th of May, at Resaca, the Confederate forces

ABRAHAM LINCOLN.

advanced under a flag so faded that it was taken for a flag of truce. In consequence of this mistake a terrible blow was given to our forces. The blow was aimed at the fourteenth corps, and shook it to the center. But Gen. Hooker, by throwing out a brigade with that marvelous dexterity in which none could surpass him, saved the Fifth Indiana Battery when on the very point of capture, checked the advance of the enemy, and held his ground until dark. The next morning the entire corps moved forward upon the enemy, now firmly intrenched in a series of lines so arranged as to make an attack very difficult. The momentum of the first charge carried it over the first line, where it gallantly reformed its somewhat confused ranks, and at once pressed on. Now came emphatically the tug of war. With straining sinews and grimmest courage, gray-haired veterans and proud-eyed youths fought on and on, gaining always some ground ; but so slowly that evening was at hand when the weary but still resolute men reached the fourth and last chain of defenses. Here was displayed as true grit as was ever known among men. So fierce was the assault that the rebels could not hold their works, and so tenacious the defense that the national forces could not occupy them; and there stood an empty fort and an idle battery between the lines, which surged and swayed and clamored around them for hours. But scarcely had the favoring darkness come, ere the Fifth Ohio boys crept to the wall, dug through, and hauled out the guns by hand.

On the 25th of May, while the second division of the twentieth corps was crossing Pumpkin Vine Creek, a bridge broke down, completely isolating those who had crossed; but their very renown shielded them from attack until help arrived. The situation was critical. No intrenching tools had been taken over the stream, and orders to recross were expected. But to pass away the time, and to deceive the enemy, the men went to work using their bayonets and cooking utensils instead of picks and shovels, to dig their trenches. But this could not long deceive the watchful foe, and while the remainder of the corps was in the act of crossing they made a most furious attack. Having checked this, the corps moved directly on the well-formed and well-defended works in its front. The fighting was desperate. Generals Sherman and Thomas were there to direct the movement, and there the fact was impressed on all, as Gen. Hooker has since said, that a good line of works, well manned, cannot be taken by infantry alone. Having lost two thousand men, the movement was abandoned, and then followed seven days of skirmishing, so annoying to the enemy that Johnston fell back disgusted with the neighborhood. No language can adequately depict the perils of that week. All felt that the welfare of their respective causes was to be made sure or gravely periled by the issue of that field. At last the Army of the Cumberland, by extending its flank, pressed the right of the hostile line back, which then retired to Dallas. The twentieth corps was now placed in reserve for six days, at the end of which time, it moved into line, relieving the fourth corps, which took position further to the left. Marching, digging, and fighting, alternately, our forces pressed on, and, finally, by the middle of June, were in line beyond Pine Knob. Here Lieut. Gen. Polk was killed and it became evident that the dearest hopes of the rebel South were doomed to perish beneath the blows of the sturdy Northmen. But none could expect the daring sons of Dixie to tamely yield their sectional claims, cherished so many years.

Valor and patience and labor and diligence and skill and blood must all be given to the nation's cause, by Sherman's noble men, and lavishly were they bestowed. It cost some of our regiments full twenty per cent of their strength to force the line at Pine Knob; but the victors went on to seek another fateful field, as light of spirit and as strong of heart as the farmer who goes to the harvest field of peace.

JEFFERSON DAVIS.

Lost Mountain having been abandoned, the Army of the Tennessee advanced several miles, and found Johnston preparing to stand. The Thirteenth New York Battery, Lieutenant Bundy commanding, coming up, attacked the enemy skillfully, and won a reputation among soldiers that will not dim while memory holds her seat. The insurgent chief was forced back once more. He then carefully selected a strong line of defense on Kenesaw Mountain. As the first division of the twentieth corps was forming its line on the right of the second, a large force was hurled upon it, which force was nearly annihilated by the artillery happily at that moment massed at the extreme front. The unprecedented slaughter discouraged the assailants, and they retired to their works, remaining in them several days.

The twentieth corps celebrated the Fourth of July in line of battle, forgetting their own crowding honors in the just glories of our hero sires of 1776. Girding up their loins, they pressed on toward the Chattahoochee with renewed courage, for Atlanta, the Gate City of the South was now in sight.

In proportion as victory cheered them, defeat carried sorrow and despair to their opponents. General Hood was sent to relieve General Johnston, whose farewell address was audible to our pickets. He instituted at once a more decisive policy, staking the very existence of his army, and requiring equal risks on the part of his opponents. Gaining the left bank of the Chattahoochee with admirable skill, Sherman approached Peach Tree Creek, where the united skill of both rebel chiefs had prepared formidable work for the intrepid travelers. On the 20th of July, the star corps, while in order of march, was assailed by the entire force then and there gathered for the deliverance of Georgia. A terrible battle ensued. The Southern troops were burning to retrieve their losses, and felt that another defeat might be fatal to their cause. Their base of supplies was at hand, and their entire force was available. The ground was well adapted for defense. Now, or never, they must crush this daring invader. To break his lines was to annihilate his army; to fail in that was to have him soon thunder at the gates. Nor could Sherman now afford defeat—it was ruin. His long line of communication could not be held a day after such an event. The immense gains of the summer's toil would all be lost. A new campaign added to the burdens of the already heavily laden nation could hardly restore what might now be secured by persevering energy and the undaunted courage that had made these men heroic.

GEN. W. T. SHERMAN.

True, their ground was unfavorable; they must stand the more stubbornly. A deep, crooked stream was before them; they must use more skill in crossing. They could not form in line; every man must be his own support. They were called upon to brave all difficulties, and they did it. They were to win success by sacrifices, and they suffered and succeeded. Peach Tree Creek was made one of the holy spots where the nation's children were faithful unto death, and victory planted there a laurel that will never fade. Two days later the Army of the Tennessee was similarly attacked with similar results, and Hood retired to Atlanta. The siege of the doomed city began at once. The twentieth corps had been under fire more than one hundred days, with only six days intermission. It had lost over thirteen thousand men, about three-fifths of its entire number, and still it retained its characteristic energy, and was a pride to its friends and a terror to its foes. Taking its place in the lines about the city, it bore a conspicuous part in that skillful siege. Meantime the lamented M'Pherson (commanding the Army of the Tennessee) fell, and General Hooker was recommended as his successor. But General Howard was appointed, and "Fighting Joe" could only ask to be relieved from duty under Sherman.

General Williams assumed his command, and by a change afterward made in the plan of the siege, this trusty corps was sent to hold the line of the Chattahoochee, guard trains, deceive the enemy, and, if possible, annoy him while Sherman flanked the great northern defenses, and approached the town from the rear. The corps, there being now confidence in every man belonging to it, stretched out in line for nearly ten miles, the men being in some instances ten or twelve feet apart. They held their position, and fully answered the expectation of their commander. When Hood left, the twentieth moved on, and was the first to enter the fallen stronghold. There it lay and recruited while the remainder of the army drove Hood to the arms of Thomas at Nashville, where Hood lost his power. Several thousand new troops joined the corps at Atlanta. Having repelled some trifling attacks at different times, here, preparations were made for another campaign. Where now? was a much mooted question among the men; but the accomplished Sherman suffered friend and foe alike to wonder and conjecture. On the 15th of November (1864) we set out for the south-east, and Mobile, Savannah, Charleston, Augusta, Wilmington, and even Richmond, were confidently named as probable points we were to reach. Very meagre were the supplies we carried, and the rebel papers we saw from time to time, were filled with the most glowing prophecies of our swift destruction. The resources of the country through which we passed were at once put under contribution. The accumulated edibles of Georgia, its numerous cattle, horses, mules, calves, etc., disappeared as by magic along our route. Too strong to be stopped or seriously hindered by any effort the foe could make, four co-operating corps swept along, and the great raid became the most magnificent march of modern history. Our experience was more like that of a band of mischievous travelers than an invading army. Destroying railroads, cotton gins, warehouses, and bridges; making roads across plantations and through swamps, and marching leisurely on with song and shout, and endless badinage; foraging, cooking, and eating alternated with each other through the entire thirty days we spent in reaching the defenses of Savannah. Our corps was assigned the direct approach by the Augusta pike, with the fourteenth as reserve, and twelve miles from the city the outer defense was carried gallantly after a very brief action. The next line, five miles from town, was its real reliance.

The complete destitution of the troops, in respect to some important supplies, caused comparative inactivity until the fall of M'Allister opened a line for supplies. Then heavy fatigue parties were employed in the raising of counterworks, which were scarcely begun before Hardee evacuated the place.

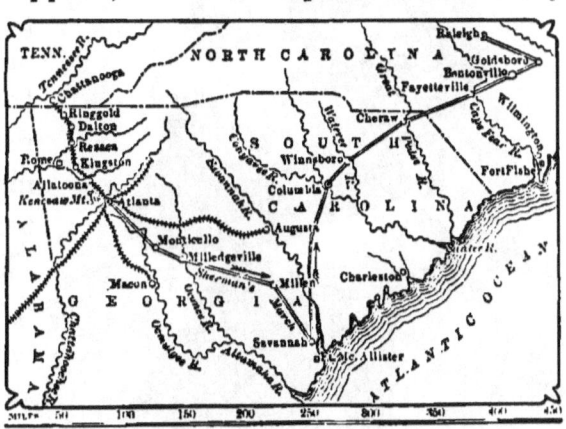

SHERMAN'S MARCH TO THE SEA.

No sooner had his sharpshooters crept away from the outer rifle pits than an enterprising New Yorker crept into them, and hurrying back, roused his officers with the welcome intelligence.

Wonderful was the forbearance of the victorious warriors. General Sherman alludes to it, in his report, as a most gratifying proof of their good discipline. The citizens, terrified by the horrible tales with which Southern editors had tried to fire the Southern heart, seemed to expect barbarities almost unendurable. Their own soldiers had wantonly murdered many negroes during the night, for manifesting joy at the coming of the Yankees. Nearly the whole day was spent arranging and stationing the usual guard, during which the city lay completely at the mercy of our men. The conduct of these sons of our free civilization in that hour, furnished testimony in favor of liberty and equal rights that the people of Savannah should never forget. The remainder of the army subsequently took position in the vicinity. On our departure, six weeks later, the reiterated regrets of the citizens was a most honorable proof of general good conduct. Earnest public efforts were made to retain the second division of the twentieth corps as a city guard. But it had proved itself too useful in the field to be excused from aiding in the great effort soon to be made.

GEN. ROBT. E. LEE.

Moving up the river in the latter part of January the army crossed into South Carolina, and entered with more than usual energy upon the work of devastation. For a considerable distance hardly anything combustible was left unburned. Neither strength nor weakness, wealth nor poverty could shield the luckless citizens of the Mother of Secession from the hot zeal of the avengers. Gradually, however, passion subsided, and a calm, quiet resolve to enforce justice and right took its place, and then more discrimination marked our deeds. By the time we reached Winnsborough, February the 20th, even Wade Hampton had learned the disposition of our men so well as to assure the citizens, by letter, that "If the twentieth corps occupy the place, private rights will be respected." His confidence was not misplaced. A feeling of mutual respect, based on profound self-respect, seemed to pervade both citizens and soldiers, and our stay there will ever be one of the most agreeable memories of the campaign. We now pushed more to the eastward, and a monotonous journey succeeded. Crossing the Catawba during a dark, rainy night, we moved on to Cheraw, crossed the Great Pedee, and three days later entered North Carolina. Here a general order was published, reminding the army of the greater loyalty of the old North State, and recommending a milder policy. A few days later we reached Fayetteville, and from that point dispatched a mail.

Much rain had made the roads heavy, and the trains were therefore sent to Goldsborough for supplies, while the main portion of the second corps was sent up the Raleigh plank road. At Averysborough the long-cherished plans of Joe Johnston were proved futile, his army badly punished, and the old reputation of our corps honorably sustained. At Bentonville the disheartened leaders of the rebellion made their last despairing, wild, but fruitless stand before Sherman's troops. For a little time their assault showed something of their ancient vigor; but, as our scattered forces came flocking to the field, their discretion prevailed, and they retired. After resting a few days at Goldsborough to refit, we hurried on to Raleigh. The foe seemed intent only on necessary flight. Here we received their very welcome surrender.

GEN. U. S. GRANT.

And now, having finished the work assigned us, and brought again every portion of our beloved country under the control of the national arms, we gladly turned toward home, loving the arts and duties of peace far better than the harsh scenes of war. Reaching Washington, the twentieth corps participated in the grand review, and won high compliments from the spectators. An impartial writer has declared the second division of the corps the crack division of the vast assemblage. A few days later the corps was disbanded, and now most of its noble members are enjoying the well earned comforts of the homes they so valorously defended. May they long live to recount their great achievements, and to perpetuate in narrative, and song the memories of their brave fellows who fell in the conflict, and who sleep everywhere from Maryland to Mississippi.

CHAPTER II.

UTAH AND THE MORMONS.

RETURNING home at the close of the war, I remained for nearly two years, a portion of the time with my father, and the remainder with friends in Madison County, Ohio. This period I will pass over without further notice.

In 1863 an uncle, my mother's brother, went to California. He was continually writing for me to come to him. I hesitated a long time. Finally he became, as he thought, permanently located in Piute County, Utah Territory. Then he again wrote me, holding out inducements so strong that I could no longer resist. He wrote to his brothers and to me of the enormous fortunes that were made in a few days (like Jonah's gourd, that sprung up in a night), and that people who would or did come there would amass fortunes ten and twenty times faster than they could in Ohio.

Consequently I could not rest satisfied until I had turned all my resources into cash, and the Fall of '68 found me in Utah, in a new mining camp located two hundred miles south of Salt Lake City. I was green in the business of mining. I had some money; but I loaned it to uncle and his friends. The consequence was, I must work or starve. This now brings me up to the beginning of a three years' sojourn in Utah.

Utah is situated in the great basin between the Rocky Mountains on the East and the Sierra Nevada on the West. Some of the valleys owned and worked by the Mormon saints are as fertile as any on the continent. They raise everything for their own use, and have considerable of an export trade with the adjacent States and Territories. But, for all that, I found it was as much as people could do to live there, for the Territory was populated with fanatics, and unless you were one of their creed, and agreed with them in their wild notions, you were liable to be forever lost unless you passed through the ordeal of Blood Atonement. You should be murdered for the remission of your sins. And they were careful that this should be done in secret. Not that the chosen of the Lord should operate with deadly revenge, on dark nights; but that the perpetrators of their criminal deeds might be the better concealed from the eyes of the Law and of the Christian world. Unless persons residing there were of their faith, or upheld them in their deeds of violence, such as murdering, stealing, and burning the property belonging to the Gentiles, they were regarded as evil doers, by the Mormon profession. Violent acts, fully premeditated, and without any cause or provocation whatever, were committed time and again; were almost daily occurrences, indeed. Numbers of instances could I mention, but they have been fully narrated heretofore by others, such as following up and murdering in the most brutal manner, one whole emigrant train of men, women, and children, who were on their way to California.

To this day their bones lie bleaching in the sun. Some claim that they did have a burial; but, judging from appearances and the manner in which I saw the bones lying scattered over the plain, it would be very difficult for Brigham Young, Haight, Higbee, and Delee, and their hordes of destroying angels to verify the statement

MOUNTAIN MEADOW MASSACRE.

that they did bury those that were massacred at Mountain Meadow.

Taking a view of the picturesque and beautiful landscapes which compose the Mountain Meadows, one would hardly think that this had been the scene of such a wanton outrage. But this was no worse than hundreds of others. Several incidents have come under my own observation. One I may mention, occurred in Manti, San Pete County. There was a young man living there who had become entangled in a love affair with a young lady of the same place. It so happened that Bishop S——, of the precinct, had had revelations; that is, the Lord had commanded him to take this young lady as his wife, notwithstanding the fact that he had several wives already. The bishop tried to reason the young lady out of having anything to say to the young man. But the fact was, the young couple were engaged to be married; and the bishop, finding that loving words to his desired darling were of no avail, resolved not to be outdone, but to seek revenge on the young man. Consequently he had a secret conference with a few of the brethren, and they decided to hold a meeting in the school-house, which meeting the young man should be prevailed upon to attend. At this meeting these plotters in a most cruel manner destroyed the manhood of the young man. He, after lingering some time in great suffering, died. Several instances of like character have taken place in Utah, all in obedience to the "revelations of the Lord," as given to those whose lives have been passed worse than brutes of the field. Another way of seeking revenge is for some one to sell horses or cattle to one not belonging to the faith. Then officers are sent to arrest him for stealing. He is certain to receive no mercy, because they will murder him on the road to trial, and make a report to the effect that he had been some desperado of the worst dye. The case of

D. P. Smith, of Piute County, is a good illustration. He bought a span of mules from a certain saint who resided in Ogden, a settlement thirty-six miles north of Salt Lake City, and took them to the mines on the Sevier River. They followed and arrested him on the charge of stealing the mules, and started to take him to the city for trial. They soon became tired of him, and, after hauling him twenty-five miles, they shot him, and buried the body in an old manure bank.

One more illustration of their saintliness. Captain Hawley, now living at Pleasant Grove, Utah, hired a young man of seventeen years of age to work for him. After the young fellow had labored six months Captain Hawley paid him off with an old horse that was not worth a cent, since good broncos were selling at only ten and twelve dollars a piece. The young fellow, glad to get anything, took the horse, and started toward Corinne. Captain Hawley waited a sufficient time for his victim to get well on his way, then got the sheriff and followed and arrested him, before he had reached Corinne, on the charge of having stolen the horse. The Mormons, being so bitterly opposed to worldly immigration into Utah, would charge any criminal offense against a Gentile already in the Territory. So it was with the young man with the horse. He was taken to the nearest tree and hung by the neck, his hands being untied. When he was swung off he commenced to climb the rope hand over hand. Captain Hawley then took a small cedar post that lay there and broke both of the young man's arms, and, after pounding him with the club until satisfied, he rode off and left the poor fellow to the mercy of some one who could show enough sympathy for such unfortunates to give him a burial.

The people in Utah who profess to belong to the Mormon Church are two-thirds of them direct from Europe (Danes and Swedes being largely in the majority), and among the most of them ignorance predominates. I have seen in Southern Utah the women out plowing with cattle, breaking up the ground, harrowing and seeding it, and tending and gathering their crops, while the men were too shiftless to either help them or otherwise to provide sustenance for their household.

Hundreds of them live in

MORMON PERSECUTION.

adobe houses. These are made by mixing black earth to the consistency of thick mud and forming it into very large-sized blocks shaped like bricks. Then they are spread over a piece of ground leveled off for the purpose, there to be sun-dried, when they are considered fit material of which to build their houses. Then they go to the cañon and there cut small straight poles for the roof. The poles are laid along the sides of the house, one end resting on a large log that is laid up for a center beam, the other on the top of the adobe wall; after which they mix more mud and water together and plaster these poles all over. This forms the roof. Shingle and all other expensive roofs are dispensed with. Here in these castles the saints have their wives brushing up their dirt floors, washing, mending, ironing, cooking and indeed providing for the support of the household, while they themselves spend their time in receiving revelations from the Lord regarding the future prosperity of Mormondom and the number of additional wives it would be necessary to take in order to obtain celestial glory.

The following illustration is given to convey some idea of marriage in Utah. A certain Mr. Buntz, who is now living in San Pete County, Utah, received a revelation from the Lord, as he claimed, that, notwithstanding he had already a number of wives, he must still increase his better half by taking to his arms and marrying three sisters who were living near by. He married all three at one and the same time with as much unconcern as if it were an every-day occurrence. Another instance I will notice. There was a certain bishop then living in Provost City, who became enamored with a married lady of one of the adjoining villages. In order to obtain his sixth loved one he went to the lady's husband, and there in pleading tones he narrated the revelations he had received from the Lord, setting forth the way in which he must do in order to receive his share of celestial glory in the world to come. The husband listened very attentively until the bishop had finished his request; then, in a good-natured way, he showed him the fallacy of such proceedings both in a moral and religious view.

But the bishop was not to be argued out of his hope of celestial happiness. That night the husband was followed and murdered in cold blood upon his own doorstep. Some who read this may think that I am overstating the facts. Indeed such is not the case; for I have given only a few instances when I could recount more than one hundred such, most of which can be verified by many who are still living in Utah, and in surrounding States and Territories.

I will next speak of the scenery. In traveling through Utah from the north-east you are constantly passing into and out of cañons with mountains on either side, towering for thousands of feet above you. These mountain sides, where not too rocky and abrupt, are covered with a dense growth of timber, while between the mountains in the canons are clear running brooks of cold water, in most of which trout abound.

In traveling along one frequently passes alkaline springs, boiling springs, and springs of almost freezing water oftentimes located only a few feet apart. Many of these springs are intermittent in their action and they are all a source of unfailing interest to the traveler and geologist.

The Jordan River and City Creek run through the city of Salt Lake, affording an abundant supply of the purest water in any city as large as this, in the world. Most beautiful trout are hooked out of the streams, by the little boys, right in the street.

After leaving Salt Lake City, going south, one is struck with the prominence of the old Wasatch range, now ascending gradually, then rising abruptly in broken, rough, and dangerous looking precipices. At other places it looks as if the country had been inundated with water, and the rock, being in some places' softer than its connecting sides, had been worn away, leaving canons of all shapes, depths, and lengths. .

The valleys through Juab and San Pete Counties are made very productive by irrigation. This is done by taking water and conducting it through ditches all over the land under cultivation. After their crops are planted, and it becomes necessary to moisten the ground, the water is turned into these small ditches and left running until the earth is sufficiently moistened, when it is shut off until it becomes necessary to repeat the operation.

BRIGHAM YOUNG.

The valleys are of a dark, loamy soil mixed with sand, and before they are brought under cultivation are covered with sage brush—a small scrubby bush that grows sometimes to the height of six feet. It is found from the British possessions on the the North to the Gulf of Mexico on the South. All the valleys and plains throughout the mountains of the West produce the sage bush in great abundance. The sage bush is the home of the jack-rabbit. Dozens of them may be seen at any time running in all directions from the traveler, as he journeys over the plains.

Some of the loftiest peaks of Utah can be seen at a distance of many miles. Mt. Nebo is as prominent as any, with an elevation of a little over twelve thousand feet. As the traveler journeys on South, through the Territory, he travels over sandy deserts, unsettled and uncultivated, except in a few places where the streams flow through from the mountains, furnishing water sufficient for irrigating purposes. Generally along these streams a few of the saints have settled in adobe houses, built after their own fashion, usually surrounded by a stone wall built in the form of a square, and often containing as much as an acre of land. Into this they remove their families, and use it as a fortress in defending themselves against the Indians, when they make their raids through the settlements.

The bench lands all over the Territory produce great quantities of bunch grass, a very nutritious grass that grows to the height of eighteen inches, and in bunches. In passing through the Territory you see thousands and thousands of cattle feeding upon this grass. The valleys are productive of no timber whatever, unless it be a few scattering cottonwoods along the banks of the streams. But sufficient timber grows in the mountains for all necessary purposes. Mahogany and cedar constitute the kinds that grow on that side of the ranges facing the South, while the pine, fir, spruce, balsam, and small scrub-oaks, with a few more scrubby little bushes, constitute the timber on the North slope.

Mines were discovered in Utah years ago; but owing to the influences brought to bear by the Mormon leaders upon their not so well enlightened followers, mining was prohibited within the limits of the Territory. But as time passed on, and people began to emigrate to the West in greater numbers, crowding full the older places, and seeking for newer fields, where fortunes might be dug from the earth, at last, and in the face of all opposition from the Mormons, prospecting and mining throughout the Territory began. So that to-day thousands of honest, hard-working miners can be seen toiling and striving for the treasures of gold and silver, and other minerals that lie buried underneath the surface earth of Utah. Notwithstanding the many difficulties that the pioneer miners of the Territory had to encounter and overcome, some of them have done extremely well. And now some who were so bitterly opposed to opening up mines there, finding it useless to resist the fast growing population of miners, are zealously engaged, themselves, in opening up some of the Territory's precious wealth.

Gold, silver, lead, copper, zinc, iron, salt, and a few other minerals are found in many parts of the Territory in sufficient quantities to leave a balance over all expenditures in running them.

At different places throughout the Territory, salt is found in the mountains, and is easily taken out and refined. Large deposits of coal are found in various places throughout the Territory.

While in Utah my home was in a mining camp

located on Sevier River. A great number of locations was recorded. The recorder was kept busy writing out and recording claims, as people would do nothing but locate and then record. I often times thought to myself, "What will this amount to?" But green as I

THE MORMON TABERNACLE.

was, I could only do as others did. I then knew no more about mining than a two-year-old boy knows about making an arasta, or quartz mill. I worked a few days and obtained a little money—enough for a grub-stake— then I went to hunting for hidden millions, along with others. I would write out a notice and post it up on everything that my ignorance claimed as a very valuable mine. It was only a short time until every bowlder and pile of rocks for miles around the camping spot was located and recorded. The recorder would most always, do the work of recording, and wait for his fees until the mine became a paying property. And I rather think that the recorder of Ohio District is yet waiting, like Micawber, for some of the miners that located there to turn up.

It would sometimes happen that two or more notices would be found on the same bowlder. Then war would be the result. A mine is of no value until a few persons are butchered over it, in an effort to determine the question as to who shall be the possessor of it.

Thousands of locations are made throughout the mountains, when work to the amount of one dollar has not been done upon them; yet the location is named, filed, and recorded, and the worthy claimant struts around and talks of his mine as though it were worth thousands, when in reality it is not worth the paper he has soiled in writing the notice. But stay with your mine, pard, you may sell it for several thousand yet. It is very easy to tell a prospector from any one else. The prospector always has his pockets full of rocks of all sizes, shapes, colors, and kinds, each piece of which he will tell you the nature of, the probability of its value, and all the different combinations of mineral that it contains, with as much ease, and all the grace of a first-class mineralogist. If he is not able to do this he is a "tenderfoot," and has much to learn in the art of mining. To prospect successfully he should send to some friend in California and have some very rich specimens of gold rock sent to him. Then, if he keeps his little tongue in the right channel, the whole camp is soon on its feet, anxious to see a specimen of the richest gold-bearing quartz rock that was ever heard of; and the next day, and for days after, the lucky miner is watched in his every movement, to see in what direction he leaves camp. He is then still watched and carefully trailed.

Miners in well doing are the most excitable of men. Often and often will they leave mines or claims that pay well, to go to a distance, led by some new excitement; and when they arrive there it frequently happens that they find nothing but disappointment and starvation staring them in the face. The White Pine excitement, in Nevada, is a good illustration. Hundreds flocked there to spend the last cent they had, and then to leave, packing their blankets on their backs; that is, they who were fortunate enough to have blankets, for hundreds had not even a meal's provisions to serve them on their exit from what a few days before was supposed to be one of the richest camps the world had ever seen.

A miner's fortune is like a mushroom—it springs up where least expected, then again it vanishes with as great rapidity as it came. I shall always remember the first mine I endeavored to work for myself. After prospecting for two months on all quarters of the compass from Bullion City, the mining town I was holding responsible for my bed and board, I at last resolved to go to work on what I supposed the best of my many locations. So

I laid in a supply of drills, hammers, powder and fuse, and hired a man to work with me for four dollars a day. Then, after spending a day surveying the location and arguing the many advantages one spot had over another for working, we at last concluded that the cheapest and best way to work the mine advantageously was to go down below the mine on the slope of the mountain and

NEW MINING TOWN.

run a tunnel in until we struck the vein, then we would be at a sufficient depth to ascertain the value of our ore. So we spent the whole day, and did nothing except to come to the conclusion that a tunnel was the cheapest and best method, and that by running in twenty feet we could tap the lead at about that or a little greater depth, and that the next morning we would begin digging the tunnel. After digging, picking, drilling and blasting one month we had run a tunnel in twenty-seven feet and had found no ledge. Then what to do I did not know, for my money was exhausted and I had been running in debt at the store for provisions two weeks. At last I resolved to have some older, experienced miners to go up with me and see my claim and give me some idea of what I should do in order to show up my vein of ore, for I was sure it was there some place, and plain to be seen on top I thought. Some said I was working it right; others were doubtful. At last one of them agreed to come the next morning and to help me work some on it from the top in exchange for work, which I accepted.

The next morning found me on the ground as usual, but not to tunnel. I was now about to sink a shaft right down on what I considered to be the vein. After spending the day in prying around large rocks and pushing off smaller ones, we were ready to begin sinking the next morning. Before noon we had sunk a shaft clear through my mine, and there was now no more of an indication left than there is on a barn floor. So I was out about three hundred dollars in time, money, and provisions, not counting my tools in, for I still had them—all because I was no miner, but simply wanted to do something I knew nothing about. This was my first out in mining.

But I remained by no means an idle prospector, showing nothing but notices on file. A company of ten of us went in on the Webster Location Lode, and we located all of the available ground that the law specified we should have and more too, and then went to work on it, some of my partners expecting to sell out in a few days for fabulous amounts. But my courage was none of the best in developing; for my first work spent in tunneling had proved such an entire failure. We had hard rock to blast, and progress was slow. At a called meeting of the members of the company, we concluded to put in the remainder of the work done in developing by sinking a shaft parallel with the vein. We got along very well with this until we had attained the depth of fifty or sixty feet, when the walls became scaly and we had to timber the shaft. Then the water came in in torrents, which had to be kept out, and the consequence was our progress was so impeded that we were two years sinking on the Webster Lode and only obtained a depth of two hundred feet. I always will think it is a good mine, could it be worked with any reasonable expense; but it can not. So there it lies yet with no one doing anything with it.

Thus it is with thousands of others who have located and worked claims until they were satisfied that the mineral extracted from the lead would not pay expenses of labor and cost of milling, and have abandoned claims that sometimes assay hundreds of dollars to the ton. In this way prospecting is going on all over the West and not one mine out of every ten thousand that is located and even put on file in the county or district clerk's office ever pays back the cost of expenditures, counting money, time, provisions, tools, and all other necessary expenses.

It can, therefore, plainly be seen that all men can not make a fortune mining; but the majority of people that are carried away by mining excitements rush in pell-mell, without ever taking time to think what they can or will do when they get there. They seem to think that the precious metals are lying around in quantities sufficient for them to amass enormous fortunes, so that they may live at ease and in luxury and splendor the balance of their lives; and all this is to be obtained within a short time and at little or no expense, merely expecting to shovel the gravel into a sluice box, or by some other method to separate the gold from the mother earth. Now, friends, this is all a mistake. Where one man reaps a fortune in a mining field, scores are retiring to hunt some other place where the chance would seem better in their favor, and they will never find it. Mining is a legitimate business, as much so as farming or any other branch of industry that one might engage in. But yet there is more chance work connected with mining than with all the other different pursuits of business. I am well aware there are a great many writing to the contrary, and I would not wish to try to dissuade any one from mining; but, on the contrary, go if you want to. There is yet plenty to learn. Hundreds will go to the West, expecting to make their mark in some profession where shrewdness and education are required. They will find all the professions full and much more so than is needed. Some want to know where to go. Bear patiently with me and I will show you where there is yet room before I come to the end of this book.

Mining, when you are on a good mine, is an investment or enterprise that surpasses all other enterprises that I know of as a high road to fortune. Thousands of dollars have rewarded the sturdy prospector in some instances in a single day. But the day is past when the miner can take up his pan and in an hour or two pan out enough dust to supply himself and friends with abundant funds. One meets hundreds of good old fellows, who will tell of the money they made in the early days of California and how they spent it, thinking there were such vast quantities lying in the gulches, that they could be possessors of all the luxuries of the land as long as they lived.

CHAPTER III.

NEVADA.

AFTER remaining in Utah Territory until I became weary of not well doing, I concluded to go to Nevada. I settled temporarily in Carson City, which, at that time, was a very small place; but was, nevertheless, bustling with life and energy. My finances not being cumbersome, I resolved to go to work at the first opportunity. This presented itself two days after, when I went to work for Yerrington, Bliss & Co., who were large wood and lumber contractors. They owned large tracts of timber lands lying in proximity to Lake Tahoe, together with saw-mills and flumes. Tahoe is a beautiful lake, about which enough has been said to justify me in passing over the beauties and grandeur of the lake, and the surrounding locality. (Read Mark Twain.)

I began work in a saw-mill, as screw-turner, and remained there until the mill closed in the Fall, which it does every year on account of cold and snow. But I had made good use of my time, and when I went down to Carson City I had six hundred and forty dollars, nearly all of which I had made that Summer. There the mining fever was raging, as it always is. Excitement ran high, and every one—men, women, and children, old and young, rich and poor—if they were able to raise only five dollars, were dealing or dabbling in stocks of the celebrated Comstock mines, which were just then receiving so much attention in the San Francisco Stock Exchange. I, of course, must try my luck, with the others. So I invested the half I had, and became a constant attendant at the broker's office, and watcher of the bulletin boards, along with the 'crowded masses of different nationalities that are always there watching every change that is noted down with

VIEW NEAR LAKE TAHOE.

the fluctuation of the stock in San Francisco.

Fortune for once, I thought, seemed to be in my favor, for during that Winter I made the little sum of sixteen hundred dollars; not by my shrewdness, however, for I declare I knew nothing about it, except that I would give Messrs. Rice & Peters my money, with orders to buy such and such stock, and in a short time I would make sale at a large profit, and buy again.

Nevada possesses some of the richest producing

mines in the world. The Comstock mines are the best in the State. Millions and millions have been produced from some of the oldest locations on this lode, with vast bodies of ore yet in sight. No one who has never been at Virginia City can form an idea of the vast amount of work that is required to carry on the mining business there. Some of the finest machinery that the world has yet produced can there be seen. This must be had in order to mine successfully in deep mines. Millions of dollars are annually spent in erecting hoisting works, quartz mills, and other necessary improvements. The water that they use comes through pipes from Marlette or Silver Lake miles away, down the mountain side, across valleys, then to ascend again, to be distributed throughout the city. The mines are always in need of vast quantities of wood and lumber, a greater portion of which comes from the mountain sides around Lake Tahoe. The lumber is sawed at the different mills along the eastern shore of the lake. A great many men are employed in this work. Some cutting logs at different points around the lake, others hauling and dumping them into the water, where rafts are formed and then towed across the lake to the mills, where they have large break-waters constructed to keep the logs from being carried back into the lake and lost. When the logs are sawed, the lumber is all piled up, each kind by itself, after which it is loaded on the cars and taken to the dividing ridge of the mountain between the lake and Carson City, where it is again piled up as before, alongside a flume.

Now, to go back a little, the Lake Tahoe Narrow Gauge Railroad was built from the lake at Glenbrook to the summit. In a direct line, the distance is a little short of three miles; but to get from the lake up, they made nine miles of road, and some of that has a grade of one hundred and sixty feet to the mile. They have two engines on the road, which run all the time, except in the dead of Winter, bringing up wood and lumber to the summit yards.

From the summit to Carson City is fourteen miles, and the distance is spanned by a long flume. The

BLUE CANON, SIERRA NEVADA.

capacity of the flume is unknown. There have been over one million feet of lumber and four hundred cords of wood sent from the summit to Carson in a single day's run of ten hours. The flume is built of two-inch plank sixteen feet in length, and twenty and twenty-two inches in width. These boards are placed the bottom of one on the flat edge of the other, and securely nailed with large spike nails, forming a V shaped box. After the flume bed has been laid with stringers properly graded, the boxes are put in place and securely supported by generally five bracket bearings to each box. The brackets are made with arms extending enough to admit of another two-inch plank ten or twelve inches in width, being placed in on either side if necessary. Then a head of water is turned on at the upper end of the flume and it is ready for operation. Sometimes fifty men can be seen throwing in wood without checking its movement in the least. When at the yard, running lumber, I have seen one hundred and thirty-four thousand feet run from the yard in a single hour. I have seen green sticks of timber forty feet long, sixteen by eighteen inches square, thrown in and run along with more ease than a boat through the water.

Miles of flume can be seen at this date extending up along the mountain sides, used to flume wood to Carson. Large bodies of men are everywhere at work cutting wood. The timber around the lake is pine of different varieties, white and red fir, spruce, and tamarack. All grow to large size. The forest land around Lake Tahoe is very rough, broken, and of no value except for the timber that is on it.

But to return to the Comstock Mines. The mines are very deep and the deeper down they go the hotter they become. Vast quantities of water are continually rnnning in and are as rapidly pumped to the top by mammoth machinery. The water is hoisted twenty-three hundred feet out of some of the deepest locations. A few years ago they claimed that they hoisted through their pumps fish without eyes; they were living when found, but, after being exposed to the cold air on the surface, soon died. The heat on the lower levels of the Comstock Lode is intense, varying according to particular parts visited, but averaging about one hundred and forty degrees. Air pumps are constantly at work, forcing down cool air, and at the same time tons of ice are being lowered. And yet it is more like traveling in an oven that is heated and still heating than in the pure breezes from off Mt. Davidson. Eight hours constitute a day's work down in these depths, where no light except the feeble flicker of the miner's candle ever shines to guide him on his narrow pathway underneath the ground. The miners' wages average four dollars a day.

The Comstock Lode and Sutro Tunnel Company entered into an agreement in 1866 to tap and drain the lode. The tunnel was commenced at what is now Sutro City, and was pushed along under the supervision of Mr. Sutro. Millions of money have been expended in the undertaking. They now think they will be able to use it by the first of June, 1879. Mr. Sutro estimates that, after the mines are drained, connections with the tunnel made, and cross-cutting under way, the average daily output of ore will be three thousand tons, a great portion of which will be first-class or good ore. The Tunnel Company expect to reap benefits in many ways, viz: by revenues they will receive for the use of the tunnel for purposes of transportation, furnishing fire-wood, timber, compressed air, water for power, irrigation, mill supplies, etc.

The climate of Nevada is cold in Winter and pleasant in Summer. All through the Sierra Nevada range deep snow falls, and covers the ground until late in the Spring, in many places not melting off entirely at all, but remaining until snow falls again.

A few years ago, in going from Lake Tahoe down to Carson City, while on that part of the road lying between Mr. Spooner's and the Flinne camp, I passed through a tunnel of snow for several hundred feet, where the snow had been shoveled out along the side of the wagon road and wood had been hauled in and burned to melt the snow. I do not know how thick the roof of the tunnel was, but I know it was on the fourth day of July that I passed through it. Large forests of the finest of timber lying between the lake and Eagle Valley have all been cut and used for the benefit of the Comstock Mines.

There are a great many horses and cattle scattered throughout the State, but not in droves and herds, such as are seen on the plains and bench lands of Utah or Colorado. Farming is not a success in Nevada for many reasons. The seasons are too short. There is generally frost every month in the year, or, at least, I found it so during my stay in the State.

Hot Springs abound all along the valley of the Humboldt. Some of these springs are situated entirely alone, while others lie very near springs of cold water.

I remember having seen a hot and cold spring so near together that the two hands could be placed one in each spring at the same time. Some of these springs are very shallow, while others extend to unknown or, at least, unsounded depths.

The valleys are covered with alkali, varying from a thin sheet to three inches in thickness. The water

HUMBOLDT PALISADES.

standing in drains, ponds, and lakes in the valleys is all brackish, containing a vast amount of alkali. In many places travelers and wagon trains, passing to and fro, laden with freight, suffer to the utmost extremity for the want of fresh water, since all the fresh-water streams from the mountains have sunk and disappeared on the bench lands, ere they reach the low lands or valleys. It is nothing uncommon to see animals of burden lying dead along the roads, killed by drinking this alkaline water. You meet travelers and freighters going and coming in all directions, with sore and inflamed eyes, oftentimes so bad that they are unable to see; lips parched, cracked, and often swollen far beyond their usual size; gums sore; throat and lungs sometimes so painful that it is with great effort the individual can eat or speak — all arising from the winds and the dust that sweep along over these alkaline plains. Nevada deserts are very bad; but I will point out further along some localities where the Humboldt or Walker River valleys would be pleasant by comparison.

CHAPTER IV.

CALIFORNIA.

IN going from Nevada to the coast, one traverses over three hundred and twenty-four miles of railroad, between Carson City and San Francisco. The enchanting views of this whole distance will awaken

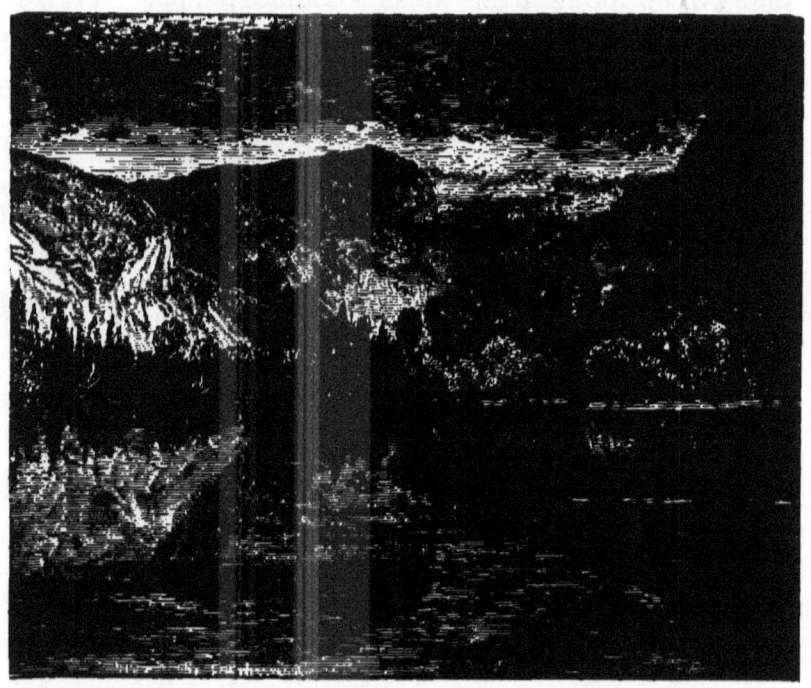

DONNER LAKE.

the traveler's keenest admiration. Donner Lake is not equaled in grandeur and picturesqueness anywhere in the East. It is three and one-half miles long by one in width. It lies at the base of the Sierra range, two miles west of Truckee. It is hemmed in on three sides by the Sierras, and a more beautiful place is hard to find. The lake is filled with fish. There are three kinds of trout and a few other kinds of fish. The lake is entirely surrounded by forests of magnificent growth.

One of the attractive places about the lake is Pulpit Rock in Echo Cañon, where the voice will be repeated so often and distinctly that it produces a peculiarly pleasing and interesting effect. This is the place the Donners perished in 1846. They were on their way to the valleys of California from Illinois. Here they became hemmed in by snow, only a portion of their number escaping and that after undergoing terrible suffering and hardship in traveling through mountains and cañons across the range, in search of some one to go to the relief of their comrades. A party finally went to their rescue, but only to find them all dead, except one, a German, who, it is said, was subsisting on a portion of Mrs. Donner's body when found, and was in a most wretched condition.

PULPIT ROCK, ECHO CAÑON.

There are a great many stories in circulation concerning Donner Lake. The Indians claim that the place where the lake now is was formerly a volcano's crater, and discharged hot cinders, fire and smoke continually. Whether this be true or not, I do not pretend to say. I was told that the Lake had been sounded to the depth of two thousand feet without finding bottom.

But Donner Lake takes its name from the unfortunates who perished there in one of those dreadful storms that pass over that region of the Sierras every Winter, where the snow sometimes falls to the depth of ten or twelve feet. Traveling is then out of the question, unless provided with snow-shoes; and then one unaccustomed to their use would find it difficult and laborious to make any progress.

Going north from here one comes to the Sierra Valley, where there is an abundance of grass in the summer; but farming is limited as the altitude is so high that it is liable to freeze any night during the Summer months. But this is still in a mining region, and mining is, directly or indirectly, the leading occupation of the settlers. Farther north we pass through Plumas, Tehama, Shasta, Lassen, Siskiyou and Modoc Counties, all noted for their mining industries. The mountains are full of holes and tunnels. The gulches have been washed over and over through strings of sluices, and still the miner is washing away with as much or more energy and ambition than in the years of '50 and '51. Sierra County has been the scene of excitement ever since gold was discovered in 1847. Thousands of dollars have been brought into Downieville day after day as a reward for the early and successful prospector. Ditches have been run for miles to convey water for washing down—by the use of hydraulic ram—whole sides of high bars or mountains, as I might term them.

I have often been asked how gold looks in the earth; in what form it is generally found, and of what size are the nuggets. The last two questions admit of a number of answers. The first question I will answer by saying that persons who can recognize gold after it has been taken from the earth, and refined and cleaned, would generally recognize it when seen in quartz rock, or in nuggets, in the sand and gravel. Gold most always has its distinctive bright yellow appearance, although I have sometimes seen it when it seemed to be covered with a coat of rust. When this is the case the color of the outside coating varies greatly. The gold I have seen so shaded has generally been where the water was saturated with different combinations of minerals.

The second question I will answer by stating that all gold is formed in quartz, and quartz (not float quartz) generally lies in veins. Where it does not, there has been a general upheaval of the earth's surface, grinding and mingling it into one conglomerate mass. In a case of this kind the quartz is in confusion and is scattered irregularly throughout the locality of such visitation. The veins of quartz are found in crevices in rocks of a previous formation. Veins are either of a different material or like that of the surrounding rock; in either case the filling-up of the vein has succeeded the formation of the country rock.

Bishop Mohr says, as to the formation of these crevices: "There seems to be no doubt that they have their origin in the rending of the crust of the earth, caused by plutonic or volcanic action in the interior of the earth, or by the formation and lifting of newly-formed masses from lower depths into higher regions, and a consequent rending of the overlying rocks. As the latter are lifted into higher regions of the globe, which have a larger diameter, these masses must of course break, or separate, and become detached from the neighboring rocks, producing chasms and crevices. The material with which these crevices are filled out has entered from below, from above, or from the neighboring strata, as a solution, either from the country rocks, or from deeper regions.

Water was very likely the principal medium, which, together perhaps with some gases, acted as a receiver for the particles of metal and other substances which lay distributed in the different strata of rocks, and deposited them, far more concentrated, by a slow and often repeated process." The uneven distribution of minerals in veins, the often symmetric and parallel texture of veins, as well as their composition, so different often from that of the neighboring rocks, seems to be proof for this explanation. Veins are usually found within those places where the surrounding country rock is in a decomposed state.

Some scientists cling to the idea that veins are formed entirely by the heating process. I will not endeavor to dispute with them. But one thing I will say, that the walls of veins show nowhere the action of fire, as would be the case where the wall-rock was of a nature difficult to fuse. Now this is where the gold in veins is obtained, the metal is distributed throughout this vein matter, and often in very rich rock or ore the

SCENE NEAR EAGLE LAKE, CALIFORNIA.

particles are so small that the eye can not discover a trace either of gold or silver. At other times the rock, or ore, will be dotted throughout with grains of gold, sometimes with golden wires woven together, and then again small nuggets can be picked from the ore with a pocket knife.

Placer mining is for gold that has been thrown from these veins where the rock has become softened and has been washed from the mother vein. The gold, owing to its very heavy nature, is left deposited along the gulches, in cañons, and along the mountain sides, and bench lands. The earth, where the gold has been thus deposited, is then washed in different ways and by different processes, until it passes away, leaving the grains of gold. It is seen, therefore, that gold in not all in nuggets; but, on the contrary, some of it is in grains so fine that the eye can not see it until it is gathered together through the washing and cleaning process. Again, there have been some large pieces found. The largest that was ever found in California was brought to light by John J. Finney, one of the Shasta County pioneers, who now resides near French Gulch. He unearthed it in the early mining times in California, about ten miles from Downieville, Sierra County. It was a chunk of solid gold that weighed five thousand one hundred and twenty ounces. This is said to be the best day's work ever done by a single miner. But John, like the most of old miners, is still prospecting for hidden wealth.

Going on to the North, from here, we pass through Lassen County. Large forests of pine and fir hem us in on all sides. We move on past Honey Lake, a picturesque place, and a sight that will be impressed forever upon the memory. A little farther on we come to Eagle Lake. There we turn and go into Siskiyou County, and soon we are at the base of old Mt. Shasta. We can then then look up to the top, where she rears her head for over fourteen thousand feet; and there she stands, with snow for a perpetual covering, and clouds dashing like billows all around her. No timber grows upon the top, of course.

The Yosemite Valley, California, is situated on the Merced River, in the southern part of Mariposa County. It is on the western slope of the Sierra Nevada Mountains, and near the center of the State, North and South. The valley is small, being but eight miles in length and three-quarters of a mile in width. It is enclosed with granite walls rising with almost unbroken and perpendicular faces to the dizzy height of from three thousand

THE TWO GUARDSMEN.

to six thousand feet above the green valley beneath. Yosemite is the Indian name for grizzly bear. This place is and will be preserved for public use. At Crane Flat there is a small grove of the mammoth trees of

Mariposa. There are two of these trees, called The Two Guardsmen, growing from the same root, which measure one hundred and fourteen feet in circumference, and are of corresponding height.

From the brink of the basin to the valley beneath measures four thousand feet. In order to get a descent at this point a trail over seven miles in length has been blasted and worked out of the rock. After the descent is made, you find yourself in what has been well called the "Garden of the Gods." Around you towers some of the grandest scenery that the world contains. The stupenduously massive walls seem, as it were, to be closing in around you from all sides. The valley in which you stand, the fertility of which is unsurpassed on the continent, is beautifully set in grass.

Here we are able to look upon Nature in all of her grandeur. The lofty walls lifting themselves to a perpendicular height of four or five thousand feet; the water gushing out of the many springs that are everywhere around you, to fall many hundreds of feet below, there to mingle with the waters of the beautiful Merced River. Looking to the east the eye rests upon the Yosemite, spreading out and falling down, like a magnificent bridal veil, a distance of twenty-six hundred feet. This is by far the highest water-fall in the world. There are numerous other falls. The Nevada Fall is seven hundred feet high. It is a grand and beautiful sight. It is formed by the Merced River, a stream several feet in depth and from fifty to seventy-five feet in width, continually pouring its waters over the cliffs into the valley.

Standing in the valley on a bright, clear day, one may well go into ecstacies over the many magnificent works

THE YOSEMITE FALLS.

of nature that crowd upon the view. Here are the giants of the forest with a circumference, at the earth, of one hundred and six feet, rearing their lofty heads over two hundred and seventy feet into the air. There is one lying prostrate, with its whole heart burned out, leaving nothing but the shell. A man can ride on horseback for seventy feet right into it, and yet have plenty of room to turn a horse of ordinary size around and come out. The surrounding country is for fifty or sixty miles dotted with little valleys in which these large trees are found all the way from thirty to one hundred feet in circumference, and from two hundred to considerably more than three hundred feet in height.

Vegetables grow to an enormous size here. I have sometimes thought I would say nothing about this, however, for I have my doubts whether the people in the East will believe the statements or not. They may think I am exaggerating when I say I have here seen single heads of cabbage weighing eighty pounds. Melons often weigh one hundred pounds, and pumpkins more than that; beets are three feet in length; onions as large around as a large pie pan; grapes in bunches weighing ten pounds.

From here we will go to the Golden City. I can not hope to say more than has been said by others, but justice demands that I shall not pass it by without a word. The first house was built in San Francisco in the year 1835. Since then a city has sprung up that to-day is the leading city of western North America. The town was not originally laid out in accordance with any definite plan, and until a few years ago people continued to build in the same irregular way. Then great improvements were set on foot by widening the streets, cutting through whole blocks of houses, tearing down the older buildings, and erecting in their stead better and costlier ones. Some magnificent buildings were erected, the San Francisco Mining Exchange, built entirely of marble, being the best and handsomest. The Palace Hotel, erected by W. C. Ralston, now dead, is said to be the grandest in the

BRIDAL VEIL FALL, YOSEMITE VALLEY.

United States. Mr. Baldwin's Academy of Music is an ornament fit for any European city. So that San Francisco is now, the hoodlums excepted, as beautiful a city as one can find among any of the port towns of the

United States of the same population, hoodlums *not* excepted.

In addition to this the city is filled with attractions of such a number and nature that one need never be at a loss for entertainment. North Beach is filled up with ancient collections in the shape of cobwebs as old as Adam would have been had he not died. The Cliff Rocks, a little more remote from the city, is a great place of resort. Here one gets a fair view of the Pacific Ocean. At this point, a little distance from the shore, are cliffs of rocks projecting out of the water. These are almost constantly covered with sea lions, rolling and pitching over another and howling incessantly.

But, perhaps, the greatest attraction of San Francisco is Woodward's Garden. This is a place of which one never grows weary. Mr. Woodward has, at a great expense of time and money, arranged and opened for exhibition a museum, containing, it is said, eighteen thousand specimens that have been procured from every part of the globe. The museum includes an art gallery, filled with the most beautiful painting and statuary to be procured in Europe and America. There are greenhouses, filled with every variety of plants known in botany. There is a zoological department, containing almost all kinds of wild animals and birds. There is an amphitheater, where twenty thousand people may sit and witness the hippodrome performances, such as racing, drills, games of various kinds, and other entertainments which may be given there. Mr. Woodward is continually making additions to his already very extensive collections. His grounds are magnificently shaded with many varieties of shade trees. Everything in the collections is arranged and labeled in the most systematic manner. Any one that can see and read may there view intelligently the productions of the world.

The valleys of California are fertile, and vegetation

A CALIFORNIA STUMP.

is thriftier there than in most any other place in the United States. Wheat has been raised, yielding eighty bushels to the acre. Thousands upon thousands of acres are sown annually. I have seen one unbroken field of waving wheat, extending for over forty miles, without a fence or ditch to separate it. The mode of harvesting wheat on the Pacific Coast is different from what it is in the Atlantic States. In the West the grain is sown either by drill or broadcast. If, after sowing, the ground is not moist enough, it is irrigated by letting on water until it has become sufficiently wet; then the water is shut off again. In this way they regulate the seasons. Harvesting wheat is done by machines called "headers," which cut the heads of the standing wheat and threshes out the grain, sacks and sews up the sacks, all at the same time. Ricks of sacked grain can be seen standing in every direction over the grain fields during the harvesting.

It may be as well remarked here that the Pacific Coast is subject to rain only at one season during the year. That is known as the rainy season. It sets in about the month of November, sometimes not until later, and closes in February. Sometimes there will be but a few days' rain during that period of time. During other seasons there may be rain for six or seven weeks. When it does rain, it often happens that several inches of water fall in a very short time.

The foot-hills of California are covered with a very nutritious grass, which during the long summer months has the appearance of being all burnt, parched and and dried up. It, nevertheless, retains a great deal of nutriment. Stock like it and keep fat and sleek as long as they can get plenty of it. Alfalfa is raised throughout the valleys with flattering success. Sometimes as many as four cuttings are procured from the same ground during the year.

Grapes do better in California than in any other part

of the United States. Hundreds of acres of vineyards can be seen growing throughout the State. Apples, peaches, pears, plums, cherries, apricots, and oranges all grow there in vast quantities and of as rich and fine a quality and flavor as any I have ever seen in the East or along the Mississippi Valley. Nuts of all kinds and varieties that I know of can be seen growing in many of the southern counties. Cotton and tobacco are said to do well also. Fish and game abound. If a well-to-do man can not enjoy himself in California, it would be difficult for him to find enjoyment anywhere on this continent.

Of course the State has many drawbacks. Sometimes an earthquake shakes up the country considerably, to the consternation of its inhabitants. This was the case when I was in the State in March, 1872. I had been at Vandalia, in Tulare County, for several days. The weather had been very pleasant and sunshiny—rather warm, with not a cloud to be seen. But at two o'clock, on the morning of March 26th, I was awakened by the windows rattling and the house cracking and shaking in a violent manner. I had not been thinking of an earthquake, neither did I realize that there was then one already at hand. The building seemed to be moving as on a wagon that was run over a hard, rough road. I did not remain long in bed, for I thought the house would surely soon fall down. When I got upon my feet I could scarcely stand. Then I was sure that the house was being meddled with in some violent manner, for it was shaking in such a way that it gave me feelings which no pen can express. For once, if never before, I was terribly scared. The oscillations were so short, and in such quick succession, that I was continually bounced about in such a manner that it was

NORTHERN CALIFORNIA SCENERY.

with great difficulty I could dress myself. There was no more sleep for me, for the shocks continued the remainder of the night; and the whole of the next day shocks could be repeatedly felt. The shocks, on this occasion, were felt the whole length of California, and into Mexico on the south, and as far east as Winnemucca, in Nevada, covering an area seven hundred and fifty miles long, by nearly five hundred miles broad. The center of the shock was in portions of Kern and Inyo Counties, including a desert country along the border line between California and Nevada.

In this part of the country the Sierra Nevada range breaks off into a number of detached ranges, so that, in San Bernardino and San Diego Counties, the range disappears entirely, as far as its distinctive features are concerned. All this region bears evidence of volcanic eruptions, some of which must have been of a very recent date. Here alkaline lakes, salfataras, hot springs, and mud volcanoes are still seen. In the north-eastern part of San Bernardino County is "Death's Valley;" said to be far below the level of the sea, while the surrounding mountains are not less than five thousand feet above it. Still further south, in San Bernardino County, north of the trail leading from Fort Mojave by way of the sink of Mojave, the Mojave Desert and River, to Los Angelos, there are numerous volcanic craters, rising to heights of from fifty to two hundred feet above the desolate plain, still as perfect as when their fires went out. The earth is covered with lava for many miles in width, and extending to the borders of the Colorado Desert. Hot mineral springs, volcanic ashes in vast beds, lava, pumice stone, and other evidences of comparatively recent volcanic disturbance, are found in abundance.

It is supposed the Dry Lakes in Bernardino County,

in the Colorado Desert, was the bed of the sea at a very distant date, and that its present condition is the result of volcanic action. The ancient water-line, which is still distinctly marked by sedimentary discoloration, can be seen extending along the side of the San Gorgonio Mountain, south of San Gorgonio Pass, for some fifty miles. At Dos Palmas, a water station on the north-

CAPE HORN, CENTRAL PACIFIC R. R.

eastern side of the Colorado Desert, on the trail from San Bernardino, by way of San Gorgonio Pass, to La Paz, on the Colorado River, in 1868, an earthquake opened a large fissure in the earth, from which flowed a stream of cold water. The fissure is but a short distance from the great hot spring of Dos Palmas, which is still flowing, but is said to have become much cooler since that event. At Fort Tejon, in the south-eastern part of Kern County, several years ago the earth was rent into a chasm.

At Lone Pine, when the terrible earthquake visited that section, in 1872, the inhabitants were awakened by a loud explosion followed by a terrible upheaval and shaking of the earth from north to south. The whole town was instantly in ruins, not a building being left standing. Colonel Whipple, who was in Lone Pine at the time, was sleeping, he says, in the second story of an adobe house; and stated that he just had time to jump from bed and get to the doorway when the house appeared to crumble to pieces beneath him, and he was buried in the ruins; but succeeded in extricating himself, though suffering from several painful but not dangerous wounds. He reports that the scenes which ensued beggared description. Screams and groans and cries for help rent the air in all directions, for nearly the whole population of the town was buried beneath the ruins. The first shock was followed in quick succession by three others. In fact, the earth was in a constant shock and tremble for over three hours. A chasm was opened extending thirty-five miles down the valley, ranging from three inches to forty feet in width. Rocks were torn from their places and rolled down into the valley.

Everywhere through the valley are to be seen evidences of the terrible convulsion of nature. Before each shock an explosion was heard which seemed to be directly underneath. Over six hundred distinct shocks were felt within fifty-eight hours after the first.

At Tibbet's ranch, fifteen miles above Independence, forty acres of ground sunk seven feet below the surface of the surrounding country. Big Owens Lake rose four feet. Owens River overflowed its banks, and shoals of fish were left on the shore for a distance of four miles. Through Lone Pine the earth cracked, and on one side it sunk seven or eight feet, leaving a wall of earth over three miles in length where formerly was level country. Innumerable cracks were made throughout the valley, and the Kern and Owens Rivers turned and ran up stream for several minutes, leaving the beds dry, and returned with swollen volume.

There had been no parallel to this earthquake since 1812, when the missions San Juan, Capistrano, and La Purissima, in South California, were destroyed.

CHAPTER V.

THE CHINESE.

FOR upward of thirty years there has been a stream of Chinese immigration to the western part of the United States. The Chinese are of a very short but symmetrical build, with a face larger in proportion to the size of the skull, than in the European race, and round instead of oval in shape. The eyes are very small, deep, and obliquely set, with a color resembling that of the almond. Nearly all that come to the coast are of a dirty brown or swarthy complexion, although you occasionally meet one of yellow, olive, or sallow color.

Their hair is all shaved off smooth and clean around the head, leaving only a small place on the top of the head where the hair is allowed to grow. This tuft is braided into a single strand, and that is lengthened out with other braiding material, so much so that oftentimes it trails upon the ground behind. While at work this queue is generally arranged in a coil around the top part of the head.

Their manner of dressing differs from the European custom. Their clothing is usually clean and tidy enough; but it is on the "too muchee loosee" fitting order, and is made after the models of their own fashions. They wear wooden shoes; but not after the Holland wooden shoe pattern, for their shoes are small and finely finished.

Their hats are made from the splittings of the bamboo tree, plaited after the manner of straw hats here, with a very narrow and shallow crown, and a rim from seven to ten inches wide.

There are now one hundred and twenty-five thousand Chinese in the State of California, the greater portion of whom live in San Francisco. Most of these people are virtually in a condition of servitude. "Why, how is that?" some one asks. The answer can be given in a few words. The Chinese who are brought to this country are of a very poor class in their own land. They are destitute of money, and even of the common necessities of life. There are in San Francisco six different companies importing them; or, in words a little harsher, making slaves of them, and that to as great an extent as ever was true of the negroes in the South.

Wages for all kinds of labor in the Chinese Empire are extremely low, amounting, generally, only to about seven cents per day in our money. In some cases the wages are a little higher. Here, briefly stated, is what is to-day causing so much disturbance in the West on this subject. These six companies have agents in the different ports of China. Whenever any new enterprise is undertaken on the Pacific slope requiring great numbers of workmen, these companies hire in China, at the low rates for labor paid there, as many laborers as can be worked—millions could be hired, if necessary—and bring them over and hire them out again. Now, some one of these companies, by virtue of the contract and agreement made and entered into in China, becomes, to all intents and purposes, the owner of the persons so imported, until they have earned their freedom according to the terms of their contract. From the terms of this contract there can be no variation. These six companies, of course, pocket the difference between what they give and what they receive for these laborers, giving their chattleman such meager credit on his account that he will be compelled to work a long time to gain his freedom.

The Chinese who emigrate to this country do not become citizens. Applications for naturalization papers have been made time and again, and have as often failed to be granted. They are called "heathen Chinese" because they have their "Big Josh" in all their temples; that is, an idol which they worship.

They have their own judicial tribunals, before which they try and punish offenders, in all grades of crime that may be registered against them. There is a secret order among them, known as the "Hoeys," the object of which is to protect their own countrymen from American or State laws, and to enforce laws of their own making. Their tribunals are held in secret, and they administer such punishment as they see fit. The penalty of death is enforced very often for the most trivial offenses, such as neglecting to pay a debt. If the culprit is not in custody when the offense with which he is charged is investigated, and he is decided to be guilty, then rewards for his assassination are offered, written in Chinese characters and publicly posted. It is with great difficulty that Chinese criminals are convicted in our courts. Officers are bribed to release them from custody, and Chinamen witnesses in court will commit perjury to get them clear, in order that they may be tried before their own tribunals. A Chinaman stands in utter fear of telling the truth in our courts, if it should tend to convict a countryman, for he knows that he is sure to lose his life if he does not aid in defeating the administration of justice to them before our tribunals. At the same time the Chinese will use our laws before their own tribunals, to prosecute innocent men, in addition to enforcing their own.

The Chinese occupy their own quarters in the city, where they live more after the manner of herding animals or swarming insects than intelligent human beings. Their houses are compact, one against the other, with very small rooms, all of which on the inside are of the dirtiest, smokiest color. Paint, whitewash, and scrub-brooms are unknown to the Chinese. Often small rooms not more than eight or ten feet square will be the abode of ten or twelve Chinamen, with bunks arranged as in barracks. There they will lie and smoke opium and gamble their hours of idleness away.

The Chinese are termed "Coolies" in popular Western phrase. That is a word used to designate all day-laborers of the East Indian and neighboring countries, where they unlade vessels, bear the palanquins of the wealthy, push and pull the clumsy two-wheeled carts, or carry such things as their employers desire in net-like bags, suspended from the two ends of a bamboo pole, resting on their shoulders. These Chinese coolies are rude in manner and noisy, but good-humored and fond of

CHINESE QUARTER, SAN FRANCISCO.

amusement. Numbers of them can be worked in very small places in ditching, shoveling, picking, blasting, working in sections in railroad cuts or in making roads, etc. They are not capable of doing as much work as Americans when put to the test; yet they generally accomplish as much or more than many Americans really like to do. Much the larger number of Chinese that are imported to this country are adult males. It is estimated that there are four thousand Chinese females in San Francisco, with a great many more scattered at various places throughout the West.

There has been petitioning and legislating in California for a long time in an effort to prevent the Chinese from coming there; but, strange to say, that is done mostly by a set of men who are foreigners by birth themselves. The more distinguished and thoughtful of our own countrymen say this: "The summary disturbance of our existing treaties with China is greatly inconvenient to the much wider and more prominent interests of the country." The Chinese question has been disturbing the minds of the Western people for a long time, and, doubtless, will continue so to do for some time to come. I think that John would have been much happier if he had never wandered away from the home of his idols.

But now let me speak a few words in general terms in behalf of the State of California. This State has been wonderfully prosperous since its admission into the Union, by reason of its great natural resources and its singularly energetic and enterprising population. It has probably more wealth *per capita* of its population than most other States of the Union, or, perhaps, countries of the world. It, no doubt, has also the materials of progress on a larger scale than has ever existed on any other similar area.

The two principal cities are San Francisco and Sacramento. The business of these two places consists chiefly in trading upon the wealth produced from the soil. The principal element of the future growth of the State will consist in the settlement of the lands by desirable occupants. The lands are naturally very rich and fertile; besides they are situated in an unrivaled climate. Southern California can boast of what but few, if any, other parts of our country can rightfully claim to possess, and that is a mean difference of temperature of 15.88. I do not know of a more healthy spot anywhere to reside in, and at the same time reap a large reward for industry. These lands have all to be irrigated. There are irrigating canals and ditches along and adjoining every ranch that is tilled.

They have been colonizing the State for a few years back, and an earnest interest has been taken in promoting the immigration of large numbers. In California the Federal, State, and County governments, the settlers upon lands, and the citizens of the commercial marts—all take a common interest in the promotion of and working for the welfare of individual and joint enterprises.

The Federal Government has several million acres of surveyed lands yet to sell in the State. The area of the State of California alone is one hundred and twenty million nine hundred and forty-seven thousand eight hundred and forty acres, of which thirty-four million acres have been surveyed by the officers of the Federal Government. Of the quantity surveyed, not more than twenty million acres have been disposed of, leaving as much as fourteen million acres of surveyed lands in the hands of the Federal Government. Over two-thirds of the State lands are unsurveyed.

The entire present population of the State is less than one million. The Federal Government has given three million two hundred thousand acres of the lands in the State to railroads, in order that the value of the whole may be improved by facilitating transportation. If a railroad company receives a grant of land for the purpose of bringing the whole within the reach of market, an irrigation company, whose object is to insure the crops of all those lands, certainly has an equal claim to aid, the more so when the canals which irrigate the lands also complete the means of transporting the crops.

I have tried to do justice to California and the good people of the State. I have traveled the State over, and, while doing so, I have met with a warm-hearted reception from all. May they ever live in enjoyment of all the bountiful blessings of peace and prosperity.

My visit here is ended. I shall now visit Oregon and see it, that I may be able to compare for my own satisfaction and that of the reader the different shades and experiences of life there.

CHAPTER VI.

OREGON AND WASHINGTON.

PORTLAND, Oregon, is six hundred and seventy-five miles, by water, from San Francisco. Oregon is like California in some respects; in others it differs from all the rest of the country along the Pacific coast. Portland is a thriving city, with, perhaps, thirteen thousand inhabitants. Along the coast warm breezes from off the ocean constantly blow inland. In Summer the atmosphere is perfectly delightful and healthy; in Winter it is colder, owing to the winds coming down from the Cascade Mountains on the east. Yet, it is not so cold as to freeze hard, except at a high altitude. Some of the valleys are very fertile, with a good depth of soil, covered with the finest grass and beautiful flowers, affording natural attractions of a richness seldom met with elsewhere.

There is splendid water and an abundance of fish in all the streams that are not of an alkaline or brackish character. The State can never have a dense population, for the valleys I have referred to above, are small and in many places settled thickly enough already. In the southern and south-eastern part of the State the valleys are not so good, and are often covered with vast beds of sand, alkali, and fields of lava. Much of this part of the State is almost a desert, with only here and there a small piece of fertile and watered ground upon which the squatter may settle. The greater portion of this part of the State is worthless and must ever remain so.

The Columbia River, which forms the boundary line between Washington Territory and the State of Oregon is one of the grandest streams in the North-west. This mighty river has cut its way through solid rock

RAPIDS OF THE UPPER COLUMBIA.

for nearly its whole length above the cascades. Here may be seen an instance of what Nature by her mysterious forces can accomplish. By the constant attrition of water, vast mountains of rock have been softened and worn away, leaving the harder portions of the rock standing in all kinds of fanciful and grotesque forms, like the ruins of some ancient castle. After passing the cascades one is soon enclosed in forests of beautiful timber, composed principally of large and thrifty trees of red-wood, pine and other varieties.

In many places along the Cascade range the mountains are barren and unproductive of either timber or other vegetation. Here are high walls of rock, sometimes perpendicular, at other times more sloping. Huge bowlders are piled up in confusion as high and even higher than the clouds. But, where the ranges are not too high and there is a sufficient quantity of soil and moisture, large trees cover the mountain sides, while there is such a dense thicket of underbrush, so filled with old logs and broken branches of trees, that there is no pleasure in making an exploration through these forests.

Hundreds of little squirrels may here be seen playing about at any time. Let a person or any other moving object be espied and they set to chattering with all their might. Sometimes five or six will be seen gathered together, viewing the same object. If the object of their curiosity ceases to move, they become more bold and will approach cautiously nearer and nearer, until they will sometimes climb upon and run over the person. As soon as they learn that there is no danger, they become very familiar, playful, and amusing. These little squirrels are found in all parts of the West, filling the woods with their constant and saucy chatter.

The lava beds of Oregon, the scene of the celebrated Modoc war a few years ago, form a very singular place. This has been at some time, ages ago, the seat or center of some large volcano. There the rock has been melted so that it would boil and run like water. The upheaval in places has been very great. The rock, in cooling off

VIEW IN THE MODOC COUNTRY.

after it had been melted and thrown out, has assumed something of a sponge-like appearance. There are holes, tunnels, caverns, caves, ridges, defiles, cañons—all running in perpendicular, horizontal and oblique directions. I was afraid to venture far into any of the openings in so much darkness, so I did not explore them to any distance.

This lava has been thrown up and is spread out over thousands and thousands of acres of land. In this region water is not at all abundant, and when obtained it is not good, having a soft, warm, brackish, disagreeable and unhealthy taste. In this part of the State the climate is hot in Summer, the hot winds and sun beating down on the pummice that covers the country, making the shade much preferable to the roads.

But, returning a little to the north again, we find some small valleys where vegetation is abundant. Cattle, horses, and sheep are found here in as good condition as anywhere, and of a finer quality than can be found in many of the other western States and Territories. No finer blooded animals can be bought at reasonable prices in the eastern States. Animals imported here from other parts of the country, after becoming acclimated, do well.

In the Willamette Valley all the way back from Portland, the climate is very remarkable. It is surprising to see here, so far in the North, such a temperature. Here they have but two seasons, Winter and Summer, each having its pleasant and rainy weather.

The grass is green in Oregon nearly the whole year. The valleys along the coast are very productive, both in quantity and quality. The yield of wheat on the

Pacific slope is good, as is generally known, and Oregon is no exception. All other grains are raised almost or quite to perfection. Small grains are perfectly at

VIEW ON THE OREGON COAST.

home in Oregon. I have seen farmers feeding peas to their horses and hogs, and the animals looked healthy and fat. It is claimed that this feed is as cheap as corn in the western States.

Fruit of all kinds is raised in the greatest of profusion, and is remarkable for its great size and excellent flavor. Although California fruit is justly in good reputation, Oregon apples are, nevertheless, exported to San Francisco, where they bring an advanced price on account of their excellence. Vegetables that come from here to the San Francisco market are held in high favor. Potatoes, especially, that are exported to the southern coast markets are prized highly, and find ready sale at an advanced price in preference to those of home production.

Washington Territory is very similar to Oregon in productiveness, though the yield is generally less per acre than that of Oregon. Even in Winter the ice never obstructs the passage of vessels along the coast. Boats and vessels are coming and leaving all the time.

Washington Territory possesses many gigantic trees of different varieties. Here lumber is sawed by millions of feet daily, and shipped to various parts of the world. Hundreds of men and teams are employed in cutting and moving these mammoth trees to the mills, where they are sawed into lumber and loaded on vessels that do nothing else but ply back and forth in the lumber traffic. In the mountains of the Territory the weather is cold—dreadful cold—and people perish every Winter.

There is an abundance of splendid fish in the Territory, and some game; but game is not so plentiful as it is on the east side of the mountains, or further south. There are still some Indians here, as in Oregon; but in both places they are disposed to be both sociable and peaceable. They live a very hard and uncomfortable sort of life, dressed either very poorly or not at all. They are too lazy either to hunt, fish, or farm. But little need be said of the Indians here, however, since I shall treat the whole subject fully in a later chapter.

The scenery of the whole north-western part of the United States is grand. There are gradually-ascending slopes for miles and miles, where the unbroken forest conceals the ground from view. Here and there, by a bold projection, the mountains lift themselves upward, sometimes to heights far above the timber line. In such cases there they stand enveloped in snow for nearly the whole year.

CHAPTER VII.

MEXICO.

I SPENT eleven months in Mexico. I found the Mexicans to be a truly democratic people, there being no distinction of caste among them. The rich and poor meet socially on the same footing, often sharing together the same sleeping apartment. However, in dry seasons, all classes seem to prefer to sleep in the open air.

The climate of Mexico is determined chiefly by elevation. On the coast it is hot; temperate on the slopes, and cold on the table lands and in the higher ranges of the Sierra Madre. Some of the valleys of Mexico are

BORDER MEXICANS.

so situated that their climate is one perpetual Spring. The coasts of Mexico produce all the plants indigenous to hot climates. The table lands produce the plants of the temperate zones, and the higher mountains those that grow farther north.

The Mexicans, though hospitable and often magnanimous, are, nevertheless, generally vindictive, cruel, and treacherous. Intellectually, they are an inferior race of people. The natives of Mexico are devoid of enterprise, and almost wholly neglect all public and private improvements. Mexico, as every one knows, is noted for its mining industries. They have good mines in several of their States. The States of Sonora, Sinaloa, Chihuahua, and Durango claiming the best, with the greatest yield of gold and silver. The Mexicans themselves have been mining in different localities of these States for long over a century. Some of their mines, properly worked, are probably capable of producing more than the world-renowned Comstock Lode, in Nevada.

But the manner in which the Mexican people work their mines is such that they would not be able to take out any great wealth in years of toil. Americans have often gone into Mexico to prospect and mine; but have as often been visited by the prowling bandits, who live in the mountains, and have either been killed or had to flee the country for their lives. All Mexicans are not bandits; but there are a great many outlaws in the mountains who make robbery and plunder their profession. There are still a few Americans interested there in mining; but they are compelled to pay well for the privilege.

One of the processes by which the Mexicans crush their rock, is to take a large rock and dress it off, first level and flat, then they crease the outer side by cutting and beveling. This rock is then placed on a solid and level foundation—and generally near some stream, so as to secure water power—after which another rock is made to exactly fit the one already in place, and so closely that with a motion of the upper rock the tailing is usually ground very fine, so that little will remain in a fifty-mesh sieve. Then, by following their tedious processes they obtain a small percentage of the royal metals which the rock contains. After this, the tailing is piled up in piles, and salted, one layer on top of another, where it is left to undergo a leaching process. While lying in this way it is occasionally stirred, and sometimes left for two or three years, when it is worked over again, and with more success than was at first obtained. But this is a very slow and tedious process, compared with the crushing and amalgamating of ores in California or Nevada.

Nine-tenths of the Mexican population live in adobe houses, built out of adobes and covered with heavily tiled roofs. From a distance, the cities and towns of Mexico have a beautiful and picturesque appearance. The buildings are low—very seldom is a *La Grande Casie* over one story in height—the walls are thick, heavy, and cumbersome, with usually grated windows. But as one enters the towns all beauty vanishes. Building after building is found to be all cracked, shaken up, neglected, and on the road to ruin, if not already in ruins. Even in the City of Mexico itself, one-seventh of the houses are uninhabited, and not fit to live in. Some of the stores, hotels, and houses of public resort are very fine, large, and commodious; but private residences are seldom more than one story high.

Many of their gardens and *campos* are deserted, and either going or gone to waste. They have been so long neglected that dense thickets of the orange and other trees occupy the ground. Some of their houses are

MEXICAN BORDER TOWN.

surrounded with flowers and shade trees as beautiful as grow in any clime.

A stranger traveling in Mexico would naturally be

deterred, by the very appearance of things, from asking for hospitality or a night's rest at most of these dwellings; but, among that small class of Mexicans who seem to take some little pride in keeping their premises neat and in good repair, I found solid hospitality and comfort. I found this class rather social and somewhat well informed. There is, in the end, but little enjoyment to be derived from a trip through Mexico, unless one is master of the language. There are very few Mexicans who can speak English, and those who can will seldom do so.

They are all very fond of their wine, or liquor (*Mescale*), oftentimes indulging more freely than they should. They are fond of amusements, and the more barbarous and cruel the entertainment may be, the better it is liked by both young and old. Horse-racing, bull-fighting, dog-fighting, sheep-fighting, chicken-fighting, and other kinds of cruelty are much sought after. Such scenes are attended and witnessed by thousands, with glee and mirth.

The Mexicans are a nation of gamblers. They engage freely in all the different games of chance or skill. Generally they do not bet heavily; but they continue the game, oftentimes, until they have lost the last cent.

They possess great powers of endurance. Even the inclemencies of the mountain rains and snows possess no terrors to the swarthy native. They are skilled in horse-back riding, often performing the most hazardous and reckless feats. In the saddle, with a lasso, they are perfectly at home, throwing the lariat with dexterity, and with such accuracy that they seldom miss the object of pursuit, whether out in the open country or confined in the corral.

The common domestic animals run wild in Mexico, and frequently become vicious. Great droves and herds of them are found in the foot hills, away from the villages and settlements. When any one or more of these animals is needed for use, the herd is surrounded and driven into some strong and convenient corral. The corral is a small piece of ground inclosed with a strong fence or barricade of small trees, usually cut in lengths to suit and placed on end in a ditch, somewhat after the manner of a stockade. After the animals are once confined inside of the corral, it is then a very easy task to throw the lariat over the heads of such as are needed. The rest of the animals are then allowed to return to their range, and they generally lose no time in going.

I might say here that this is the method of handling stock throughout the west beyond the Missouri River. Horses are known by various terms, such as mustangs, *broncos*, or *ciyuse*. Cattle in Mexico are known by the following terms: *souaves, toros, vacas*, and so on. Lassoing those wild, vicious animals, where so many are corralled together, is attended with danger. None but a daring, resolute, self-reliant man dare enter a corral full of wild Mexican stock for the purpose of making selections. After the lariat has been thrown and the animal is ensnared, an exciting scene takes place. The lassoed animal goes rearing, plunging, running, struggling, and snorting through the herd at a tremendous rate, dragging the would-be captor after it for a time, it may be, at a comparatively easy gait, and then again lifting him, by a jerk, several feet through the air. By this time the animals all become frightened, and around

MEXICAN BORDER INVASION.

and around the corral they go until assistance enough has arrived to hold the animal, or else the poor beast gives up from exhaustion.

If the animal be a horse, he is led out and a saddle securely fastened to his back. A bridle, that needs to be seen for it can not well be described, is also put upon him, when some *buckarier* advances with a spur on either foot, with a rowel as much as two inches across, and locks attached to the center pivot, making as much noise when he steps as a little boy with a parcel of bells. The horse is held, generally, until the rider is seated and ready. Then commences another ordeal, in which man and beast are generally both severely tried. The Mexican horse is small, but yet possesses great strength. He is slender limbed, well-muscled, and very active. They very seldom weigh one thousand pounds, unless crossed with eastern horses. They can be ridden or driven further than any eastern horse could go in the same time with the same treatment. They usually get no grain, and even when in use are picketed to a stake, driven firmly into the ground, in some convenient spot, near camp, producing the greatest amount of grass. These horses have often been ridden one hundred miles, and, in some of the Mexican incursions during the border troubles, one hundred and thirty miles in a single day.

Horses here and in southern California are very cheap; whole herds can, in some instances, be bought for from eight to twelve dollars per head. An extra good riding horse of native stock can be had for from twenty to thirty dollars.

Mexico is a beautiful country. The climate is delightful. The scenery is picturesque, and the forests are immense, extending along the sides and into the gorges and cañons of the old Sierra Madre range, and overlooking the beautiful valleys beneath. Some of the low lands in the valleys are covered for miles each way with lagoons. A lagoon is a very shallow lake, covering, sometimes, thousands of acres of land. In the northern part of the Republic there are large deserts, or plains, where there is no vegetation, neither can wood or water be procured.

Chihuahua is the State lying in the northern part of the the Republic just south of Arizona and New Mexico. This State is very thinly settled by Indians only, and they not civilized. The valleys are small, and, in some parts where there is water, very productive. The country shows unmistakable signs of having once contained large cities and towns, the ruins of which are now leveled to the ground. The valleys are of a sandy soil, which washes very easily. In this shifting, sandy soil there are found covered, or partially covered, ruins of old chimneys and walls, and vases and pottery of many varieties, mementoes of a bygone race. I have there found some specimens of earthenware in almost a perfect state. But, generally, time has told upon it and it is found in scales, not entirely separated, but still hanging together, showing that it has been ages in existence.

Near the head of the Rio San Miguel, in Chihuahua State, there is what is called the Casas Grandes ruins, that, no doubt, have been standing for hundreds and hundreds of years, but which to-day can be examined as easily as if built but yesterday. Some of the buildings are still partly standing, while others have nothing left to mark the spot they once occupied, except a rough pile of earth and rock. At this place I have found earthen pots with the ornamental figures upon them as perfect apparently as when they were first made. The vessels, however, showed great age and rough usage. I, with others, have dug into several of these heaps of ruins to see if we could unearth anything. We found nothing different from what was to be found on the surface. We found abundant proof, however, that at some time, at a very early day, there had been a city there over a mile square in extent. There is evidence of some magnificent buildings.

The inhabitants of these ancient cities must have been of a race far superior to those found there to-day. Many large, polished blocks of stone are found. Portions of whitened walls are still standing in perfect shape. Earthen-ware vessels, large enough to hold five gallons have been discovered. Hundreds of flint arrow heads are found. The parts of walls still standing have been built of stone. Where the walls have been protected from the storms and sun, they show such neatness of finish and workmanship as shows the painstaking efforts of highly-skilled workmen. There are many places in Mexico, where ruins similar to these are discovered. Northward we find traces of ancient cities. In Arizona there are innumerable remains of villages, towns, and cities that have long since crumbled away.

In the cañons in the northern part of the Territory, and in places on the Rio de La Mancas, in Arizona, and on the Piorere, and in the country of the Rio Virgin in Utah, ancient dwellings are found high up in the cliffs. On the Rio Virgin and Rio de La Mancas these dwellings are deserted, and have been for a long time. In Arizona the Moqui (pronounced *Mo-kee*) Indians inhabit some of the caves and rocky houses of the ancient cliff-dwellers. I found in and around the ruins of Chihuahua pottery of the same material, character, manufacture and flowering as is found in these cliff villages. It would seem, therefore, that these may have been one and the same race of people. Some have thought that the pre-historic races of Mexico and Arizona were two distinct races of civilized beings. My idea is that they be-

ARIZONA SAND PLAINS.

longed to one and the same race. The fragments and ruins are all similar, with only this difference: at the ruins of the Casas Grandes I found remains of polished walls in a few places. These I saw nowhere else.

The Moqui Indians live in villages or houses, some of them five, six, and seven stories high. These structures are built from sand, rock and mud. The lower story has a strong wall, in some places eight feet in thickness. The roof of the first story forms the floor of the next, which is entered by a ladder from the outside, and, when necessary, the ladder is pulled up inside. The inside walls are whitewashed, and, though their houses on the inside look rather strange, yet they are neat and tidy.

Arizona is a dry, barren country, with little water and less vegetation, unless it be the prickly pear, which covers the whole face of the earth. No soil but sand, which lies in one broad expanse of heat and sultriness. Consequently the Moqui Indians are not farmers and producers from the soil to the extent that some writers have represented. They have in places little gardens, perhaps two rods square. Their houses are away up in the cliffs, like sparrow nests. In some places they are as much as eight hundred feet above the level of the valley beneath, and they can only reach them by the aid of ropes made generally from raw-hide. These Indians are fed, clothed, and supported by the Government through its agents.

It is supposed by many that they belong to the ancient New Mexican race, called "town-builders" or "cliff-dwellers," who first lived in cities on the plateaus, and, as they became less numerous from war and disease, removed to the cliffs, so as to be the better prepared to resist and take advantages in attacks that were from time to time made upon them by other savage tribes.

There is a legend to the effect that they are descendants of the Scotch. For myself, I am better prepared to believe the legend than to think they descend direct from the Indian, Spanish, or any of the northern tribes. The language spoken is different from that spoken by any of the other Indian tribes in the West. Many of their words have that peculiarity of accent so noticeable among the *broad*-speaking Scotch people.

The Moquis are highly sociable in their rude way, and show ready hospitality to the stranger. Among themselves they are most wantonly cruel. They are very superstitious in their belief, and worship a fire-god. If one is evil disposed, and steals, murders, or commits an offense which they consider of a very serious nature, he is burned in a furnace. They are very ignorant, yet they seem to have sensitive feelings. They wear woolen clothes, partly of their own make and partly such as the agents issue. They are lovers of the chase, and continually at war with other tribes. I traveled through that part of the country, helping to make a government survey.

In the next chapter I will give a somewhat extended account of this little known part of our country.

CHAPTER VIII.

ARIZONA.

WE found Arizona the worst country we ever saw; heat oppressive, sand ankle-deep, and no timber to be had to build fires for cooking, except in some places small quantities of "grease wood," which is a little thorny bush that, in Arizona, only grows about ten or twelve inches in height and not to exceed one inch in thickness. We had to carry our water with us, often carrying enough to last us, if used sparingly, for two days.

I believe Arizona has some good gold and silver-bearing mines; but very little prospecting has been done there. Traveling through the Territory has a few delightful features, but many more of a disagreeable character. On the whole, when the prospector once gets there, he is so harrassed by Indians, a lack of provisions, water, wood, and other things, that his next move is to retrace his steps, or to get away in some other direction as soon as possible.

There have been some great excitements gotten up in order to induce people to go to Arizona. Great stories of rich mines of gold and silver have been published. It is said that a Mr. Janin even went so far as to buy up a large quantity of diamonds in London and induced people to go to Arizona by representing that he had discovered vast diamond fields there, from which he had obtained the diamonds which he exhibited. He stated that rubies, emeralds, opals, garnets, sapphires, and diamonds were there in abundance and that, if he could get a good number of men to go there, millions of wealth were in store for them. He sent specimens to the Savage Mining Company to be tested, who pronounced them genuine. Others were sent to lapidaries in New York City for testing. The decision was, of course, every time satisfactory, since the gems submitted were all really genuine. This, naturally, soon caused a terrible excitement throughout the mining communities of the West. Hundreds went rushing into Arizona from all directions, only to find, when too late, that they had been disastrously hoaxed. A great many perished on the road out for want of supplies. The remainder soon left, for there was nothing for such a vast crowd to subsist upon.

Perhaps miners will some time learn to take these great excitements for what they are worth, and remain where they are. I never was carried away by one yet, without returning poorer than when I started. And so, in a large majority of cases it is with the rest of them.

A man, to prospect properly anywhere, must lay in a full supply of blankets, provisions, a prospecting outfit of tools, and utensils necessary for cooking. When he adds to these his gun and ammunition, he has much more of a load than he can carry. He is, then, compelled to procure a pack-horse or two, or not to go at all. Mexican *burros* are plenty and cheap. Good ones can be bought for from fifteen to twenty-five dollars, while inferior ones can be had for the taking away. These *burros* are small, sorry-looking animals, with ears nearly as long as their legs, and heads as large as their bodies. The foot is like a mule's, only very small, not much larger than a trade dollar. When the *burro* walks, you must be near him to be sure that he moves.

These animals will carry a load weighing from one hundred and forty to three hundred pounds. They carry these loads across the mountains, over trails and through places where it is impossible to use conveyances of any other kind. There are saddles made on purpose for packing. These are formed of four short square sticks, two in front crossed, and two behind in the same way. Then there is a board the length of the saddle on either side, and on the inside of the sticks, to keep them from hurting the *burro's* back. This pack-saddle is fastened on a horse in the same way that any other saddle, by "sinching" or girthing. A rope is then attached to the front cross-stake of the saddle, brought over and allowed to remain across the saddle double.

Now we are ready to begin packing. One man generally works on either side. The first two bundles are as near the same size as we can make them. One of these is placed on each side of the saddle, and the rope on the saddle is taken and tied over both, to stay them until the load is made up. We now have plenty of room to pile on the remainder, consisting of our bed, flour, meat, sugar, coffee, beans, fish, cooking outfit—

consisting of a bake oven, frying pan, and coffee pot—
and our prospecting outfit, consisting of a sledge, pick,
shovel, gold pan, etc. By the time our *burro* is packed
he has a rather heavy weight on his back. A canvas
cover is then thrown over the whole load, and then
everything is lashed on with a long rope, kept for the
purpose, solid and tight. The animal might roll down
a mountain for a half mile without losing a single
item. A train of packed *burros* contains about twenty,
and is usually run by two men, called packers. A
prospector, however, seldom uses
more than two *burros*, and gen-
enerally rides a mustang, or walks.
Though the *burros* are good all-day
animals, they do not travel far.

A TRAIN OF BURROS.

Prospecting in Arizona is attended with so much danger from
Indians that the country has been
explored but little. One may
travel there day after day without
meeting any one except Indians
and half-breeds, and these not always as friendly as
they might be.

Prospecting, besides being very laborious work, is
very injurious to the health. The prospector goes climbing up the sides of mountains, winding around through
cañons, traveling over the *macas*, through sand, and
over burning rocks, sometimes holding on to bushes, or
clinging vines, and again catching hold of rocks, pulling up precipices—all for the pleasure of finding hidden

wealth. The unexplored mining ranges are in such rough, broken-up belts of the mountains that it is impossible to travel through on horseback where the prospector wants to go. Consequently they get as close as they can with their horses and pack-animals, and then leave them picketed to stakes on the best grass, to remain there until the neighboring country has been prospected on foot.

It has often happened in the southwestern States, that the Indians have been watching every movement of the prospecting party, and, as soon as they leave camp, down they come and

PERILS OF PROSPECTING.

take their horses and everything about camp, leaving the miners to hunt for meat and to foot it out of the country; that is, providing they are spared to enjoy that privilege, which is not by any means always the case.

Arizona has some mines worked, no doubt, centuries ago. There are tunnels that have been run and are now nearly full of loose and decomposing rocks and earth that have fallen in; at other places there is every indication of vast expenditures of labor having been made, in ditching and in scraping off the bed-rock where they have found it. There are shafts that have been sunk on the bars until they have been forced to abandon them. Hundreds of these old mines, showing evidences of having been worked long ago, can be found throughout the Territory. No one of the present day can know with what success these ancient miners prosecuted the work.

As every one knows, Arizona Territory is inhabited chiefly by the lower classes of Mexicans and an Indian population. Every day in the week is marked by similar scenes and occupations. I dare say one-half of the people do not know when Sunday comes, and the other half do not care. In fact, if Sunday is observed at all it is by the special devotion of that day to the gambling table and horse-racing.

Their villages are generally lined on each side by a row of gambling dens and miserable billiard and drinking hells. Passing the open doorway of one of these places, you can hear the voice of some one calling out something at regular intervals, and can see a deeply interested crowd standing or sitting in the interior. This proves it to be a gambling house. Now just step inside. The game may be keno. (They play many different kinds of games.) If so, the caller stands at a small table facing the open doorway, and has in his hands a hollow tin cylinder containing dice. These dice bear figures representing different animals and vegetables, counterparts of which are supposed to be on the cards in the hands of the players. A few vigorous shakes of the cylinder and the game and sing-song commences. So intent are the players in listening to the words falling from the caller's lips, and in watching the cards lying before them, that the entrance of a stranger into the room is unnoticed, and consequently attracts no attention. A crowd of Spanish or Mexican men, women and children fills the room. All are intent on the one object. Here they spend the last cent they have.

CIVILIZATION IN ARIZONA.

The few Americans and people of other nationalities who live in the Territory are as bad as the others. As far as I could see and judge, gambling is the leading topic of conversation, and the foremost thought of the mind. .Here you see men make themselves, many of them, so degraded that they leave all enjoyment of that which is right, reasonable, and just, and seemingly are contented only when around these places of resort. However, there is no other resort here unless it be to view Nature in solitude.

Let us go out and proceed a little further up or down the street. Here we encounter Indians congregated before the very corner saloon where they have undoubtedly obtained the liquor that has intoxicated them. With disheveled hair, foaming mouths, and disordered and dilapidated garments, they present a very disgusting and pitiable sight, while their discordant voices, joining in some Indian song, grate harshly upon the ear. Similar sounds come forth from the open doors and windows of the adjoining houses, indicating the presence of others in a like condition. In another portion of

AN ARIZONA SCRIMMAGE.

the town, in front of some crumbling adobes, we see a number of game cocks picketed at regular intervals apart. By and by these will afford amusement to their owners and the spectators by being pitted one against the other. They also provide a means by which the insatiable desire to gamble, which seems to have taken such firm hold of the native western people, may be gratified. It seems to be almost a mania with the most of them to take sides by betting in all games or trials of chance.

Perchance a hand to hand fight closes the day's orgies. I look upon these facts, which portray in the average citizen of Arizona so much of worthlessness, ignorance, and vanity, and speculate upon the probability of his reformation with a feeling that any rational person might experience if gazing upon a greased elephant which he had been commanded to swallow! There is no hope. Civilization can do nothing with a people so ignorant and self-degraded; so lawless and so vain.

CHAPTER IX.

NAVAJOES.

IN 1874, twelve of us started on horseback from Fort Defiance, in the western part of New Mexico, near the eastern line of Arizona, to go to the junction of Green and Grand Rivers, in Utah, to a place known as the Old Mormon Fort, of which I will speak more fully after we have reached it. Our intention was to travel across the country of the Pueblos and Navajoes, since by that route it was some six hundred miles nearer than it would be to go around.

We had an Indian trail nearly all the way. I carried a compass with me all the time, and had been with a surveying corps, establishing Government boundaries, for three years. I had, also, a good knowledge of the mountains, and felt confident that I could pilot a company of men through the Territory without the least danger of getting lost, if not molested or interfered with by the Indians, who are as thick in that country as grasshoppers in Kansas. It being so much nearer across, no one belonging to the party would hear of any other route being taken, and all insisted that I should be the leader of the party.

We expected to be able to make the trip across in twenty days. We procured riding and pack animals, and laid in a twenty days' supply of provisions. We took no more than this, since we had no doubt but that we could procure provisions in Utah as cheap as in New Mexico, and cheaper than in Arizona. We did not want to be encumbered with so many pack ani-

SCENE IN THE SIERRA DEL CARISO RANGE.

mals and so much stuff. We had bedding and every thing necessary for camping out comfortably. We carried, also, good rifles, revolvers, and plenty of ammunition to use on our way, if occasion should require it.

The first day we traveled through sand and some alkali. The next day traveling was a little better; we got on higher ground, and could move along without being wearied to death with the alkali and sand. When we came to the Sierra del Cariso we traveled through portions of the range of great natural beauty and grandeur. The mighty mountain crags lifted their jagged crests to dizzy heights toward the deep blue of the distant heaven. In many places their summits were lost to view in the midst of masses of fleecy clouds that cling around their snow-clad slopes, while midway up the sides of some of these mighty mountain peaks were stunted pines of a green and verdant hue peeping from out of the midst of the eternal snows around them. A little lower on the slopes is an occasional tract of pines or firs, often acres in extent, with the trees all dead—some standing, others leaning ready to topple over with the slightest push, and a great portion lying in confusion, just as they had been prostrated by the fires from Indian encampments, or the winds had thrown them.

The valleys lying between the hills were here covered with a peculiar grass, such as is seen no where else in the Territory, in a dead and dried-up state. The noisy rush of the swollen mountain streams (for there had been recent rains) as they went rushing down their meandering courses through the deep cañons, the far away mountains veiled in the hazy enchantment of distance, the charming little mountain parks, breaking in upon the view here and there, threaded by pure rivulets, sparkling with trout, and shut in by arrow-like quaking asps, balsams, and firs, altogether made a scene which awakened the liveliest emotions within us, which found vent in animated conversation and song. Yet, on the other hand, the grand sublimity that enveloped the higher peaks as they stood in the majesty of primeval beauty, snow-crowned and half hidden in enfolding clouds, often hushed us to silence.

It had been stormy weather, as we could see before we ascended the mountains, and, as we approached the summit, we knew there was yet more in wait for us, for, as night drew near, it grew darker and more dreary. We selected as our camping place a cluster of trees with a small strip of grass near by. This furnished feed for our mustangs, while the chaparrals afforded some protection and shelter from the wind; but not much from the rain. We made our horses fast to stakes driven into the ground. We protected our packs from the rain, that was by this time falling in torrents out of the darkness above us, by piling all up in one large heap, and covering this up with canvas. We had no tents, and there were no houses nearer than those we had left some two hundred miles behind. No cooking could be done, for we could not build a fire. Everything was wet, green, and soaked through.

After several unsuccessful attempts had been made by different ones to light a fire, and all the paper and kindling material that we carried had been consumed to no purpose, and a good share of our matches had been wasted, we concluded to do without fire. We made a very light supper of crackers and raw meats. We made preparations to camp for the night by cutting some of the largest chaparrals, and placing two on end in the ground opposite each other, allowing the upper ends to stand up four or five feet high, with a ridge pole resting on them. The two posts were placed just far enough apart to allow a double blanket to be stretched over the ridge pole, thus forming a tent and making splendid shelter for the night, where four persons could sleep very comfortably.

The storm lasted all night, and until ten o'clock the next day. We then built a large fire, and dried our clothing and blankets, and, at the same time, prepared something to eat, for we had eaten but very little since the morning before, and we were all feeling hungry, and none the better for the poor rest of the night. After breakfast we cleaned and dried our guns and revolvers; then saddled our animals, and packed up. Proceeding on in the afternoon, we found every gorge in the mountain full of water, that went roaring and pitching down its sides, washing before it everything that was loose enough to be moved. Whole trees could be seen floundering and bouncing and crashing along over precipices and around the rocks, turning sharp angles, swept on by the mighty torrent to the valleys below.

We pushed forward without any road or trail to guide us, the rain having completely obliterated it. We encountered streams and bodies of water continually during the afternoon, a few of which we could leap over, but most of which we were compelled to ford. About four o'clock we struck a trail bearing in the direction we wanted to go. We followed it the remainder of the evening, until we came to a splendid spring of water, bubbling out of the rocks. There was grass near by, so we camped for the night. But we could find no wood. We gathered old moss and such stuff as wild animals gather together for beds in the neighborhood of ledges of rocks. We managed to make fire enough to boil our coffee and fry our meat, which two articles soon disappeared.

FOLLOWING A MOUNTAIN TRAIL.

The next day we followed the mountain trail, which still led in the direction we were going. It was barely wide enough for a horse to travel on. It went winding around cliffs, often on the very brink of precipices hundreds of feet deep. Should a horse fall, he would be dashed to pieces on the rocks beneath. Not relishing the idea of such a death, the most of us led our horses along the most difficult, narrow passes.

That night we camped in a large forest. From every side all manner of strange noises could be heard. The screaming of panthers and wild cats, the screeching of birds, and the croaking of innumerable frogs, made up a concert that was novel and lively, if not agreeable. One who has never spent a night in a mountain forest can form no just conception of the strange and unearthly noises which make the hours of darkness hideous. Oftentimes, while one is asleep, some wild animal will come up and smell around your couch and, perhaps, give some terrifying howl that will cause you almost instinctively to clutch your gun and bound from your bed. Looking around you behold the glaring eyes of some wild beast fixed upon and watching you. It may be a panther, mountain lion, grizzly bear, Mexican jaguar, American tiger, wolf, or some other of the hundreds of wild beasts that inhabit those wildernesses. You may hear him snuff the air and walk away, for the chances are it will be so dark that you can not shoot. These wild animals, however, seldom attack a man, unless goaded by hunger or wounds.

The next morning when we got up all were complaining of a sleepless night, and some of sore limbs and aching heads. After everything was ready for the march, we descended to the valley below, thinking to travel up the valley, as we would have easier traveling and, at the same time, be out where we could see what was going on. This last object was quite desirable, for we were now in an Indian country. The pony and mocassin tracks of the Navajoes could be plainly seen on all sides. We kept our rifles constantly in front of us, ready for instant use. The day was passed, however, without seeing an Indian, though we were constantly on the alert, for we knew that the Indians were numerous all through this section of country.

We halted before sundown, ate supper, and smoked awhile. Some of the boys were just saddling up to proceed onward, I was taking a little stroll from camp and smoking along at my leisure, when suddenly and, after all, unexpectedly, I beheld a traveler, clad in buckskin, hastily making his way toward us. He carried a Henry rifle in front of him, and a pair of huge pistols and a hunting knife in his belt. His belt was well filled with cartridges. He seemed to be peering around, and watching every moving object, and listening keenly to every sound; but seemingly intent, nevertheless, on coming to us. After he came near enough, I could see that he was a young man, thirty-four or five years of age; and, upon forming his acquaintance, I found him to be a light-hearted and jovial fellow. He was, however, one of those sons of Kentucky, whose early education had been sadly neglected, for he could not read nor even write his name. He was gifted with a good share of caution, and was firm as a grizzly—two qualities which we much needed afterwards as you will learn, for Bennett and I remained chums for the next eighteen months. He had carried the United States mail for over a year through Arizona, and was at this time off duty.

After the usual salutations were passed and our visitor had sat down to a supper one of our boys had prepared for him, the general conversation in reference to business and matters generally,—"What are you doing, and where are you going?" came and went at random, as is usual on such occasions. But, to cut the story short, Bennett was persuaded into the notion of going with our party into Utah Territory He had been out at one of the agencies, and was then on his way to California District, in Arizona. He had seen us as he was crossing one of the divides, and had come down to see who we were. He said the Indians were watching us as he supposed, or else we would have seen plenty of them before we got to the heart of their country, as he had seen numbers of them that day, but none in speaking distance. After supper we again made ready, and were soon on our way to find a place to camp for the night. During the evening I gave Bennett to understand what our business was— that we were a company of prospectors, going to the Elk Mountains, at the junction of Green and Grand Rivers, to hunt for some of the hidden wealth that was supposed to lie there in chunks as large as hogsheads. Bennett went with us until we changed our minds and concluded not to go through. About nine o'clock we camped for the night, all lying down to sleep except the man on guard. We had no fire, as that would be seen a long distance, and would reveal our whereabouts.

The next morning we had brought our horses close to camp, and were just ready to pack and saddle, when one of the men on the lookout, sung out, "Injuns! Injuns!" Immediately the camp was in the midst of a terrible excitement, and though everything was lying near at hand, yet some of the men could not see their guns. There were two in the party who could find nothing they wanted, or that belonged to them. I gave these two and another one orders to attend to the horses. One of them grabbed an ax and went to driving the picket pins down tight, so as not to let our horses be stampeded and get away from us. Up to this time none of us except the sentinel had seen the Indians. I gave orders, that if we had to fight we should scatter out, so as to protect the horses, and at the same time, for each one to look out and secure safety for himself. I then took my gun and ran up on a little eminence, a short distance from camp, so I could get a better view, and ascertain about how many there were of the Indians; and whether we seemed to be the object of their attention, or not.

Having gained the eminence, I could see twenty-seven Indians, not more than one quarter of a mile away, coming down upon us with their horses on a full run. They were painted up in the most warlike manner. I had scarcely gained the eminence before I was observed. They had been coming in single file; but now they commenced to quicken their speed still more, and to scatter over more ground, so as not to expose so many to the same range. As soon as I got sight of them I knew we would have to fight, or fare worse. I looked around for some place where I could run for safety. I saw the boys going it in all directions, hunting for the best holes to creep into. I noticed a

ATTACKED BY NAVAJO INDIANS.

rock, as I supposed it to be, between where I was and the horses, a little to the right of the direction from which the Indians were coming. I broke for that; but was terribly disappointed when I got to it, for it was nothing but a sand heap the ants had piled up. But I had no time to run further. The Indians had already gained the eminence, and were coming down on us as fast as their horses could carry them, and making a more fearful noise with their yells than ten times that many coyotes possible could make. I had run a considerable distance and their horses had gained on me until they were not over one hundred yards away.

The boys had all scattered, so that none of them could be seen except the three who were holding the horses. The others had gone, as I said, every fellow for himself, and not a shot had been fired until I reached my ants' nest, when, as I threw myself behind it, a whole volley of bullets went singing over my head and into the sand above me. The Indians then made a break to capture or stampede the horses. Up to this time I had heard but two shots fired by our side. But as soon as they made for the horses then they were brought fairly into view, and a stream of leaden bullets was poured into their midst from all sides. Horses and riders went careening and falling together. They could stand it no longer than about ten minutes, when they started on a retreat. They almost ran over me, when retreating. One of them certainly would have done so had he not been killed on his way.

They lost ten of their warriors and six horses. One of our men who was holding the horses was killed, and another shot through the ear. This, together with the general frightfulness of the situation was enough to make a man feel scared. The Indians seldom leave their dead upon the field. But we got six of these, and only four were carried off. The reason the dead bodies are carried off the field, is because the Indians generally tie themselves to the saddle by a strap that comes over the thighs and holds them on tight, enabling them to lean themselves from either side of a horse, and pick up an object from the ground, the horse being at the same time on a dead run. These ponies are accustomed to running together, and will keep together, rider or no rider, if let alone. So that if an Indian is killed his pony will take him to camp, there to meet a burial after the customs of their tribe.

We buried our dead comrade by wrapping him up in his blankets and placing him in the sand about three feet deep. We threw the bodies of the Indians into a shallow ditch and pushed some sand over them. This might be considered a little rough; but such is the custom of the country. This is far better, moreover, than the Indians do themselves, as I will show soon. The Indians retreated in the direction from which they came, none of us following them. It was not our intention to molest them, or to interfere in any way with their interests, if only permitted to travel through their country in peace.

We now packed up and moved on, as we wanted to get through as soon as we could, and not to give them a chance to murder our whole party. This, I remember, was as lovely a day as I ever saw; but yet we were depressed, and felt sad on account of our dead comrade. His name was Charles Willett; he was from Illinois—I do not know from what part of the State. He was twenty-seven or eight years of age, and a very fine young man; and was well liked by all of his comrades in the West. About noon, or a little after, we came to some splendid water and grass. Here we halted and let the mustangs rest and eat, and provided dinner for ourselves. After resting awhile we moved on to the mouth of the cañon where the mountain is traversed by the San Re Nado Pass.

We had traveled perhaps two miles up the cañon when the Indians again set upon us. They were behind rocks, on top of the bluffs, and, in fact, they were everywhere it was possible to hide. Not an Indian had we seen since morning—not even an Indian sign marked the way. The first warning was a volley of bullets coming from the bluffs, from every rock and hole to the right, to the left, behind, in front, and above us; every place was filled with the noise and alarm of the Indian rifles, and they so well concealed that not one was to be seen. We saw at once that we were lost; for in such a place there could be no salvation for us if we went any further. Some of our comrades had fallen at the first volley, and more were falling now. We beat a retreat as fast as we could. When we got out of reach of their guns we found that we had lost seven men and all of our pack animals, food, blankets—everything except such things as we had in our pockets.

There were only four of our original party left.

These, with Bennett, making five of us, were left to beat our retreat as best we could. We had been only seven days out, and eight of our comrades were

AN INDIAN AMBUSCADE.

already dead, and the rest of us in the greatest danger. There were Indians on all sides of us, whithersoever we might go. Only a few moments before we had felt very jolly and confident of getting through without further fighting. Now there was no hope; the best we could do was to beat a retreat, back the way we came, as best we might without provisions. The Indians followed us all that evening. We traveled all night, and all the next day and night. We halted long enough, at places where there was water and grass, to let our horses rest and feed awhile, for everything depended upon them.

We were of course getting hungry and tired ourselves; but the Indians were still in sight, pursuing us. Signals could be seen in all directions. We knew that they were following us up as fast as their jaded horses would permit. We could occasionally, from some of the high points we were passing over, see them in the distance coming toward us as fast as their ponies could be urged along.

For two nights and better than a day we had not tasted a morsel to eat. We knew of a small stream of water a little farther ahead, which we had crossed over on our way out, where we had seen some fish. We had not seen any game that day, or the day before, to kill; and the fish were our only hope of relief from several days more of hunger and suffering. We struck out for the stream, and fortune favored our efforts for once, for we encountered no Indians on our road, nor at the creek. We went to work with a saddle-blanket for a net, and were not long in catching more than we could eat of the nicest kind of small trout, from three to six inches in length. We wasted no time in cleaning them and roasting them on sticks before the fire, without salt or anything else, unless it was smoke, for seasoning. We thought them excellent; as good as we had ever eaten.

After resting a short time longer we moved on higher up the mountain. Here we found a small park. We picketed our horses and took the first rest we had been able to enjoy for some time. Our feet were all swollen, and we were tired and sore from riding so far and sitting so long in the saddle. Our horses looked wretched. They were worn out. Their feet were very sore and tender. Their limbs were all scratched, bruised, bleeding, and swollen, and they could scarcely walk. We took them to a little spring near by, and washed their backs and limbs all over with cold water, which we dipped from the stream in our hats. We then rubbed them dry, and tied them to stakes where they could be allowed to eat grass. They soon seemed much revived. We washed and bathed ourselves as best we could by taking turns, some keeping a lookout all the time lest the Indians might try to come on us unawares as before.

After all were done bathing, and we were feeling considerably refreshed, we went to work, and soon gathered a small quantity of dry, quaking asp limbs, and built a small fire, being very careful not to make enough smoke to be seen at any distance. We roasted on sticks the remainder of the fish which we had brought with us. We then took turns in guarding the horses through the night, while the rest would sleep. We did not get much sleep, however, for the night was cold, and we had no covering, except the small blankets used under the saddles. These were damp with the sweat of the horses and full of hair. We did not dare to build a fire, as the light would reveal our place of camping a long distance away, and show the Indians our exact locality, and none of us were desiring another fight. We were thankful that we were alive.

We formed a sad little group as we huddled around close together, telling one another how near we came to being left with our comrades in the San Re Nado Pass. The Indians would, no doubt, have a big pow-wow and war-dance over the scalps of our brave fellows. Such things may be read of, perhaps, without causing much, if any, emotion of feeling; but no pen can paint the picture; no tongue can tell of it; no idea can be conveyed to a person who has never been where the dreadful war-whoop sends terror to the strongest heart, and a shudder even to the very depths of the soul, of the feelings one has under such circumstances.

Even now I imagine I can see again my comrades as they conversed together around the camp-fire, or sung their merry songs, while traveling over the desolate wilds of the West. Again I see them in the fierce struggle for life or death with the red men, falling dead or mortally wounded, to be a sacrifice to the knife of the dusky warriors. They take no prisoners. No mercy is shown the white man that is unfortunate enough to fall into their hands in time of war.

Our sleep on this night was none of the soundest,

for, besides the cold, perhaps by the time we were commencing to doze, some wild animal would utter some fearful scream, striking new terror to our hearts. Such was the first night's rest we had taken for some time. At three o'clock we saddled our horses and started. It was well for us that we did so, for the Indians were on our trail as soon as it was light enough to see to follow it. But two hours of travel had given us a good start, and, when we had crossed a small valley and were on the last slope leading to the Rio Puerco, we could see the Indians, by looking through Bennett's glass, on the slope between us and the slope where we had camped.

We reached the Rio Puerco that evening, where we found a party of prospectors, who were returning to Prescott from an unprofitable expedition in search for rich mining ground. They gave us all we could eat and shared blankets with us, so that we got a more comfortable night's rest than we had enjoyed for some time.

Perhaps the reader would like to know the names of some of our comrades who were killed. I took down all their names and the places from which they came as far as I could remember of their having told me. As everything had fallen into the hands of the Indians in the San Re Nado Pass, I am unable to tell where they were all from. William Fleming, aged near forty, of Philadelphia; Chris. Olten, of Indiana; George Goodhall, of Indiana; D. P. Wheeler, of either Dayton or Springfield, Ohio; George Brady, of St. Louis; William Carlton, and one more, who went by the name of

"Arkansaw," because he had formerly been a resident of Arkansas. His name I never knew. The four who escaped with me were: A. Bennett, of Kentucky, still alive; George Bales, of Keokuk, Iowa, now living in Nevada; J. T. Taylor, now somewhere in California or Nevada, and John Middleton, now in Leadville, Colorado. From Prescott, Bennett and I went to Pioche, Nevada.

CHAPTER X.

THROUGH THE COLORADO CAÑONS.

IT was my fortune to spend three months in the mountains along the Colorado Cañon. The Grand Cañon extends from the mouth of the Little Colorado River down to the mouth of the Yampa. The Colorado River runs through cañons from the mouth of the Dirty Devil, in Utah, to the Rio Virgin, in Nevada. I am unable to say how far this is in miles; but I know that from the mouth of the Dirty Devil to the mouth of the Rio Virgin is twenty days' hard riding by the shortest trail you can go.

The main Colorado Cañon, including all its curves, is over one hundred miles in length, and the river runs through cañons for over four hundred miles. The Colorado is the mighty river of the West. The Green, Grand, Cottonwood, Convulsion, Little Colorado, San Juan, Uncompahgre, and a large number of other streams, all pour into it the water from the melting snows in the mountains, and form a mighty river.

I joined a company of forty-one young fellows (Mr. Bennett was one of the company), who started out from Nevada—most of the company from Pioche. The principal object of our expedition was to prospect the Buckskin Mountains. Most all kinds of stories were afloat in reference to this locality, among the rest, that

THE GRAND CAÑON OF THE COLORADO.

this was where an expedition from California under Col. Baker had gone and found such vast leads of rich deposits of gold. But the Indians had killed all the party except two, Baker himself being among the missing. The two that did escape did so merely by accidental circumstances.

One fine morning our company all met together at a point between the Dry Valley Mill and Bullion City, and started off to try the chances of newer fields in the Buckskin country. Some of us were mounted on good animals; others on hungry, lean looking mustangs and mules. With our traps and accoutrements, our pack and riding animals, we formed an ideal group of frontiersmen off for an expedition, or, a scout after Indians.

I had heard much of the place we desired to reach and of the kind of country we would have to travel through; but I afterwards found that I had gained my information from men who knew nothing about the matter. There are always a great many ready to tell you all about the Buckskin Mountains and the Grand Cañon of the Colorado. But nine out of ten of them never saw that portion of the country.

As for a road, there is none. The only way to go is to follow trails, sometimes of Indians, at other times of some wild animals; and sometimes you must leave the trails entirely and go across the mountains, which are so abrupt, barren, and desolate, that you wish greatly for the land of civilization once more, long before the day passes into night. After we arrived on the Muddy River, in Utah, we then changed our time of traveling from day to night, as we thought that plan would be the safest.

Sometimes we were in narrow valleys, at other times on top of mountain ranges, traveling across them or lengthwise as the case might be, always keeping to one course as nearly as we possibly could. In one place the top of the range was a vast sheet of lava. We traveled over it for two days without wood or water, for neither was to be found. After we had gone two days without water, and were almost perishing from thirst, Bennett, four others and myself started in search of water, taking all the canteens with us. We must have gone fifteen miles when we found a small supply in a hole in the rocks. There was no way of knowing how long it had been there. It was alive with little wigglers. We took a pocket-handkerchief and strained the water through it from one tin-cup into another, thus procuring enough to fill our canteens; but at the same time throwing a larger bulk from the handkerchief than we were putting into the canteens. I have tasted a great deal of bad water; but that supply was the worst I ever met with. When we arrived back at camp again, we found there had been a mutiny, and that fifteen of our party had gone off in another direction. They had taken, it was claimed, more than their share of the supplies, and some were growling and swearing about it. Others were in favor of following them up and reclaiming a portion of the supplies. Everything was suggested, but nothing was done.

As for Bennett and myself, we had made up our

minds to go to the Colorado Cañon at least, or to lose our scalps on the way. So I spoke to the men, telling them that none of us had ever been there; that we had talked the whole matter over before we left Pioche; and at that time we were all of one opinion. We were at the start well aware that we must stand together for the sake of our mutual protection, or else not go at all. I acknowledged that we were then in the worst country I had ever seen; but I had not known that it was so bad before I started. But I supposed that we were now over the worst of the road, and I thought it

THE SEARCH FOR WATER.

likely that we would soon arrive where there was plenty of water and game.

But some of them seemed very much down-hearted, depressed, and to be feeling very sore about something, I knew not what. They were growling and complaining, and one of them came to me, and said, if I would give him rations to last him on his way back, he would leave us. Then I got mad and told the party, that if there were any who felt timorous or afraid, or did not want to go, they were at perfect liberty to take provisions, and leave us in peace. But, if they would leave a proper share of the provisions for Bennett and four more of us, we were going through, if such a thing were possible. Some said they would see us out; others could not make up their minds as to what they wanted to do for a long time; but finally all came around and were willing to go on.

Everything went on all right until we had our animals saddled ready to start, when another mutiny broke out, which lasted for over an hour. I then gathered together from the supplies what was my own, and took care to take my full share. Bennett did likewise. Some still said they would see us through. "No," I said, "I do not wish any man or set of men to see me out of danger that I voluntarily run into. You all know that I did not raise this company. Hess and others were the leaders in raising the company, and now, if they want to throw the responsibility on a few who only volunteered to go, I for one will not travel with them. But I will go through alone, if no one wishes voluntarily to go with me." Bennett and I had plainly seen that they were endeavoring to throw the whole of the responsibility upon our shoulders, when we really had nothing to do with organizing the expedition at all, having merely volunteered to accompany it as members.

That evening eleven of us started on, leaving the balance to go where they pleased, so they did not travel with us. It was threatened before we left that we would be fired upon. But we had had our say, and at the time I fully expected that we would have a fuss, which would have been very bad for all of us. The other party outnumbered us, but were divided among themselves. But we were as determined as ever men were not to let them get the drop on us, and if a muss did break out, to put it through in the shortest possible way.

We got started off, however, without any one being hurt, and a merry little crowd we were. There was quite a difference between our little party of eleven, as we jogged along side by side, and the big, noisy, boisterous crowd that started out together at first. The flying moments passed unheeded by as we rode along, engaged in mutual exchange of thought and feeling. And we were just flattering ourselves over having gotten rid of the worst part of our crowd so easily, when five of those whom we had left behind overtook us. They reported that the others had gone back. But that they would go with us as long as a button remained to their coats.

That day we camped in a secluded spot at the foot of one of the peaks, where we found a little water for our horses, which did them a great deal of good, for they had been without water for three days.

I was on guard that morning, in the first watch. I concluded to go to the top of the peak and make some general observations of the country. Armed with my rifle, revolver, knife, and Bennett's spy-glass, I started to make a circuit of the mountain for some distance, so as to find some place to climb up. I had not gone more than a couple of hundred yards, scarcely out of sight of camp, when I heard a noise, as of a stone rolling down the mountain. I stopped, and looking in the direction of the noise I saw a small stone, as large as my fist, rolling down the slope. Looking up in the direction from which the rock had come, to ascertain what had started it, I beheld, not more than twenty yards to my right, and a little above me, a monstrous grizzly bear, in the act of raising himself in a sitting posture. I suppose that he took this attitude in order to see, think, and determine whether it was best to hold his position or make a retreat. The old fellow did not look so wonderfully savage, for he wore more of a smiling look about his eyes than that of the most ferocious of wild beasts. He sat perfectly upright, and not a muscle or a limb did he move. His forearms were drawn up upon his breast, and I could see his paws, with their tremendous claws drooping in front. I could see but little to encourage me in my suddenly perilous situation, when I came to fully appreciate my danger. He sat there in front of me looking entirely calm and collected, free from all show of excitement,

CORNERED BY GRIZZLIES.

and as firm as a rock. I well knew it would need only one blow of his paw to knock me into eternity; for the strength of the grizzly is greater than that of any other animal of similar size in existence. He is king of the brute kingdom. The hunting of the grizzly bear averages more disasters than the hunting of any other animal. Hunting some of the smaller and more inoffensive animals is followed with enjoyment, and affords recreation and amusement to thousands, who are, in pursuing these animals, in no danger of being killed, crippled, or maimed for life. But there are very few who desire to hunt for the grizzly bear, and though often seen by travelers and scouts when passing through the hills, canons, and forests of the Rocky Mountains, he is generally left to pursue his journey in peace.

Oftentimes the scout runs up against one as I did this one, and has no chance to retreat, for a grizzly can out-run any man. On a mountain side they can out-run a horse. A horse might out-run a grizzly in the valley, or in rolling country; but *there* there is no grizzly. He is an inhabitant of rougher regions. In the rough country of California there are hundreds of them. They subsist principally on acorns, berries, and toolie roots, of which they are very fond. These toolies grow around lakes, ponds, marshes, and lagoons, sometimes higher than a man's head, with roots in the muck and soil similar in looks, except smaller and thicker, to the swamp dock of the eastern ponds. Here the grizzly bear and wild hog feed and keep themselves fat. The bear stays in the mountains all day, and comes down to feed at night. After feeding awhile on roots the grizzly generally goes out to try to finish his feast with a young colt, or a calf, pigs, geese, or anything he can kill and carry away. I have never known them to molest grown cattle or horses.

Often you will see them chained to posts as pets. These have generally been caught while young. I have seen a great many pet grizzlies; but I never saw but few that I could handle. They are most always cross to strangers. You cannot strike one, for he will sit upright, and either take your stick away from you or knock it out of your hand. When you make your pass at him he will not show the least fear, but rather the more determination to thwart your every move. If you shoot at and only wound him, then the grizzly is a most dangerous animal. At such a time the most perfect nerve is required. He will then charge on his nearest foe, mad with pain, and with more than ordinary strength. I have seen large, rough-barked trees where they had torn the bark away, clean into the wood, from a space ten inches square at one single stroke of the paw, and this, too, in their last dying struggles. Even after the animal is fatally wounded he often has strength enough to make an attack. Then all depends upon courage and coolness, and upon rapid and careful shooting. The great danger, the renown incident to the capture of so ferocious, and, when wounded, so blood-thirsty a beast, the nerve required, all combine to lend an extraordinary zest to hunting or attacking the grizzly bear. When a tender-foot first comes West he yearns to encounter a grizzly. And generally when he does get sight of one his courage fails him, and Mr. Bruin is allowed to depart in peace.

When, on this morning, I beheld this grizzly so near at hand, sitting upon his haunches and looking at me, I, in a moment, took in the dreadful and dangerous character of the predicament I was placed in. I was sure to be overtaken if I should run. My only safety, that I could see, was in my rifle. Then I wondered if I was cool enough to take a steady aim. I thought I was; but, at the same time, I knew if I failed there would not be time enough for me to load and shoot my rifle the second time, since he was above me and would immediately charge down upon me at such a rate that I would no doubt get very nervous, and even did I again shoot, it would be with a poor aim, and I would only enrage him the more, and no doubt be torn to pieces by his powerful claws, before assistance could arrive from camp. I looked at him but a moment, and in that moment a profound sense of my great danger came over me. But I hastily put my fears aside, and, dropping the glass lightly at my feet, I brought my rifle down and fired. I used an ounce explosive ball. My shot was well aimed, and struck him under the fore leg. As he sat a little quartering to me, the ball ranged towards his back-bone, completely smashing it. When the gun cracked I was certain my ball had taken mortal effect. But to make assurance doubly sure, I gave him another shot. Then I heard the boys coming from camp, on double-quick, as I could tell by the way the stones and gravel were thundering down the mountain side. But, by the time they got to me, the fun was over, and Mr. Bruin was my meat. He was very large. We estimated that he would weigh nearly or quite eight hundred pounds.

After the usual complimentary remarks of the occasion had been passed, we left our king of the forest, the boys to return to camp, and I to proceed to the summit of the peak. After I had gained the summit, which was through no little exertion, it being very difficult and hard to climb, I could see a great distance on all sides of me. The bright sun was shining on the many different colored peaks. The calm solitude of the place caused strange feelings, indeed, in my mind. I sat on that peak for six long hours, viewing the many different and curious formations of nature. I noted the many different colors of the rocks, as the sun would reflect upon their surface. I could see wild animals of various kinds in the distance, such as coyotes, deer in herds, and others which I thought were antelopes. And once I saw a band of Indians; they were a long distance off; but I could make out that they were not hunting, but traveling. Perhaps they were going to new hunting and fishing grounds. I could see in what direction they were going, and that was all-important to me. I could not tell how many there were; I could see a large party.

I was not sorry when I was relieved from the guard, for the warm sunshine had made me sleepy. I did not speak to any one of having seen the Indians, for I considered that they would be none the better off for knowing it; and there was no need to alarm the lads any more than was necessary.

I lay down as soon as I arrived at camp, and was quickly lost in sleep—dreaming of the girl in a far-off, friendly land; or the one whom I had never trusted enough in my own native home. At such times the light of the world, for the dreamer, dies out, and only disappointments crown his efforts until at last he loses all hope. Alone in a strange place, without one of his kindred near to know his wants, or to learn even one of the many different conjectures that pass through the brain. But, hold on here! I find I am leaving my subject entirely. Should I keep on in this strain some kind-hearted people will think I am in love, or in as bad a condition as if I were.

Well, when I awoke, the sunlight had become as dim as twilight, struggling in only here and there, through the branches of the small trees. When we had finished supper, which was then ready, and were sitting around in a circle, lounging against the trunks of the quaking asps, which grew in great numbers there, we then gave the subject of our journey a grave consideration. Each held between his lips a wooden pipe. The smoke that issued from them went rising above our heads, forming many-shaped curls to be lost sight of in the low boughs above. Our plans had been formed, and the swift darkness of night was falling around us; already the gulches, hollows, and ravines were shrouded in impenetrable gloom, and the black shadows were creeping up the mountain sides when we emerged from our place of repose, to saddle and pack, and jog along.

I was riding in the lead, with no trail, no road, nothing that we could see to follow. So we took a star to guide us and on we went, over gulches and gullies, up mountains and down again, to then climb others, perhaps worse than those already passed over. We had traveled nearly all night in this way, when, about three o'clock in the morning, we came to a place, that baffled us for a long time. It was one of those places, which are to be found in many parts of the West, where the water has left standing perpendicular precipices of rock to fence in the little valleys along the river bottom. Dismounting, I was leading my horse along the edge of the precipice that I might find some place to get down to the valley below. I had gone in this way as much as a mile, trying to find a trail leading down, when I found one as I thought. So, calling one of the boys to hold my horse, I started down the trail to see where it went, and to discover if it were possible for a horse to follow it down. I could see that the bluff was very steep, and if I fell I would fall a long way without any chance of preservation. I wished for daylight, for a balloon, or some flying machine—anything to help me down to the valley below. I knew there was water there, for I could hear it. So, continuing on in the little bit of a trail, that one could scarcely walk in for the unevenness of its bottom, I had made good progress, and was, I thought, half way down, when suddenly, just a few feet in front of me, and a little below on the trail, a wild, terrible howl or scream rang out through the darkness. I knew at once that I had a panther to contend with, and that is an animal to be terribly dreaded, for it is large, quick, muscular, and powerful. I brought my rifle to position as quickly as ever gun was brought to readiness, I imagine. Scarcely had I done this, when the animal gave vent to another howl, more terrible than the first.

What should I do? I could not run had I wished to. I was then standing on a little, narrow trail of rocks, with a mighty chasm below me, and a precipice of rocks above me. I doubled myself down as close to the trail as I could, and at the same time drew my knife for further defense. When I got close down to the trail I could see the panther's eyes glistening like two coals of fire. I had hesitated for a little spell. I was afraid to shoot, for in the darkness a shot is uncertain; and, if the animal should spring upon me there, I would certainly fall off. I thought of jumping off; but I did not know the distance down. Then again I knew, if I did anything I must do it at once. So I threw my gun forward and pulled, aiming at his glaring eyes as near as I could. But my gun failed to go for the first time since I had owned it. I drew my pistol, which was a Smith & Wesson forty-four. While I was doing that the beast again gave utterance to a howl that pierced me through, and made me feel that my fate was sealed. I thought that he was stealthily drawing nearer and nearer to me. His eyes were glistening with penetrating brightness. I could feel myself shaking from head to foot. I was terribly frightened. I had been on many battle-fields, where men were falling all around me, and the groans of the wounded rent the air; I had heard them plead in vain for assistance that was beyond the power of man to give; but never before in my life did I feel as I then felt. I knew my last chance depended upon my pistol. I could see the long, lithe form settling for the fatal leap. Then, holding my pistol out, resting the barrel and cylinder along my finger, I aimed at his eyes, and pulled the trigger. He bounded into the air, and fell downward into the darkness below. I heard him when he struck; it sounded a long way down.

I could hear one of my companions calling to me from above to know if I was hurt. Answering him that I was not, I went on down the trail, and found it about the same thing all the way. So I hallooed for my companions to come down carefully. When they had all got down, we pitched camp for the day. We had not long to wait for the morning, as day was fast coming out of the sombre darkness. After daylight we found that we were in a beautiful little park.

I was interested to know whether I had killed my animal or not. I did not know whether I had hit him, or only frightened him, and made him jump. Three of us went to see if we could find any trace of him. We had not long to look, for we saw him lying on the slide rock, where he had stopped rolling a good bit before we reached the place. He was a nice, sleek, large-looking animal, over seven feet long from the point of the nose to the end of the tail. He had fallen over sixty feet from where he was when I shot him. I often think and wonder what would my fate have been had he made the spring upon me. I found that the reason my gun would not go off was because I had got a very small twig fast in front of the hammer, so the needle could not strike the cap.

While at this place the boys

IN THE COLORADO CANONS.

caught plenty of nice trout. Some of them would weigh a pound or more. We were all delighted with the place. After a time I lay down to sleep, but only fell into a disturbed slumber, which was worse than wakefulness, for it was haunted by such terrible dreams. I was dreaming of wild animals howling, and roaming about all night, or else of the savage Indians, and that one of these was in the act of lifting what little hair there was left from the top of my head. I finally awoke, screaming for the boys to run for their lives, as the Indians had me and would soon have the balance of the party. To sleep again was impossible. I was soon up, therefore, to take a view of the country.

The air had been fresh and nice before sunrise; but now the sun was sending its scorching rays upon and all around us in that little valley. The sky was intensely blue, and without the smallest cloud to break its monotony. I spent the afternoon in visiting some of the different peaks, and examining the general character and formation of the ledges that crossed the gulches, and projected from the sides and summits of the main ranges. When the afternoon had been spent in sight-seeing, and in visiting the many little caves, and examining the numerous particles of quartz that we discovered, we then took our gold pans, and tried the creek. We raised the color; but we could do that any place in the mountains. Take a pan of dirt from the top of a range, and wash it out, and you see a little shiner. The mountains, however, afforded us much study here, for they were filled with various classes of rock, such as the prospector delights to find, and exhibit in his collections.

We again start on our way. The sun has set in a tremulous golden glory, and the twilight has already deepened into night. The red and white sands, the silent castles that were by daylight seen rearing their jagged crests far above the surrounding country, have now all disappeared in darkness. We traveled all night without any special adventure.

CHAPTER XI.

THROUGH THE COLORADO CANONS.

[CONTINUED.]

THE morning found us on the verge of a mighty precipice. Before us opened a mighty chasm in the earth, in some places over a mile in depth, and appearing as if it were closing together at the top. You think you can throw a stone across to the other side very easily. But in this you are mistaken. Try it. Ah! see, the stone drops downward out in space far short of the other side. As you watch it on its steady journey downward, a sensation creeps through you that you too are falling from these giddy heights above to the mighty depths below; thence to be borne away by the mighty river that goes rushing onward beneath you; boiling, splashing, and frothing, white with madness. Here you see it pouring over a perpendicular precipice over fifty feet in height, and over hundreds of others not so high. See it strike and divide against that large bowlder. Thousands of rocks can be seen, projecting their dark-colored heads, as you look up and down the river, above the white, splashing spray.

"Now," says some reader, "where are you, and what are you describing?" I am sitting upon the mighty precipice, overlooking the grand Colorado River, upon the brink of one of the longest and deepest cuts in solid rocks that Nature has ever made. Moreover, I am now seeing what few white men ever have seen. There are a great many men who claim to have seen the Grand Cañon of the Colorado, when really but few have ever seen it.

The river runs through a rough, broken, alkaline range. The first morning we arrived at this cañon, there being neither wood nor water, we moved back a short distance, where there was some alkaline water, standing in holes in the rocks. We had no wood, and grass was scarce. Neither our horses nor ourselves fared the best. Some of us followed the edge of the cañon down the river, while others went up stream (leaving some to take care of the camp), to see what the chances were for crossing. The Buckskin Mountains proper are on the eastern side of the Colorado River, though I have seen them represented on some maps as located on the western side. The Indians call the four peaks that stand up so prominent, and which are seen for a long distance, lying on the eastern side of the Colorado, between Colorough Lake and the Grand Cañon, and forty miles north of the Yampa, the Buckskin Mountains.

We wanted to get across the river, and were unable to cross there. At that time none of the party knew at what part of the cañon we were. We tossed up a four penny bit to determine whether we should go up the river or down. Mr. S. Jones tossed up the piece, which came down heads up, deciding that we should travel up stream until we could find a crossing. We thought that a rough journey was before us, whichever way we might go. We struck up the trail that had been marked out by the ponies of the savages in their wanderings up and down the cañon. We felt sure the trail would lead us aright through the, to us, unknown regions.

We were very fortunate, for we met with no Indians on our way up the cañon. All the difficulty we had to contend with was the lack of water and the roughness of the mountains. It was so rough that we now changed our time of traveling from night back to day again. At times we were close to the brink of the precipice; at other times we were entirely out of sound of the river, in some deep gorge or ravine, or behind some mountain. At times we were traveling directly from the river, and then climbing and sweating and working our way back again. Sometimes when we looked down into the cañon, it was impossible to see down to the water. The vapor or mist that was rising from the water looked like a cloud or thick smoke ascending. Again, when we could see down, we could see in the walls on either side caves, rooms, and openings that the water had formed in its downward cutting. In some places the cañon walls are much farther apart at the bottom than at the top. While at other places the top of the cañon will be more than a mile in width; but the walls are so steep and rough that nothing can get to the water below without falling down, down for hundreds of feet. For fifty miles we got down to the water's edge but once, and that was by following down

SUNSET IN THE COLORADO CANONS.

a dry gulch that started from the mountains a long way back from the river. While traveling down this gulch one has a feeling not easily described. You are going down all the time, either jumping down from perpendicular declivities in the rock, or groping your way over and down from large bowlders. This gulch is very narrow, not more than seven feet wide at the bottom. It is hemmed in with perpendicular walls in places. At others the walls project over until they meet or lap at the top. As you approach the river the higher these hard rocky walls get to be. You look up from your low position, down deep between these mighty walls, and in many places see them closed above your head. Again there are places where you are able to see the top. That is where the top of the cañon has some little width.

It was a bright, sunny day when we went down. Ever and anon I would try to see the top. I well remember how I felt, but can find no words to express what I would like to say. Imagine yourself for a moment way down, down, down for thousands of feet in a deep, narrow gulch, walled in with rock, which time and water have worn smooth as glass. Then you will have the idea, if not the realizing effect. As you move on down towards the river, the roaring of the water gets louder and still louder as it goes beating, knocking, splashing, bounding, and rebounding on its course, for here the cañon is very deep and narrow; and consequently the mighty force of the river must exhaust itself upon the confining walls. The noise in this narrow confinement became so great that I did not hear the loudest hallooing that was, as I was afterwards told, shouted in my very ear.

The Colorado River does not appear to be very wide here. But take into consideration where you are; see the mighty, dark-colored walls all around you, and far above, covered here and there with moss; see the mighty river rushing past you with steep descent, and solid rock for bottom. I cannot say that it was beautiful to me; but it was marvelous.

We continued on our journey up the river until we arrived above where it enters the cañon, when we came to a small tract of bottom land lying nearly as low as the river. This valley is a little more than one mile in length and is half as wide. Then the river is again confined in a narrow cañon.

In this valley we found the ruins of buildings, with portions of the walls yet standing. In several places the walls are yet eight feet in height. As I mentioned, when speaking of the ruins in Arizona, and the Casa Grandas, in Chihuahua, Mexico, pieces of plate and other articles of earthenware are found here also, scattered among the ruins. A large spring flows out high up in the rocks. The water comes tearing down through the little channel it has cut and then goes rippling through what has at one time been an inhabited town.

This little secluded place affords an abundance of grass, which was thickly set and as high as our ponies' knees. The country all around is made up of high, mountainous lands, with little or no vegetation. In this little valley the river widens out. At the upper end the water runs in a smooth sheet, denoting depth. At the lower end, or near it, the fall is greater, and the water goes at a much more rapid rate. This we found was our only chance to cross the river. By entering the water well up towards the upper end of the valley, our horses could swim over very easily, without drifting into the rapids below. If once swept into these rapids there is no chance for man or rider to be saved. We met with splendid success in crossing, and lost nothing of any value. We got wet, of course, but soon dried ourselves.

On the eastern side of the river the country is still broken with ravines, gulches, and cañons. The mountains are fully as high as on the western side; but hardly as barren and sterile as the range we had come up. There are some small streams and one good large creek between where we crossed and the mouth of the Little Colorado. At the last mentioned place we camped for two days and prospected for gold. The place looked more favorable for deposits than any we had seen since leaving Nevada.

We found some very fine specimens of float quartz, and also some veins of quartz, but generally barren; that is, quartz that carries no metals of value. While here we were blessed with plenty of venison and fish. With a single hook one man caught, in an hour, more fish than, together with some venison, we ate during our stay. The next day we crossed and camped on the Little Colorado, which is at this place a beautiful stream; but having a valley of no width.

Here a party of Apache hunters came and camped with us for the night. They were very talkative; more so than common. Of inquisitiveness they undoubtedly had more than their share. They soon warmed up toward us and then wanted to swap guns, as we had arms superior to theirs. We might have done well in the way of a trade, to have swapped our rifles for their guns and horses; but we did not care to do this. We divided our "baca" with them, and the next morning they moved up the Little Colorado; but not before they had warned us of "heap bad Injun at Buckskin Mountains. Ma-be-so see 'em to-day heap bad Injun. We heap good Injun. We no care for white man catch

PROSPECTING IN THE COLORADO CANONS.

'em fish—not too many—eat 'em. Kill 'em deer—eat 'em. Heap white men shoot 'em Buckskin, poom-poom—no eat 'em. *Kots bueno* (no good). Ma-be-so (holding up one finger) sleep see you. Ma-be-so (holding up the fist with fingers closed) see you Buckskin Mountain. You *siguea?*" "Yes," I say. "Me heap good Injun. Buckskin Mountain no good Injun." After warning us in this way, and passing the friendly salutation, they went their way, leaving us on our way to the Buckskin Mountains.

This country we prospected as well as we could under the circumstances. We found several gold and silver-bearing quartz leads. How valuable they may hereafter prove to be, I do not know. We found some gravel claims that I always will think, if properly worked and under the right kind of management, will pay. I have taken as many as twenty pans of dirt and washed it out and I never got less than three cents to the pan. In one pan I got one nugget that weighed seven dollars and sixty-four cents, at the First National Bank of Utah. I sold it for that to Mr. Warren Hussey, president of the bank. He said it was of a good quality of gold.

I have often been asked why I did not stay there. I will here say that we were not prepared to stay long at this time. We had nothing to work with; no saws of any kind, and we could not saw lumber without a whip saw. Neither did we have provisions enough to last us long. Our company had only sixteen men left. The others, you remember, had taken a skip and left us.

I tried to get there once afterwards, of which I will speak further on. We reached the Buckskin Mountains without any resistance from the Indians. A few of them were friendly, and a great many otherwise. As we kept a guard out night and day, they offered no violence more than some abusive epithets which were not resented on our part. We prospected the ranges all through that section of country. We found gold, silver, iron, lead, copper, bismuth, and cinnabar in various places. But whether in paying quantities or not, I do not pretend to say. We also found bench and bar claims; but nothing to justify any very heavy outlay or expense.

We then pushed on to Callville, below the Yampa, the highest point of navigation on the Colorado River. From here some of the party went to Pioche. Four of us went to Salt Lake City. We traveled over an abundance of alkaline and grease-wood land, where nothing else was to be seen; not even a jack-rabbit, an animal of which I have already spoken.

We called at a Mormon house occasionally, and bought milk or butter, which they were very ready to sell for cash, and at a much more reasonable figure than we could buy at in any of the other Territories. I may mention, in passing, that at Callville we were ferried over the river by John D. Lee, who has since been shot on the scene of the Mountain Meadow Massacre of the Kansas emigrants, which he superintended in person. It is said that he took an active part, personally, in the slaying of the unfortunate children that belonged to the train. I am told that, in one instance, two sisters, small children, were begging for mercy that they might be spared; and some of the blood-atoning followers of Lee and other Mormon saints were about to spare them; but Lee dashed in, revolver in hand, and shot them both, with the remark, "They are too old to live." I have been told often by men, some of

EXECUTION OF JOHN D. LEE.

whom now live in the Territory, and do know whereof they speak, that until only a few years before Brigham Young's death, he rode in the carriage that was captured by his murdering this train of emigrants. He was not there in person, of course; neither does a President need go in person to quell a rebellion; but yet they can act as instigators or accessories to the act of having it done. Other things, such as clothing, wagons, guns, etc., went to the highest bidders in Cedar, Parowan, Beaver, and other settlements. Such live-stock as the Church could handle was considered as Church property, and found its way, a lot of it, to the Church Island, where no one ever went except those intrusted with the care of that kind of property. Church Island is an island in the Great Salt Lake, where a good portion of the stock of the Co-operative Company is kept.

CHAPTER XII.

MONTANA AND IDAHO.

MONTANA and Idaho, like California, were settled originally by gold-hunters. At first they neither knew nor cared whether the Territory possessed any agricultural advantages or not; but when the easily skimmed cream of the placers had been gathered, and more difficult and permanent quartz mining succeeded, the pressing needs of a settled population turned the attention of a large number of the people to farming. The country was then found to be as rich in agricultural as in mineral resources.

Montana is celebrated for its many large productive valleys. The Gallatin Valley is situated in the southern part of the Territory, and is one of the largest and finest grain-producing valleys in the West. Some very nice little orchards have been set out. Whether these will prove productive or not, I am unable to say. In Jefferson, Madison, Bowlder, Prickly Pear, Bitter Root, Marias, Milk River, and a number of other valleys they raise magnificent crops of wheat. Although Idaho is south of Montana, the valleys are as cold as those of Montana. They produce no better grain, neither any greater variety.

Estimating from what I could learn, about one-half of the population of these two Territories is engaged in agricultural pursuits. The other half, in mining, stock raising, and other branches of industry. The roads are generally lined with freight and immigrant wagons. The larger part of the best land has been taken up. There are a great many quartz mills. Some are idle; but many are doing a thriving business.

Before the Pacific Railroad was built, all goods for Montana were sent up the Missouri River—in the Spring—to Fort Benton, which is at the head of navigation. The distance up is thirty-one hundred miles, along a most tortuous course, requiring very careful piloting. Steamers would consume from three to four months in making the trip. Their progress depended greatly upon the nature of the current, and the depth of water on the almost innumerable shoals. This difficult and exasperating method of transportation had nothing to recommend it except that it was the best then within reach. Very little freight is now sent by the river. The great bulk of it goes over the Union and Central Pacific Railroads.

At present all goods for Montana, whether from the East or West, go to Corinne, Utah, on the Central Pacific Railroad. It is thirty-one miles west of Ogden. Ogden is the junction of the Union and Central Pacific Railroads. Corinne is four hundred and seventy miles south of Helena, the chief town of Montana. The two places are connected by a wagon road, over which there is a line of fast stages, fast and slow freight wagons, and innumerable mule teams. Since the great Washoe teaming business has been discontinued, there is no other Territory that gives employment to as many freight teams as Montana.

The largest freight warehouses in the West have been built at Corinne for the storage of merchandise for Montana. They are always well-filled with goods. Dozens of teams are constantly to be seen at the depot, either loading up with freight, or waiting their turn to be loaded. The freighters generally drive mules and horses. During a brief portion of the year, in the summer months, cattle may be used with advantage.

From Corinne to Helena is a hazardous road. A good portion of the year there is snow on many parts of it. When the snow melts, streams of water continually run across or along the road, making it very difficult for heavily-loaded teams to move along. They are either mired down in the mud, or fording ponds and streams of water one-half the time. The other half is spent in winding around and up over ridges and mountains, turning sharp curves, climbing steep mountain grades, and skirting along the edge of lofty precipices. Sometimes wagons, horses, goods, and every thing go rolling over the precipice, and pitching down the steep mountain side, to land at the bottom a total wreck. Goods are scattered the whole distance down; the wagon is smashed to fragments, and the animals killed or hopelessly crippled. Hundreds of skeletons of animals line the road on either side the whole distance.

In the summer there is plenty of grass along the route, so that animals have good grazing. But during the greater part of the year they must be full fed with grain, such as chop feed, rye, oats, barley, peas, and corn. If none of the above can be had, then wheat is used, which is an excellent feed for horses or mules. Hay commands a good price at all times, sometimes as much as eight cents a pound. Before the Pacific Railroad was built, at times everything sold at enormous prices in some of the mining camps where provisions were scarce. Eggs have sold for fifty cents a piece. Flour seventy-five cents a pound, and at one time one dollar and fifty cents a pound. Tea, coffee, and a great many other such things were not to be had at all. Tobacco retailed for two and four bits a chew, a bit being twelve and one-half cents.

Californians, are called in Montana "Self-risers," to distinguish them from the "Pilgrims" or "Tenderfoots," who footed it into Montana from the south-western States. The "Self-risers" largely monopolize the mercantile and mining interests, while the "Pilgrims" generally guide the plow and handle the hoe. A great many people who have gone to Montana have done extremely well.

CHAPTER XIII.

LAKES AND SPRINGS OF THE FAR WEST.

THIS chapter I will devote exclusively to the waters of the West. There are in the West many kinds of water, with different qualities and properties. There are waters of many colors. Water, we all know, is found in Nature in three forms, vaporous, fluid, and solid. Science teaches us that water is a compound of one part of hydrogen, and eight parts of oxygen. Water is never pure, but always impregnated. Take the waters of the wells, springs, rivers, etc., east of the Missouri—they are mostly fresh. Take them in the mountains west—they are saline (salty), alkaline (some mineral being held in solution), and often caloric (that is warm or hot).

The Great Salt Lake is situated in Utah Territory in the great basin. The water of this lake is saline, with one part out of four salt. There is no living thing in this lake. Bear River, coming down out of Idaho, empties in on the north. This is, commonly speaking, fresh water, where splendid fish are caught in large quantities. There is no outlet to Salt Lake that I know anything about, and I have been told there is none. It has been stated that there is an underground outlet, and that the water at a certain place out in the lake is continually in a whirl, caused by the suction from below. This, I think, is a mistake. I was often on the lake in 1868 and 1869. I have talked

GREAT SALT LAKE.

with different individuals well acquainted with the lake, all of whom deny the assertion.

The water of Great Salt Lake is rising all the time. When the Mormons first settled there, all the available fertile land around the lake was fenced to the water's edge with post fences. Owing to the presence of large quantities of salt in the soil, the posts have been preserved from rotting. And now the fences are still standing, but are under water, in many places entirely out of sight. Whole fields that once were cultivated are now under water.

People often go into **Salt Lake** bathing. If they have sores, cuts, or broken flesh, their sufferings are severe. When they come out there is a saline coating all over the body, so that they have to bathe in other water to wash the salt off. The lake spreads over a vast scope of land, and is in some places deep.

Lake Tahoe, or Lake Bigler as some call it, is in Nevada. The former is an Indian name; the latter is the name of the first white man of any note in that part of the now State. This lake is called fresh water. There are hot springs boiling up out in the lake. At Hot Spring City they began at the bottom of the lake, and built a wall around one of these springs, and continued the wall until above the surface of the lake. This wall is solid, and keeps the water separated. The lake water is cold around the outer side of the wall, while the water on the inner side is hot.

Fresh water is much lighter than salt water. The water of Lake Tahoe is undoubtedly the hardest to swim in I ever tried. It is almost impossible to swim in it even for a short distance. It would be a great place for

Captain Paul Boyton to experiment in. Another feature of the Tahoe water is, that if a person is unfortunate enough to be drowned in it, as has been the case of several persons, his body is never recovered. Bodies have never been known to rise to the surface, nor have they been found drifted to shore. This water is very transparent, and is said to be the clearest water in the world. You can see down in it to the great depth of over one hundred feet. It is so transparent that it does not appear to be over ten or fifteen feet deep. Near the shore, while rowing in a boat, you feel sure you could wade it, when at the same time there will be twenty feet of water beneath you. Large trout are caught in Lake Tahoe, weighing often over twenty pounds.

Crystal Lake, west of Tahoe and distant two miles, is a small lake of like properties to Tahoe. It is about one mile long and half as wide. It is very deep. Some claim that it is deeper than Tahoe. Large numbers of fish are caught in this lake. Schools of them can be seen sporting and swimming down deep in the water.

The river water in the Winter, in many instances, tastes as if free from minerals. But as soon as Winter is over, and the water gets warmer, then it tastes strongly of substances held in solution.

Water is found in the West at every temperature, from the freezing to the boiling point. It appears in various mineralized forms; sweet, sour, sulphurous, siliceous, chalybeate, and other forms.

Throughout the West hot springs are numerous. Some of these springs are of great depth, while others seem to be entirely on the surface. All around a hot spring the surface of the earth is heated, and is generally mound-shaped, sometimes several feet higher than the surrounding surface earth. Sometimes the spring runs out from the side of a mountain. The earth below is all crusted over with sediment-rock varying in color. This crust of rock is formed out of the substances the water contains.

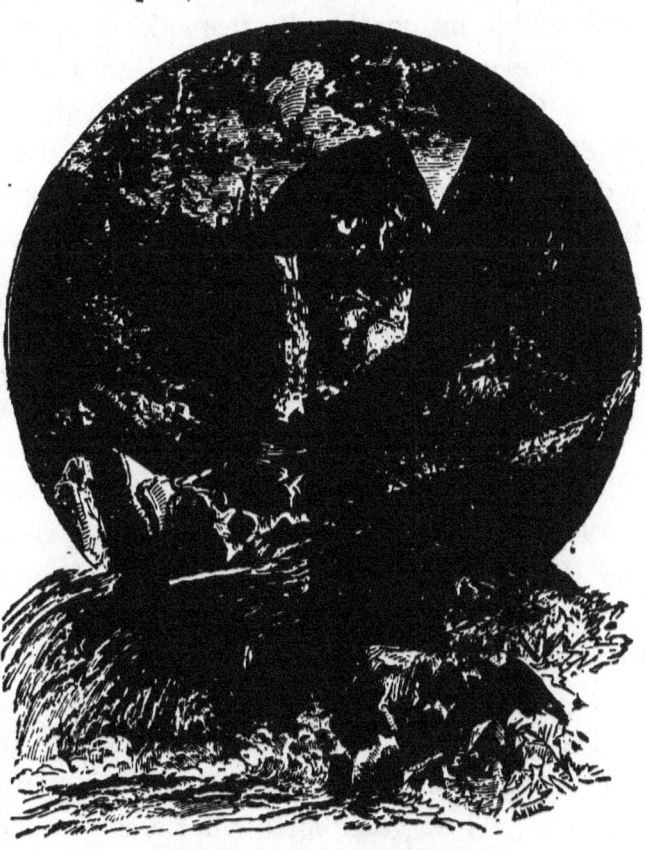

VERNAL FALLS, CALIFORNIA.

Often it partakes of the nature of burnt brick, or clay. In some places it is compact, and in others it is not, but is in globular and sponge-like form. Sometimes it is of a white color.

When mounds are formed as at the hot springs in Ouray Park, Colorado, these mounds slope off gradually, until the surface earth is reached. The Pecoshia Springs are similar to these, but larger and grander. These springs are boiling hot. The water will boil and bubble up continually from the bottom to the surface, like water boiling in a vessel on a fire. The water in the Pecoshia Springs is nice, clear, and as pretty as any water I ever saw. Looking at the water, you would not suspect it to be so hot. A large stream of hot water flows continually from the spring, and retains its heat for a good distance before it finally cools off. Hundreds of these hot springs are found throughout the West, in Colorado, Utah, California, Arizona, and the States of Mexico on the north.

The largest warm spring I ever saw was close to Ojo Caliente, in Mexico. It is over forty feet wide and very deep. It had no outlet that was visible; neither did the water reach the surface, as is generally the case where springs are perennial, and constantly discharging their volumes of water. A great many of these springs show no diminuition in the seasons of longest drought. Fresh-water springs are intermittent, depending entirely upon the prevailing character of the seasons. They gush forth after heavy rains, and flow freely for a time, and then fail to flow in continued dry weather.

Now allow me to lead you to the Yellowstone, to behold some of the natural wonders of that place. Here, far up the valley, we come to an ebb or tide spring that flows at intervals or seasons. Part of the time the water gushes from one side of the knoll formed around it, and runs off in a little rill; then, ceasing to flow on that side, it bulges forth on the other. It never, so far as I was able to discover, runs from both sides at the same time. I was told, by an old gentleman who had long lived with the Indians there, that this spring would run for five or six months from one side, and then would shift to the other. In very dry seasons it would dry up. This is called a tide spring, and is singular in its way of running, and its like is seldom

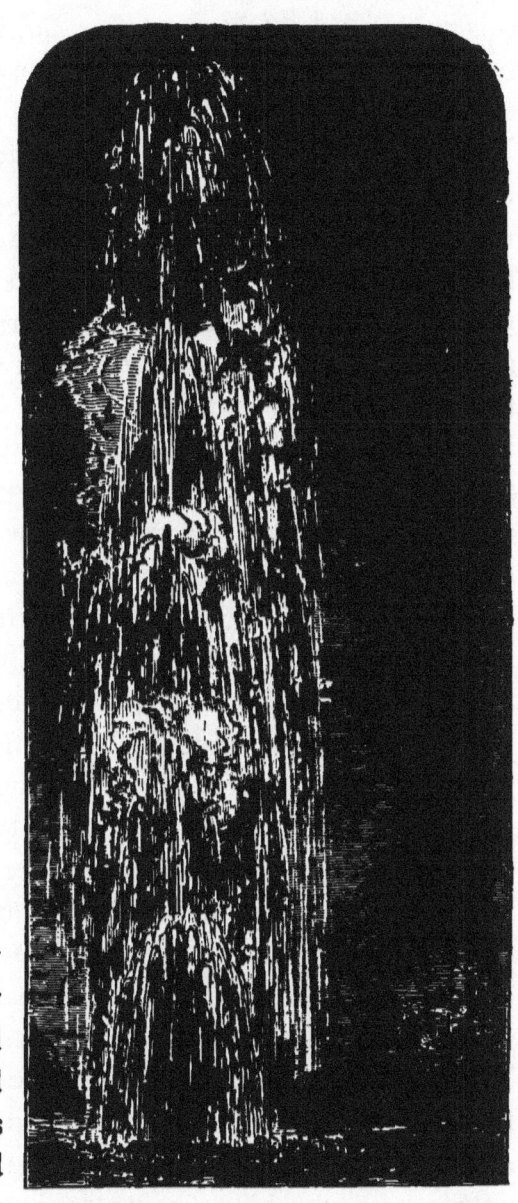

"GIANTESS," BIG GEYSER OF THE YELLOWSTONE.

seen elsewhere. Why the water changes its course in this way I am unable to say. Some say this is caused by the action of the tide. It may be, but I do not think so. I do not think the tide has anything to do with it, for this reason. This place is shut off from the ocean by two distinct ranges of mountains on the west, and a large extent of mountainous lands on the north and south. We are over seven thousand feet above sea level. Now if this spring is governed by the action of the tide, why does it not flow continually from the same side of the *butte*. But it does not, as I have been assured by the Indians themselves. I leave this, as I came to it, in my own mind—*nonplussed*.

At some distance from this, lower down, we have a mud spring. This is not a spring that runs mud, neither is it, as I could see, a spring that runs water, although there is water in it, and that to an enormous depth. It has a natural wall formed of sediment, compact and solid as though hewn from rock itself. It was thirty feet to the water when I saw it, and I could not touch the bottom with two lariat ropes tied together, making nearly one hundred feet of line. This spring is in a little valley to itself, and is not only curious, but marvelous. Seven miles below this mud spring is what is known as the Steamboat Spring. It works upon the principle of an exhaust to a steam engine. The water recedes from the surface of the earth around the spring, and then comes rushing up clear out and above the surrounding surface; then it recedes again to gather more force and come again. The time between each two discharges is as much as four minutes. The temperature of this spring is one hundred and forty degrees. There is a vast amount of sulphur in it. The air for a long distance around is full of the odor of sulphur.

In the valleys there are numerous alkaline streams, in some of which the water is so strong that nothing can drink it. They often dry up, when the alkali is left deposited along their beds, sometimes for two or three inches in depth.

We are unable to trace the intimate connection of hot springs, and the discharging of hot water, steam and gases. Yet it is impossible to doubt the direct relationship of these different phenomena and their mutual dependence upon one grand cause, namely: A high temperature prevailing in the earth at an unknown depth below the surface. No doubt this is the original cause of earthquakes that burst forth with deep jarring noises from below, without warning, and open up fissures, and rend the rocks apart. Evidences of this is seen in volcanoes, as on the Sandwich Islands, where there is a large opening all ablaze, like a lake on fire. Around these springs the earth seems to be only a crust hollowed out underneath. So that one is treading as it were upon an arched bridge over the cauldron below.

CHAPTER XIV.

LA PAZ.

I WILL devote this chapter to giving a bit of my experience while connected with the surveying party in Arizona. We had halted at Fort McDowell. I had expected to meet some friends from California at this place. When we reached the Fort, my friends were not there; but I found a letter requesting me to come on immediately and meet them in La Paz. La Paz is a small town in Yuma County. I therefore bustled around and was soon ready, and waiting for the "Jerkey" to take me through. I was jolted, bounced and bumped about in the stage all day, all night, and next day, without sleep or comfort.

Let my readers for a moment imagine themselves in some cramped-up, little, crowded-to-death corner of one of these overloaded stage-coaches; the seats are all filled with passengers; the space between the seats is filled with trunks, valises, blankets, bedding of all kinds, new blankets and old blankets, half-worn blankets, torn blankets, and bedding of the same description; prospecting outfits of picks, shovels, pans and provisions; arms and ammunition, enough for an arsenal. The boots are full of mail sacks, packages and papers. The passengers are of all kinds, grades and nationalities, and crowd full every inch of available room inside and on top of the coach. Now you are to be whirled along at a most reckless rate over a rough mountain road. At one moment, passengers and traps are all piled up in confusion in one end of the stage, to be suddenly thrown the next moment to the other, there to be jostled, now to one side, then with renewed force to the other; and thus you go on bounding and bouncing over rocks, through ruts, hollows, holes, wash-outs and everything else that is met in the road. This description gives but a faint idea of stage riding. However, stage-coach passengers, especially in the Territories, are not supposed to have any feelings.

The expressman knows by name every one he meets along his route. He is continually tossing letters, newspapers, periodicals and bundles from the top of the stage. His legs often appear in frightful proximity to the rapidly revolving wheels, for he is climbing on and off the coach while it is going at a sweeping rate. In gallantry, energy and knowledge he is generally superior to all the other passengers. He will answer the questions of a whole group of persons and attend to some matter of business, all at the same time.

When I alighted from the coach at La Paz, I was like one paralyzed in all his joints and limbs. I could scarcely stand, much less walk.

I looked around at the adobe walls and the deserted houses with walls, windows, roofs, floors, everything from garret to cellar, from pavement to rear fence, all going to decay. I thought the Mexicans here much worse off than those in other localities. Very rough-looking customers were to be seen in front of saloons, groceries and in groups on corners. I could not but think that a great many of them must be common vagrants, with no means of support. The word ragged conveys but a feeble idea of their miserable dress. These poor wretches all carried six-shooters, and knives sticking out boldly and defiantly from their persons. Verily, they were hard-looking specimens of the human race.

I gathered my things from among the bundles that had been tossed pell-mell in a heap together from the stage, and went to the hotel. The only one then in the town was kept by an American. I stood gloomily clutching my things, waiting until my host should give me checks for them. Some how or other, he had got his checks mismatched, and I thought he never would find two of a corresponding number. He did finally, however, fish up the checks from some quarter of the house, or out of some of his pockets. Giving me one, he tied the remaining tag to my things. Being relieved of my baggage, I turned and took a seat. The landlord then began to ply me with questions. "Do you desire a room for the night?" "Where did you get on the stage?" "Do you want supper?" "How are the roads?" "Any road-agents at work down about the Fort?" and so on, until I wondered if he would ever come to the end. He then offered me the drinks, which I politely declined, telling him I had never drank any in my life, and could very well get along without it now. "Well, then, do you ever smoke?"

"Yes, sir." So I accepted a cigar that was certainly made from some weed worse if possible, than tobacco, and that would not draw any more than a piece of iron-wood. I soon tired of such enjoyment as an effort to smoke this afforded. I threw the cigar aside, and went out and took a wash. After this, I felt in a better humor in mind, and considerably revived otherwise.

After I had taken a survey of the people, and the things inside of the house, I was not very favorably impressed with my stopping-place. Everything and everybody seemed to be suffering from a severe attack of hard times. The windows and doors were all cut and scratched; various calculations and reckonings had been scrawled upon the door and window casings and walls, and names had been written everywhere, until there was no available room for more. Every thing was disagreeable and uninviting. I felt doomed to dreariness. Everything to intoxicate and degrade was here. There was the "valley tan" flavor of uneasiness hovering over the whole place. Here were men who long had outraged every law of Nature, gathered in groups around circular tables, gambling. Others went staggering around the room, or were lying prostrate under the influence of liquor.

I went to the door, and looked out on the street. The sight was appalling. Here were men swearing in a jargon of Spanish and broken English, with now and then a plain-spoken English phrase, for there were some Americans in town. Some were betting on horse-races; some on cock-fights, bull-fights, foot-racing, jumping, wrestling, and future chances in general. Some were stripping for a fight; others fighting, chums taking sides either actively or with a great deal of harmless bluster. Some had pistols drawn, and the whole town seemed to be in a riot. The tumult and racket sometimes lulled for a moment, only to break out again afresh in new groups quickly formed elsewhere. It seemed to me that boarding in this place would only be from the lack of a better place to go to.

While I was standing, contemplating the different faces before me, the landlord announced that "hash" was ready. As I entered the door, a number of persons (I suppose, regular boarders) made a rush for the dining-room, and engaged in a general scramble as to who should get seated first, just as if there was not enough for a mouthful a piece. I got a seat, finally, at one end of the table, but really I would have preferred to have had my portion handed out to me, that I might have eaten it under some tree, and there made my dinner in peace. Every fellow was going for what he could get, as if it were the last meal that he ever expected to eat, and as if he had not partaken of a mouthful for several days.

After the meal was over, we went back to the saloon, (for this was also the sitting-room). The crowd immediately arranged themselves around the stove, some with their feet on the stove, and leaning back in different positions; others with their legs hanging over and resting upon chairs, some smoking, others chewing tobacco, as if they all were trying to get the taste of the meal out of their mouths. Thus, they resigned themselves to indigestion. The landlord was a short, heavy-set, good-looking specimen of a frontiersman. His every action and whole manner showed him to be a man accustomed to but one single thought, and that thought was to get all he could, regardless of the method employed. I sat and talked with him awhile and found him perfectly at home upon the different topics of conversation. He told me several stories, all bearing a strong flavor of the roughness of the place. He told me also what a wilderness of a place it was when he first moved there. I could but think while he was telling me this that it must have grown worse instead of better, since it was settled; for, though I had seen rough civilization before, I had seen none to compare with what I saw that day. He told how he had killed several "Injuns," and several times was nearly scalped himself. All this he told with much candor, but, as I thought, with a good deal of braggadocio.

I after a little left the bar-room, and went to the post-office. There I found a letter, informing me that my friends would not be in town for three days yet to come. I then took a stroll through the streets, if streets they can be called. Here I beheld numerous specimens of the "Greaser," dark and swarthy, and well named *Greaser*, each jabbering to his friend in "Mexicana." I saw the freighter loading up his teams with hides, to take to some of the coast towns in California. I found the saloon-keeper everywhere, with his sign up above the door, and, perchance, he himself standing as conspicuously in the door-way, inviting those who would to indulge in drink. I whiled my hours away, strolling about until time to return to the hotel.

After resting a while, I prepared to retire for the night. Preceded by my redoubtable hero of a host, and a flaring candle, I followed up-stairs to my room. It was the only spare bed he had, he told me. The room had a cloth partition on one side, and large holes through the wooden partition on the other. It was unfurnished, nothing in it, except the spare bed. It had a very small window on one side, which rattled fearfully every time the wind came against it. From the bar-room came one continued uproar of profane epithets and drunken orgies, all night long. I tried to sleep, but could not. I covered up my head, thinking to drown the tumult. Everything I could do failed to let me have a moment's relief from the gang of gambling and drinking fellows down stairs. The night was long. I thought daylight would never come. I arose early in the morning, and was told that I could get no breakfast until seven o'clock. I had firmly resolved to leave this boarding-house that morning, provided I could find another. So killing time as best I could, until breakfast was over, I started in search of another hotel. Any place I thought would be better than that one.

After searching the town over, I at last found a place which I thought would suit me. It was a small, two-story adobe house, kept by an old lady and her two daughters. After all arrangements had been made, and it was settled that I should take up my stay with them until my companions came from Los Angelos, I went back to the hotel to get my things. When I arrived, everything was still in an uproar. One big Texan, beastly drunk, was lying flat on his back in the bar-room, with a large dragoon revolver in each hand, shooting at everything in the room he could get sight of. He had frightened everybody out of the room, so that he was like Robinson Crusoe, monarch of all he surveyed. He had the large looking-glass that was back of the bar shattered to pieces with bullets. I suppose he had been trying to kill himself, or the fellow that looked like him in the glass. There were pictures with holes shot through them, holes in the ceiling over head, holes in the windows. The stove was lying on its side, broken up in his amusement. He had done a great deal of mischief in a short time. I told my host I would settle my bill and take my things. He was sorry, as he expressed himself, that I would not remain longer, but I had not an insurance on my life, though I would have taken out a policy at almost any price, the way I was feeling just then. I settled up, and gladly took my departure from that ill-managed house.

The idea of going where I thought there would be a social family circle, was particularly pleasant. This would naturally be the case with most any single man like myself. I had been tumbling and pitching over pumice rocks in the wilds of Arizona, with a load of surveying apparatus upon my back, for the season past. I pictured to myself the sitting-room and dining-room with the old lady and two buxom, grown daughters, bustling around to make the place sociable and comfortable. But how often our imaginations prove delusions! I shouldered my things, and off I went to my new boarding-house. I had my mind fixed on how I would act, and what nice things I would say to the old lady, and how sweetly I would talk to the daughters. I heard them bustling around in the house, when I knocked at the hall door. My knock was answered by the eldest daughter. I was told to walk in. I was just commencing one of my sweet sentences, and had just got out, "How ha—" when my foot caught in a hole in the carpet. I never finished my sentence, for I went falling into the hall, over the young lady, upsetting her and knocking down the hat-stand, making a dreadful racket and crash.

The noise brought Mrs. Pierce and her remaining daughter to the scene, to behold my things strewn along the hall. The eldest daughter had regained an upright position against the wall, and was no doubt wondering what kind of a boarder they had got, and I was trying to regain my equilibrium in another part of the hall, with all my sweet words withered and forever lost. Mrs. Pierce had her sleeves rolled up to her elbows. She had been making up the bread. Not a smile was visible on her countenance. Her daughter with a dusting-pan was close by, wondering no doubt if I was drunk or had taken a "conniption fit," which last, I presume, was most likely. Her sister was evidently frightened almost out of her wits. My position was to me more embarrassing than amusing. I blurted out some kind of an apology. I do not remember what I said. When I had gathered my things together I was ushered into a small room, certainly not very well furnished, which was used as a sitting-room. Here I was left alone to wonder what they thought of me. I heard the daughters say to each other, "How clumsy he is!"

"Yes, he is so. I wonder if he is drunk."

"What a stumbling way he has of coming into a room!"

"I should say he had. Did you see him? He fell over me and knocked me down. He frightened me so I could hardly get my breath to speak. I wonder who he is, and what he has got in his valise, and how long he intends to stay here," etc., with innumerable other questions and comments, until I thought my position rather unenviable and unpromising.

I had not been there long, before dinner was announced. When I went in to dinner, I found the table had been laid with care, and that I was the only boarder present. Mrs. Pierce headed the table, and the two daughters sat opposite me, eating in a lazy manner, and occasionally casting inquisitive glances across the table at me, (a sort of Arkansas courtship). I was dreadfully hungry, and it seemed to me that they were counting how many chops and what amount of other things I ate, so that they might calculate the expense of my meal. I was ashamed of my appetite, but I determined to eat as much as I could. Toward the end of my meal, for the others had finished, the eldest daughter arose and donned her hat and shawl. Having given her mother some instructions in reference to supper, and bade us "Good afternoon," she took her departure. I heard her slam the door after her as she left the house. I took the hint and stopped eating. I betook myself to the country for the remainder of the day. I saw nothing worthy of special notice, only a dry, barren, desolate-looking plain, dotted all over here and there with *buttes* of black rock or lava stone. When I returned to town, the sun was sinking from sight behind the dark-colored mountains in the west.

After supper I strolled around over town again a little while, to see, as on the previous evening, crowds assembled to again pass the night away in gambling, drinking, and carousing. But this time there were to be more serious results. There was quite a lot of soldiers in town this evening for some purpose, I know not what. All the gambling houses were filled with soldiers and natives. They spent the evening in gambling, until it became monotonous, as I suppose, when soldiers and citizens changed the sport into shooting and cutting one another. Two men were killed outright during the night, and others were badly hurt. This drunken and gambling carousal was going on as long as I remained in La Paz. Horse-racing, chicken-fighting, dog-fighting, and everything involving the principle of chance was sought after for gambling purposes. Every occasion of this kind generally ended in a row, to be settled with the pistol or knife.

After I had seen enough of their rioting, I returned to my lodgings. I was tired and sleepy, and soon went up-stairs to bed. I have seen better beds in Ohio. This one was filled with bed-bugs. The walls of the room were filled; the floor was full. They were of all sizes and colors. They all wanted to be in the bed. I could see them, and smell them, and could hear them falling from the ceiling upon the bed. They ran all over me. They bit me with an energy that could only have been inspired by much previous fasting. I suppose I was a stranger, and they enjoyed a change of diet. Sleep was out of the question. After I had lain for, perhaps, half an hour turning and twisting frantically, trying to keep the bugs out of my ears and face, I began to wish I had not gone to bed. I regretted that I had come to La Paz. When a restless hour had been spent with the bugs, I got up and dressed myself, swearing inwardly at La Paz and the whole country.

There had been a fire down in the sitting-room. Perhaps it was still burning. I had brought a small piece of candle up-stairs with me, but no matches. I opened my door and groped my way along the passage made doubly gloomy by the whistling of the night wind. In feeling for the stairway, I got to the wrong end of the opening. There was no railing around it, and, groping along in the darkness, I stepped off into space and fell down through the opening, hard enough to have broken every bone in my body. The memory of that fall makes me laugh even now. I do wonder if other people ever fall down stairs. It gives one curious feelings, to fall down stairs in a strange house. I picked myself up as best I could at the foot of the stairs, and entered the room. I found the fire still burning a little. I was very much jammed and bruised, and was bleeding in several places where I had been hurt by the fall. I stirred the fire up, and, drawing a chair close to the stove, was just falling into some serious meditations over my situation, when the door was opened, and the eldest daughter looked into the room in a frightened way. She had heard me falling down stairs, and, wondering what could cause so much disturbance, she had gathered up courage enough to come down and see. I tried to explain the situation by telling her that the bed they had given me to sleep in was already taken with hungry occupants, etc.

We fell into a conversation, and I learned many particulars from her in reference to the history of the family. There were only the three of them at home. They had a sister married, and a brother in the Fresno Mines, in California. Mr. Pierce, their father, had been killed in a row two years before at one of the mining camps north. We talked until I was sleepy. I then asked her to give me a spare blanket, if they had one. She gave me a number of them. I then made a bed on the floor, where I enjoyed as good a sleep, as I ever had, for I was tired and sleepy. I did not awake until the sun was shining brightly through the window. I remained in La Paz and vicinity for two more days and nights, when my friends arrived. I slept on the floor each night, in preference to any of their beds.

Before I leave I will sum up my impressions of the place briefly. The sun blazes down upon the town from the cloudless skies day after day in succession, until one's weary eyes long for relief from the dazzling light. There can not be found a hotter place on the American Continent, taking the year around, than Yuma County, Arizona. The natives of La Paz are principally Mexican Greasers. Their stock in trade is horse-racing, whisky, cards, tobacco, cigarettes, a knife, one and often two revolvers, a lasso or lariat, with a few other like articles. It may be that it would be more gracious, and more to my credit, did I not find so much fault with the natives of Arizona. But I spent some time there, and all the scenes I have narrated, and will yet speak of, took place. Consequently, I am profoundly of the opinion that a good part of the natives need to be enlightened and civilized.

I went back to the Fort again on the stage, as I came. We went first to Los Posos, a Spanish town; then, from there, we went across over the South Granite Mountains. The next station we halted at was Deep Well, where we cross the Mass Kampa River, which is one of the northern tributaries of the Gila River; thence to White Tanks, and thence to Fort McDowell. Fort McDowell is situated on the Francisco River. This stream empties into the Solado River, and the Solado runs into the Gila. Fort McDowell is hemmed in on all sides by low, broken hills, much lower than those a little farther distant. These side hills produce but little vegetation. Scarcely any grass could be seen on them. At the foot of these hills, in some places where there is water, as along the river bottoms, there is some very good grass; but it is not as plentiful, neither is the soil as productive, as where the climate is cooler, and there is less drought. Even if it rains hard in Arizona, the water soon disappears in the sandy soil. The Fort is situated midway between Prescott on the north and Tucson on the south.

I was glad enough to arrive back again, where my companions were awaiting my return. It was about eleven o'clock at night when the "Jerkey" wagon drove up. I was tired and hungry. My appetite flourishes with exercise in the open air. But I had a good supper of venison, fish, potatoes, bread, etc., followed by an hour's talk with those who had not yet retired to sleep, but had been awaiting the arrival of the mail. The remainder of the night, spent in sound sleep, put me in good shape again, and I felt better than I had at any time since I had left there to go to La Paz. Roughing it is very pleasant, of course; but I would not advise anyone to try it on. In this experience you must meet with various, unexpected, and vexatious misfortunes, seldom thought of or met elsewhere. It is only the man of rare good fortune that in such a life as this meets with sufficient reward to justify and compensate him for all his loss of comfort and enjoyment.

CHAPTER XV.

STOCK-RAISING.

AMONG all the various enterprises in the West stock-raising ranks first. With many of these western settlers it seems as natural and easy to raise stock successfully as it is for the farmer of Illinois to raise corn. Some men are always more successful in an undertaking than others are who may have equal, if not better, advantages; and they generally succeed, too, with more ease, less attention to business apparently, and with a certain don't-care, go-ahead kind of spirit that seems, to a beholder, to border closely upon recklessness. The ease and success with which this business is prosecuted, depends principally upon the number of cattle one has in the herd, and the locality and situation of the range. As in other enterprises, the more attention bestowed upon it, and the greater care exercised, the greater the profits. To start into the cattle business a man must have money. He purchases a brand for marking his stock, which is generally the initials of his name, or sometimes an imitation of some instrument. This brand or mark is recorded at the nearest county clerk's office.

The man that goes into raising stock must content himself to live along the frontier, away from all society, except of a few frontier neighbors. He is shut off from all communication with the world at large, away from railroads and post-offices, sometimes as much as three hundred miles—in earlier days, much further than this, indeed. Stock-raisers generally go into the foot hills, because there they find pasturage and water. The foot-hill and mountain bunch grass is excellent food for stock. The herd consists of cattle of all kind and all ages. After these are all properly branded, they are turned loose on their respective ranges. Some of the stockmen who have been in the business a long time have enormous herds. These are left in the hands of herders, or, as they are called in Texas, "Cow-boys." These herders are a very rough, uncouth, and untidy class of fellows.

When an animal is sold from a herd, then the former owner brands it with what is known as a vending brand. This vending brand is recorded like the former. It is used to cancel the former brand. When this is applied to an animal, it indicates that the former owner relinquishes all right and title to said animal. When an owner's whole stock is purchased, then the purchaser generally buys the brand also, and that saves canceling. All the animals that can be found bearing the former owner's brand, belong to the last purchaser. When animals are bought and driven away, it is customary to give a bill of sale, which bill is recognized and respected by law.

In early days an owner of cattle could drive his herd where he liked; but now there are inspectors in nearly every county in which a large business in stock-raising is carried on. Before stock is taken from the county, it is inspected by the County Inspector. Then the owner is permitted to pass with his stock where he

A WESTERN FRONTIERSMAN.

pleases. When stock is on the ranges that the owners have assigned for it, it is left entirely in the hands of herders, or cow-boys. These look after the stock, stand guard over it, and, if any animals wander away, they look after and hunt them up. Oftentimes several owners of stock join together, and let their herders run the same range. Some of the herding grounds are as much as fifty miles square. The cattle are allowed to run at will on this large scope of territory. The herders remain on the outskirts, where they ride around from post to post, keeping the stock within the proper bounds. A good range consists of any territory away from the settlements, with sufficient room, plenty of good grass, a supply of water, and plenty of shelter, either timber or bluffs. The herder is allowed sometimes as many as five or six ponies, which he rides by turns while herding.

The most work the herder has, is when a herd is removed from one range to another. Then great diligence is required from the herders, until the animals become accustomed to their new range. This may take some time, as some animals are naturally much inclined to wander. If some start from a herd, a great many more will follow. If animals leave the herd, and the direction they have gone is not known, which is often the case, then the range is circled until their tracks are discovered, when they are followed up and brought back. If stock is taken to a new range in the fall of the year, and is fed and salted occasionally, until they can get good grass, they do not then incline so much to rambling. Stock is very seldom fed in the West, where herded. Work cattle and milch cows are sometimes fed in bad weather.

The stock-men have certain times when they make what they call "round-ups." Then all who are interested in stock-raising, turn out and round in their stock. The calves are all branded and marked by their respective owners. This is an exciting time. The long-horned Texas and Mexican cattle, the fullbloods of that breed, wild and vicious, come pitching at horse and rider with all their mad and enraged strength. They will run right over one, if possible, and trample and gore him to death.

Here is Mr. Rust's description of the cow-boys, and their customs: "There are various rules and customs among stock-men. Some of their practices are in diametrical opposition to the statutory provisions and common law. Cow-boys are said, in the way of laudation, to be brave, bold, free-hearted and true to their friends. In the fulfillment of the above specification, they take pride, even though not in strict obedience to law and order. Yet, the services of the expert cow-boys are indispensable, and they must be tolerated, although they arrogate to themselves superior powers, and at times set law at defiance. There is practically no appeal from their decisions, they being out of the reach of law. They defend themselves most vigorously against what they may deem any encroachment upon their sacred rights. Arrests or apprehensions are seldom made on their grounds. They, like the Mormons, keep the law in their own hands.

"When a new cow-boy enters a camp, a few of the boys propose a hunt. All agree. A part of the campers, including the new one, wheel into rank for the hunt. They make a half day's ride out to some convenient hunting ground, where they prepare a camp. They leave here a proper number on guard, of which number the new comer is one. This guard is to give an alarm, in case of a surprise by Indians. Another party, from the main camp, in full Indian costume then comes rushing upon the camp about midnight. They fire twenty or thirty blank shots, and give the war whoop. The sleeping hunters awake, and raise the cry of 'Indians, boys, Indians! Run, run!' All, Greeny included, rush pell-mell into the bush, leaving the horses. It often happens that the new one is never seen again. I do not mean to insinuate that there is ever foul play used on such occasions. The new comer has simply gone off after a stock of courage."

There are many such tricks resorted to, for the sole purpose of testing the courage of a new hand. These cow-boys, or stock-herders, are bound by the sacred ties of brotherhood to defend one another. These, with the Indians, are about the only neighbors one has on the frontier.

Often you will find men with small herds, which they look after themselves; they seldom venture as far away from the pale of society as those with larger herds, who have a number of cow-boys in their employ.

The life of the frontier herder is one of continual danger. Indians are supposed to be either on reservations and peaceable, or back from the frontier. Yet, they will often come swooping down like an eagle after

READY FOR A RAID.

its prey, and kill the herders, and drive the whole herd away to their retreat. And this is so common an occurrence, that it happens every day in some part of the West. Whole settlements have been left destitute of horses, cattle and sheep, in a short time, as the principal part of the frontier-man's wealth consists of stock. When this stock is run off, he is in a very poor condition. Frequently, hard fights follow, to recover property from the Indians, where whole settlements are sometimes either murdered or driven away from their homes entirely. Of this I will speak again, further on.

CHAPTER XVI.

STOCK-BROKER AND FREIGHTER.

NEW Year's Day, 1877, found me in San Francisco, California. I had for some time been dealing in mining stocks, and, like the majority of people who dabbled in stocks that winter, I had been unsuccessful. I had bought Ophir, Mexican, Union-Consolidated and Sierra Nevada stock at a high figure. The Board of Brokers in the Stock Exchange is divided into two factions, one the opposite of the other. These factions are known to the public by their well-earned titles of "Bulls" and "Bears." The object of the "Bulls" is to keep stock up to a good price; while the "Bears" do their best to break the market by large sales of stock, often going so far as to sell stock that is not in their possession.

During the Winter both factions had taken a very active part; but the "Bears" finally won the field, and the "Bulls" had been compelled to retreat in confusion. The market had gone down, until mining stock was a drug. Previous to this time stocks had fluctuated more or less, and generally stood at fair prices. A person of shrewd judgment could make fair profits on quick sales, often doubling the money invested in a week's transaction of business. I remember that in the early part of the Winter I made a purchase of several shares in one of the leading Washoe mines, and in ten days I sold out for nearly four times what the stock cost me. But, about January 1, there came a depression. To double up stock now was only to lose, and to double on a margin was sure destruction. I with hundreds of others found myself losing daily. I could see no better way out than to sell, and save what I could by putting it into my pocket. I did so. I then found that I had lost about two-thirds of the money I had when I began. Out of the eleven thousand dollars I started in with, I saved three thousand.

I continued watching the market closely, and often thought another investment in such and such stock would prove a splendid speculation. But I was afraid to invest. This was my situation, when I received a dispatch from my uncle in Utah Territory to come on there immediately. He wished me to invest some money in teams, and to go with him as a partner to Colorado with flour. We could buy flour in Utah for three dollars a hundred. In Ouray, Colorado, flour was worth fifteen dollars a hundred, and we could readily get that price for all we might take there. We would have a good road all the way, but it was through the Ute and Piute country. The road was traveled but little, since few persons cared to undertake such a hazardous journey. My uncle had just come over the road in company with some others, and thought that we could make the trip in thirty-five days with freight teams. Having been a heavy loser in California stocks, I thought this looked like a *big thing* for me, and that

I would not be likely to find any better opportunity to redeem my shattered fortunes. I sent a letter to my uncle, asking for full particulars, and meanwhile began to settle up all my affairs, preparatory to joining him. My letter was delayed for some time on the road. I did not get an answer until near the end of the month. When the answer did come, it was sufficiently satisfactory to induce me to make the venture and see what we could do. So, on the fourth of February, I

SALT LAKE CITY, 1857.

left San Francisco for Salt Lake City, which place I reached two days after. The city of the Latter-Day Saints presented a bustling, thriving appearance, having grown from a mere straggling village in 1857 to a Mormon metropolis of some 15,000 inhabitants in 1874. I found Uncle there, but by no means ready to start. Here I met with a number of persons I had known when I first came West. Some of them I now found in good circumstances. Others were evidently rather the worse for hard luck; a great many of them in very poor circumstances, without money or property of any kind.

I was there several days, waiting to see what was to be done, for I had learned on my arrival that there were to be three partners in the undertaking. I amused myself by going to the theater in the evenings, and by hunting up and talking with old acquaintances during the day. I went one day to see Captain Bogardus kill his forty-four birds out of a possible fifty. The Captain gained celebrity in San Francisco in the sport of shooting. He is considered the crack shot of the world. The boarding at the Salt Lake House, where I stopped, was wretched. I could not stand it. I slept there, and went to the Arcade Restaurant, where I could get a good meal, for fifty cents, of anything I called for.

On Thursday, the 15th, we went to Lowell & Co., in Salt Lake City, and bought wagons, and a complete outfit of everything pertaining to them, as bows, covers, etc. The next day we shipped these, *via* the Utah Southern Railroad, to York, at that time the terminus of the road. It is nearly one hundred miles south of Salt Lake City. We went to York the same day, unloaded our wagons, and set them up. They were all large, four and one-half inch thimble, Fish Brothers' wagons, made at Racine, Wisconsin, with high beds and broad tread. We staid in York over night, and the next morning hired a man to take the wagons to Fountain Green, a settlement in the northern part of San Pete County. We went to Salt Creek by stage, and staid all night at a Gentile hotel, owned and managed by a Mr. Seely. There were a great many miners and others there, all Gentiles.

Mr. Seely being a Gentile, the Mormons would not put up with him. They preferred to stop with Mr. Foot, who kept a Mormon house. He is the man who has attained considerable notoriety from having taken so active a part in sheltering and deceiving the two wounded men who had escaped and made their way to his place, more dead than alive, from the horrible butchery of their party on the banks of the Sevier River, south of Salt Creek, by Brigham Young's infamous "destroying angels." After these two poor fellows had remained some days with Foot, they endeavored to procure transportation to Salt Lake City. An old wagon was furnished them by one man, and after a little time they found a Mormon, who agreed to hitch his team to the wagon and take them to the city. Foot had taken possession of their revolvers, and would not give them up. He, by the way, has one of them yet in his possession, a very handsome revolver, mounted in gold. When they had gone a short distance from town, the driver halted under the pretense of watering his horses. The two poor fellows were again immediately set upon by some of these hellish rascals, who were lying in wait for them, and shot with doubled-barreled shot-guns. One of them fell dead in the wagon, and the other on the outside. Their bodies were then taken to what is known as the Bottomless Spring, close by the scene of the tragedy, and there weighted with rocks, and thrown in; the cold-blooded murderers thus hiding in this spring the evidences of another of their most foul deeds. This same Foot is still keeping a hotel in Salt Creek, or was when I was there, and the rest of the perpetrators of that deed are running at large.

At Mr. Seely's, I met with a number of persons I had formerly known. Among the rest were the Gilson brothers, owners of a large herd of California horses, which they kept in Castle Valley. Sam Gilson was United States Marshal in Utah. These brothers are large, strong, daring and resolute men, each standing over six feet in height. They are very well liked by the Gentiles, but feared and held in dread by the Mormons, who repeatedly make assaults on them. They are all scarred and cut in many places on their persons, but, like cats, they are very tenacious of life.

The next day we hired a man to take us to Manti. This is a settlement in San Pete County, and entirely Mormon. The Mormons are erecting at this place another temple, similar to the one in Salt Lake City. Here we went to buying work-oxen of the Mormons. We wanted fifty yoke of cattle, so that we could work six yoke to the team, and have two yoke as extras. Six yoke of cattle and two wagons constitute a team, with one driver. We were in Manti until the morning of the twenty-fifth. We had not yet bought a sufficient number of cattle. We took twenty-four yoke and went to Fountain Green, to Mr. Dougall's flouring mill, and loaded up fifty thousand pounds of flour. There was no trouble in driving the cattle up to Fountain Green, for they were all loose, and traveled as fast as we wanted to go.

I had never driven cattle in my life, but I did not see anything to hinder me from driving. I thought about all there was to do was to walk along and keep them in the road, and, if an ox shirked a little, to touch him up with the whip. But that word "whip" brings to my memory the many painful cuttings and slashings that I inflicted upon myself. I had a whip with a lash eighteen feet long, near two inches in diameter at the largest part, and a stock about four feet long. This whip worried me. I could not crack it like other ox drivers did. I was continually trying. I wondered how they could make their whip crack so. I thought there must be some slight in it. My companions in the profession had been driving before; they had had experience. They tried to teach me. I would try, try again; I kept trying, and all I could accomplish would be to slash the tail end of my whip around my head and neck. I would then try the under hand lick; would succeed in cutting myself most unmercifully around the legs, or else in getting the lash all coiled and entangled about my feet, almost throwing me down. I would stop and uncoil it, and get it all straightened out, and then try to swing it over and around my head, but there was something wrong with the whip, for the snapper and my head were continually coming in contact with each other, bringing the water to my eyes. I was, of course, angry, and out of patience, but I kept my sufferings to myself. Myself and whip afforded much amusement to the boys. I was vexed to think I was outdone. I would steal out with my whip where I thought I would be unobserved, to practice striking at some object. But the boys were wide-awake fellows when there was any prospect for fun. They would steal a march on me, and lie concealed and watch me cutting and slashing away with that whip in very dead earnest. When they had laughed until their sides were sore, and their cheeks were wet with tears of amusement (and mine, meanwhile, with tears of anger and pain), they would then laugh outright, and make their presence known to me. Then I would invariably wilt.

After our flour was all loaded, we then set to work to yoke up the cattle. That was another job I dreaded, and the more so after we had the cattle corraled in a large pen. I was nervous, I have no doubt, for some of the cattle had horns; and, oh! what horns! —nearly as long as the rest of the body; they looked frightful. Some of the cattle were wild, very wild, while others were friendly, in fact, too friendly, for they would come as far as they could get their horns through the corral fence to meet us. I do not know why, but somehow or other, it became an understood thing, from the start, that I was to help yoke and tend the cattle. I cannot tell the experience of others, but my first lesson in yoking up convinced me of several things. First, that Texas and Mexican cattle have horns, and that they are not particular how they use them. And, secondly, that each one of them is in possession of a pair of hind legs that a mule might be proud of. Probably the only thing that kept me from using my revolver, which I was carrying in my belt, was that such action might be fraught with much more danger to the persons around the corral, watching, laughing and joking, and to my companions on the inside, than to the particular ox which was just then the object of my ire. Some of these cattle were easy to yoke. We had to lasso others of them, and draw them up to a post. We would put a yoke on the one caught, and then lasso another and draw him up beside that one. We used the gentle ones for leaders, and would drive these around in front of the wild ones, and fasten them together by a chain, before we let them loose.

After a long time had been spent in yoking and hitching up, we drove out, starting back to Manti, where we expected to get more cattle and more freight. The roads were very muddy. In the settled portion of Utah, there is a ditch on either side of every street and road, and many cross-ditches, so that water is running in every direction, to be used for irrigating and other purposes. These ditches are seldom, if ever, bridged, and the mud is much deeper than the water. Whenever we came to one of these settlements, we would put twelve yoke of cattle to one wagon, and then a number of drivers would range themselves on each side of the team, and whoop, and cut, and slash, until we got through town. All the people in the village would run to their doors, and stand in groups through the streets, watching the fun. Sometimes a chain would break; it was sure to break when the wagon was in the worst place. Then we would put on more cattle, sometimes we would have twenty yoke of cattle to one wagon; and, by this time, if it was in town, the whole population would be gathered around, looking at the team and wagon, and laughing and passing remarks, not the most complimentary. We would then try again, all hands assisting, by pushing the wagon, and endeavoring to roll the wheels. Everybody not engaged in whipping the cattle or pushing the wagon, would assist by shaking their hats, and yelling at the top of their voices; and the poor cattle would by this time be so terribly frightened, that, if a chain did not break, they were sure to run out with the wagon. In a scene of this kind, the drivers were very apt, accidently of course, to let some of the bystanders feel the weight of their whips, which action always added not a little to the confusion of the moment. I was very willing at such times to give up my whip, and go back in the mud and water, and push, for, had I tried to use the whip, no one else could have come near the same side of the cattle. Neither was I safe from a whip in my own hands.

I remember, the second day of March, we had got to Parley Allred's place, in San Pete County, Utah. There we stuck in the mud about noon. We worked until twelve at night, whipping and slashing, until there were, I know, as many as three hundred people around, pulling and pushing, and helping us through a mud hole that was not over three hundred feet across. Here I fared roughly, for, in the early part of the afternoon, I had gone in among the cattle to fix a chain, when one of them kicked me, knocking me down in the mud, with which I was completely covered, and, while I was trying to get out, he struck me another lick, knocking me back against the off-pointer. He was an ugly brute. He made a pass at me with his long horns, but I was so close to him that he only struck me with the side of them. He knocked me clean out of time, however. I landed, not as one usually sits down, but on the flat of my back in the mud. Then and there I swore vengeance upon that ox. To find myself crawling out of the mud in this pitiable plight, looking more like a hog that had just been wallowing in the mire than the well-dressed city lad I had been but a few days before, was more than human nature could endure. I rebelled. If I could have had my money back that I had already invested, I would have given up the freighting business on the spot, and would never have tried to drive another ox. But I was like other men often have been, and will continue to be; I had got my foot into the mud, and must either push through or stick fast.

We got back to Manti on the night of the fifth of March. The roads had been muddy all the way. Here we remained for two days, buying up more cattle, to fill out our teams. We also filled out our loads, making ten thousand pounds of freight to the team.

On the morning of the eighth, we had everything in readiness, including beds, clothing, guns, provisions for two months, and a cooking outfit. The roads were heavy, and we made but a short drive the first day.

We were now on the road for San Juan, Colorado. We intended to follow the old road that Captain Gunnison took his soldiers over in 1855. It had never been traveled over since. It will be my endeavor to describe the route, as I go along, the best I can. I think that I have had a better opportunity to view that section of country than any white man that ever was there before me.

Our train was arranged as follows: William Johnson Black, of Manti, drove the lead team. I was second. George B. Kelly, of Salt Lake City, next; William Stringan, of Manti, fourth; Albert Stevens, of Salt Lake City, next; Charley Manser, next; Neals Mortison, of Salina, Utah, next; and one of the young Taylors, of Utah, last. Each one had his regular duty assigned to him. Charley Manser did the cooking. I attended to the cattle when unyoked; saw that they got water, and were put on feed for the night, when I could find any. Then Dave Mortison took them off of my hands, and herded them until morning. Dave herded at night, and slept in the day-time in one of the wagons. In the morning I would saddle the horse I used, and go and help to round up the cattle, and drive them to camp, preparatory to yoking. The others attended to getting wood, water, greasing wagons, and other things that were necessary. Mr. Hess was the "boss," or had charge of the outfit, and as he had been over the road, or part of it at least, he was supposed to know more about it than the balance of us. I had never been east of Salina through the country, and it was all new to me.

The first night we camped at Six Mile Creek, and the next on the bend of the Sevier River, Wasatch Mountains. The third night we reached Salina; this is the last settlement we will pass through in Utah. Salina is a small place, only a few Mormon families living there. There were at one time nearly one hundred families there, but they were frightened away, or killed by the Indians. Salina is in a very nice location, at the foot of the Wasatch range.

SEVIER RIVER, WASATCH MOUNTAINS.

On the south is an elbow of the range, that shuts off all view from town in that direction; on the east is the main range; while, about one-half mile to the west of town, is the Sevier River, which runs into Sevier Lake, and then disappears.

Salina Creek runs through the town in irrigating

ditches. We found a great many of the houses deserted, and falling down. There was an old stone fort near the center of town, at this time used for a corral. There is a post-office and one small co-operative store. The houses are well made of adobes, with dirt roofs. The place presents a gloomy and dismal appearance. The land all around this place is sandy, and better adapted to raising potatoes than anything else. Children do well here, I suppose, for they are very numerous.

From this place we go into Salina Cañon, and follow it to its head, which is the summit of the Wasatch range, for we are now wanting to get to Castle Valley. Six miles before we get to the summit, the cañon widens out and rolls gradually away on each side, for two miles or more, thus forming a small valley. In front the range becomes more steep. We find a small stream of water running through this park, and a small cabin built of quaking asps. This is used as a shelter and camping-house, by Mr. Jennings' herders. Mr. Jennings, of Salt Lake City, has taken up and located land here, and has had others to locate lands for him, until he claims here a large stock ranch. He has hundreds of cattle here running wild, including all ages from sucking calves to old, full-grown animals, and they are scattered all over the country. We found two young men here herding for Mr. Jennings.

Here we came to snow, the first we had seen on the way. It was six miles to the top of the range, and about the same distance down the other side out of the snow. The ground was very muddy underneath, where it was not rocky. In some places the snow was fifteen feet deep. We had to shovel a road through the snow. Our hands got wet and soft, and blistered all over the palms. We were compelled to wade through snow and mud all day long. None of us expected such obstructions on the way. It was a terrible undertaking to work our way over. We took

HERDERS' CAMPING HOUSE.

up one wagon at a time, and the rest of the party, not needed in keeping the wagons up, were continually shoveling snow. Our faces were all burned to a blister, and our eyes presented a frightful appearance. There was but little feed for our cattle, as the herded droves had consumed all there was in that region. We kept teams hauling hay from the settlements by contract, until we passed the summit. Mr. Jennings had a large corral in the park, to which we drove our cattle after the day's work was done, and fed them upon the hay. In this way, for five long, hard weeks, we labored to reach the summit, Then commenced another task of getting down, for the snow was as deep on one side as on the other. But, on the west side, the mountain was very steep. We rough-locked all the wheels, then cut pine trees, and chained them by the top to the hind end of the wagon. We used a single yoke of heavy-wheel oxen to guide and keep the tongue straight in the road.

Allow just a word of advice to any who may be contemplating traveling over that road. Go on horseback. Take pack animals and plenty of provisions, and not too much baggage. You will not go far before you find baggage a great nuisance, and wish you were rid of it. Take but few dishes in your cooking outfit, as they are a nuisance. You will soon learn that the fewer dishes you have, the fewer you will need to wash, and, if they are no women in the party, you will find dish-washing a burden. It is impossible to keep warm in camp, on the summit of the Wasatch in March. The wind is continually blowing, and the snow flying and drifting, so that you can not see, and can scarcely stand.

Around our meals we would console ourselves with the thought that we must expect the bitter with the sweet. But before we get through with shoveling snow, pushing wagons, thrashing cattle, and climbing up and down that mountain, we concluded that we were getting far more than our share of the bitter.

The clouds had hung low and black nearly all the time we had been crossing the range. Enough snow kept falling to make matters still more uncomfortable. We were six weeks making thirteen miles, and we worked every day, Sunday not excepted. This was less than one-third of a mile a day. Our cattle were nearly starved.

SHOSHONEE INDIANS IN THE SEVIER VALLEY.

They were fat when we started, and already they were reduced to skeletons. Complimentary remarks would often be passed about the thinnest ones, such as propos, als to tie knots in their tails, to keep them from running through the bows of the yoke. From Gilson's ranch it was difficult to realize that we were in a straight line, only twenty miles from Salina. But such was the case. After passing over the summit and coming to Gilson's, we saw rolling country ahead of us, as far as the eye could reach. Upon inquiry, I learned that we would not go on in that direction, however, but would turn to the left as soon as we reached the valley still lower down. There was little snow here, consequently the cattle got plenty to eat. Here was a splendid stream of water also. We moved on down the cañon to Ivy Creek, and were then sixty-seven miles from Manti. The country is very dreary, and is uninhabited, except by straggling bands of half-starved Shoshonee Indians. It is very seldom that a white man visits this section. In the following chapter I will speak further of our experiences on this journey.

CHAPTER XVII.

IN GREEN RIVER VALLEY.

WE reached Green River the eighth day of May, having been exactly two months on the road. We had now passed through Castle Valley, so named from the numerous castle rocks that can be seen in all directions. Hundreds of rocks can be seen rearing their heads in dome-like or spiral shape, high above the mountains that encompass the valley. There is no one living in this valley. Not a house is to be seen for one hundred and fifty miles west of Green River. White men are seldom seen here. There were two brothers, white men, living on Grand River, of whom I will speak again later. They were killed while we were on Green River. With their exception, we were the only white men in this part of the country. There are a great many little streams running across Castle Valley into Green River. Ivies Creek has clear, good water. The next is Salaratus Creek, seven miles from Ivies Creek. The water in this is not fit for man or beast to drink; it is so strong of alkali. The next is Convulsion Creek, eight miles further up. This is a dangerous stream, narrow, with high banks. The water runs with a very swift current.

The next stream is the Quickapaw, two miles further on. This water, like that of Convulsion Creek, is not good. The next is the Muddy, a very dangerous stream of muddy water, and where we crossed with a quick-sand bottom. We had to strain the sand and mud out of the water, and then allow it to settle before we could drink it. This is brackish also. From the Muddy to the Ferrons is nine miles. This stream is of clear, brackish water, between high banks. From the Ferrons to the Cottonwood is ten miles. From the Cottonwood to Huntington Creek is three miles. Huntington Creek is of fresh water, and is a pretty stream, with high banks and gravelly bottom. We turned to the right at Huntington Creek, and went on past the Rock Wells. The first wells are eleven, and the second fifteen miles from Huntington Creek. From this point to the Green River is thirty-five miles. It is one hundred and sixty-four miles to the settlements.

Castle Valley includes an area of several thousand acres, but it is not very valuable for agricultural purposes. There is some little grass, but it is nearly all alkali grass. The soil is full of sand and fine gravel. The mountains on either side (until we get near Green River), are of sand and sand rock. There are large bowlders and fragments of sand rock scattered over the lower end of the valley. Hundreds of sand *buttes* are to be seen scattered about here and there. Time, the rains and the wind have crumbled and washed down their sides, until they stand up like tall pyramids, hundreds of feet in height. We could climb to the top of some of them by a very easy and safe ascent. Others are so perpendicular that the top cannot be reached without the aid of some mechanical contrivance. From some of these giant points of sand rock, we could look out over the many lower *buttes* standing in the valley. The place appeared very much as if you were standing in the center of the plain, overlooking an immense ruin.

Rock Wells are well named from the place in which they are located. They are not wells of water fed from below the ground; they are merely holes in the naked, black rock, which is found here without dirt enough on a square mile of it to cover a bushel of potatoes. It is a large, bare plain of smooth rock, dipping in all directions up and down. There are holes in these rocks, from one foot to hundreds of feet in depth. It sometimes rains very hard here, and these holes are then filled with water. When we passed through, we suffered very much for want of good water. What we got from these holes had to be strained, and then boiled, before we could use it. It was full of little animals, from the minutest size up to as large as a man's thumb. After we strained the water, we had a larger pile of these than there was bulk of water. The cattle fared worse than we did. We watered them from buckets, and then turned them loose, to hunt over the mountains for what feed they could find growing out of the crevices in the rocks, which was so very little that they almost starved.

Going down this mountain, we traveled for miles over the solid bed rock. Sometimes we would have all the wheels of the wagons locked. Then we would go for a little distance with the locks all off, and then again would be compelled to double up the teams for a hard pull. After we got over this, we came to an alkali sand plain. The alkali is so thick that it looks like snow. This is a wretched place through which to travel. The sand is so loose that the wagons cut down to the axles all the time. The dry alkali flying in the air soon blinds both man and beast. We were white with dust. Our flesh burned and smarted with an itching and pain. Of all the alkali plains in the West, this is the worst I ever traveled over.

When we reached Green River, we found a most beautiful valley. It was so different from any thing I had ever seen, that I pronounced it at first sight one of the prettiest places in the West. Beautiful grass was waving on the river bottoms, and the trees were all out in leaf and bloom. Green River Valley is narrow at the point where we entered it. The river runs crosswise of the first bench lands. The bottom lands are a half mile in width. On either side of the bench lands, the river runs through cañons, with rugged, rough mountains on either side, towering up higher than the timber line. The cañon is here separated by a valley eight miles in width, so that the length of Green River Valley is the width of Salaratus Valley, the valleys crossing each other. Green River Valley is ninety feet lower than Salaratus Valley.

When we reached the river, it was so high we could not ford it. We tried a raft, but failed to get over in this way, as the swift, running current would sweep a heavy log raft into the cañon below. The river was eight hundred feet wide between the banks, which are high and undermined in many places with the water. They are on this account continually falling in here and there, making a terrible noise that can be

CAMP IN GREEN RIVER VALLEY.

heard a long distance. After we tried to cross by a raft and failed, we had to send a man on horseback back to Manti for a boat, and the rest of us remained to guard the train and herd the cattle. I passed away part of the time in hunting up and down the river. We had a beautiful place for our camp. This was the first perfect camping place we had found. There were beautiful groves of large cotton-wood trees along the river bottom, furnishing plenty of wood for fires; no mud, some sand, abundance of grass for our cattle, and plenty of fish and game. This abundance of good things was enough to repay us for much of the hardship thus far encountered. There were some in the party who seemed to have no idea of the beautiful. They might travel all over the country, and see all its beauties, and after all would pick out a well-filled cupboard as the prettiest sight they ever met with. They never could understand how anything was to be gained by such a journey as this, though through such grand and beautiful scenery. Their idea of traveling would be to follow the valley roads, and feast with their Mormon brothers over night.

We had all started out with bright anticipations of a two months' trip. We had now been over two months out, and were not yet across the first river; and there were several wide rivers yet to cross. But there we were, and I determined to get all the enjoyment possible out of this journey. I was very thankful to be out of the cold and chilly storms of the Wasatch. The skies were blue, and the days were as warm as in summer.

After having rested a day or two, I concluded to go up the river to the cañon, about five miles distant. So taking my gun, I started early in the morning.

Near the river were patches of brush, so thick that it was impossible to pass through. In addition to the brush were numerous sloughs full of water, some of them deep. These sloughs were covered with ducks and geese, which would fly from one side to the other as I approached near them. I saw deer and antelope feeding in large numbers. They would bound away upon my approach. I went back farther from the river, and got upon higher ground, out of the brush. There I found the ground cut up with deep gullies. After traveling a number of miles, I came to the mouth of the cañon. I found it narrow, with steep and rugged mountains on either side of the river, which is very narrow, and runs with a much swifter current here.

NIGHT SCENE IN GREEN RIVER CANON.

I concluded, as it was yet early, to climb to the top of the mountain, and take a view of the surrounding country. I found this a difficult undertaking. I would climb awhile, and then rest. I could look back and see the river twisting along in its course to the cañon below, there to be lost sight of in another range of mountains, separate from the one I was then climbing. This is an uninhabited region, and has never been marred by the hand of civilization. The members of our party are the only white men on the river. Flowers of the richest hues, and of endless variety adorned as with a robe of beauty the extended valley below, while the distant green groves, dotting the banks of the river here and there before me, appeared like emerald isles floating in a sea of glory. I could but gaze with rapture upon the magnificent scenes, the beauties and sublimities of nature as they lay unrolled before me. I was far above the valleys on either side of the river, and could see far out in the direction we desired to go.

I kept climbing higher and higher until I wondered if I would ever reach the top. I would sometimes come up plump against the steep sides of a ledge. Then I would have to meander up and down, and around, to get to the top of that, and there, most likely, come up against another one. I saw numbers of mountain sheep, and shot one of them. These sheep are as noble-looking and as pretty a wild animal as I ever saw. They are harmless. I have been told that they will jump off of precipices, and strike on their heads, on the rocks below, and then go bounding off from danger. This may be true, but I never saw them going through such any unpleasant performances. The sheep are natives of rocky places, so I think this locality exactly suited to them. Their horns are at the largest part six inches in diameter, are tapering and curved, and from ten to fifteen inches in length.

I found the mountain barren of vegetation, and with many deep wash-outs. The cañon was very deep and narrow, as far as I could see. When I returned to camp I carried with me a quarter of the sheep I had killed. I was tired and hungry when I got into camp, but plenty of fish, bread and venison had been prepared in good style, and I was soon seated on the front end of the wagon, feasting as sumptuously as a king.

Beaver and otter are very numerous at this place. Dozens of them could be seen in the evening carrying sticks to form their houses or dams, or swimming in the water, or climbing up the steep banks. All along the river where there are little groves of trees, the marks of their cuttings can be seen. Trees over one foot across have been cut down with their teeth. I have seen as many as three, all cutting on the same tree. They are very cautious and cunning. The least noise will drive them to the water, to be seen no more for hours. They have their trails from the water to their cuttings. Their slides in places are worn down several feet in depth, on the edge of steep banks. When the beaver travels on land, his trowel-shaped tail is so heavy that it drags the ground, like a board dragged along by one end. When swimming along in the water, the least motion or noise will cause them to dive suddenly, striking the water at the same time with their flat tails, making a noise similar to striking on the water with a long paddle. At night they keep up a noise the whole time, fighting, squealing and slapping the water with their tails. They are sixty pounds and upward in weight. They are easily trapped, if the trapper understands his business, but unless he does know how to go about it he will not catch any except by accident. It is interesting and amusing to watch three or four beavers cutting down a tree. They sit down, and twist their heads a little sidewise, and then with their broad, chisel-like teeth, they cut deep into the wood at every bite. They cut round and round, equally on all sides. In many places in the West, beavers are very numerous, but a great many are caught every season. Their houses are generally formed by burrowing in under the deep banks, and then filling up in front with huge piles of weeds, mud and sticks.

Here, on Green River, is the worst place for snakes I know of. I did not see them corded up in piles, as large as some people write about, and scores of feet in length, but for numbers and varieties this locality can not be surpassed. Often when one is not thinking of them, they frighten him terribly by crawling up against him. I am not afraid of a snake, but then I do not like to be social with them.

The snakes live in colonies on Green River. I have seen them crawling in every direction at the same time. Some of them are very large, as much as seven feet long. Rattlesnakes are numerous, and of all sizes, from tiny ones up to three and one-half feet in length. Some of these have lived to a good old age. I killed one three feet long, that had twenty-two rattles, and a button on the end of his tail, so that if I am informed correctly, he was twenty-three years of age. It is said that a rattlesnake has a button on the end of his tail the first year, and for every succeeding year a rattle. I think this is correct.

When we would start out to look after the cattle, we would cut a good, heavy club before we went far, with which to kill snakes. I remember that one morning I was out looking up the cattle. I had a desire to climb to the top of one of the rocky *buttes*. I had not gone far up the hill-side when I could see snakes lying coiled up, or stretched out in every shape, sunning themselves on and among the rocks. I think these were all rattlesnakes. I had not yet come close enough to arouse them, for I saw them before they began to rattle. I counted over twenty, without moving from where I stood. I moved on toward them, keeping a careful watch at my feet. They were soon aroused, and, coiling themselves up, there was immediately a great rattling along the lines on both sides of me. Their eyes were glittering, and their forked tongues protruding, and every one warning me that I was then trespassing on forbidden ground. They seemed to be more numerous on this slope than I had ever before seen in any mountain country. In Rattlesnake Gulch, California, there are thousands of them, but this

Green River slope leads in snakes. I retreated and left them in possession of their stronghold. This was but a small, rocky knoll or knob, rising about two hundred feet above the plain, and covering perhaps, two acres. There must be thousands of snakes there. On the river bottom, a long, yellow-spotted snake is found in great numbers. This species can run like a racer. These are called bull-snakes, I believe.

At another time I had occasion to go to the top of one of the peaks; for, if cattle are not in sight while you are standing on the plain, they may often be seen from some elevation, feeding in the distance. I was sitting on one of these high points one morning, early. From this position I could look to the east, and at the foot of the *butte* running east, was a deep depression. The *butte* had been rather difficult to climb, and I was halting a little to rest my lungs, as a person finds

PEAK IN GREEN RIVER VALLEY.

some difficulty in breathing, when climbing one of these high peaks here in the mountains. This, however, was a high peak in the valley between the mountains. I could hear the distant howl of wolves in various directions. I noticed that they seemed to get nearer, and more numerous. They soon were howling all around me. I wondered what was up. Soon a number of them came in sight. I now saw what was the matter. They had started a deer, and were chasing it down. It was out-running the wolves, but there were too many closing in on all sides. They were at the far end of the basin from me, but I could see the chase very plain. The wolves took turns, running and heading off the deer, until they finally succeeded in capturing it, when they became so eager after the poor thing's carcass, that I could hear their teeth snapping together two hundred yards away. There were twenty wolves taking part in the feast.

When a hunter, wounds a deer, and, darkness coming on stops the chase for the night, should it be renewed next morning, he will often find where the deer has been caught and devoured by wolves. They can scent blood or fresh meat a long distance away. When chasing game, their howling is very different from that at other times, and is of such a nature that they apparently all understand what is going on, for they seem to come running together immediately, and to form themselves into a circle. Once, later, when I was in the Dolores country of Colorado, I remember seeing them chasing a jack-rabbit. They would take turns running. A single wolf would not run far at any one time before he would be relieved by a fresh animal.

And so among all these varied scenes, and amid the varied scenery, each successive day brought with it some novelty, and such scenes and incidents as kept up an unabating and lively interest in the minds of our party, until the boat arrived from Manti, which was not until the eleventh day of June.

CHAPTER XVIII.

VEXATIOUS DELAYS.

THE boat having arrived, we began to unload, and to take the wagons to pieces. The boat was small, only three and one-half feet in width by fourteen feet in length. It was flat-bottomed, built of three-quarter inch pine lumber. With close packing it would carry twelve hundred pounds. Everything had to be adjusted very carefully, or else the boat would list to the heavy side and become unmanageable. We got along very well, however, carrying over two wagons and their loads in a day. We left the cattle until the last. We undertook to make them swim over by tying a rope around the horns of one of them, and attaching the other end of the rope to the boat, and thus towing him over. One of us would row the boat, while the rest would drive the other cattle into the water, and then whoop and halloo until our throats were sore, and throw clods and sticks and stones at them, trying to make them follow across. The cattle would go well enough until they struck the main current; then they would begin to "mill," the current carrying them down stream all the time, until they would finally strike back for the same side they had started from. The current would beat them back against the high banks, where they remained struggling in the water, scattered nearly all the way down to the cañon. Then we would have to go to work and dig down the banks, so that they could get out.

In this way we kept on trying, never getting over more than six at any one time, and often only the one that was towed over. We were two days getting all the cattle over. Some of them, while being towed, would dive apparently straight down, and come up almost under the boat. Towing the cattle across the stream was a dangerous undertaking, for the little boat was too light to hold them, and they could nearly master the oarsman. I got out of patience, and tried to ride some of them over; but all to no purpose. My uncle and my other companions kept advising me to be patient. Patience is a very good thing, and all well enough; but how any man can have patience for many days while trying, as we were, to swim cattle over Green River, with the mosquitoes eating him up all the time, is more than I can tell.

We had everything safely over by the 23d of June. We were very busy all that day fixing things in readiness for moving on the next morning. But during the night a grizzly got down among the cattle where the herder was tending them on the river bottom, and frightened them off in all directions. Two yoke jumped into the river, and crossed back to the other side again. We could not see them, but could hear them on the opposite side of the river, splashing in the water, and bellowing. At this time, however, we did not know how many had crossed over, but we felt confident that these were some of our cattle. So we unloaded the boat from the wagon, where we had it packed up to haul to Grand River, and carried it down to the river, and hunted up a lot of ropes, and some shovels. Then four of us struck across in the darkness for the other side, which we soon reached.

We felt sure that the cattle were below where we landed. The banks of Green River are so undermined in time of high water that there is a constant caving in, and a consequent splashing and eddying of the water, and a variety of noises. This seems to be particularly the case when you are hunting for cattle in the darkness that you know are in the water and needing assistance, and are compelled to find them by hearing, instead of seeing. This was our situation at this time. I was keeping down close to the bank, while the other boys were keeping off considerable distance from the river. The noise of the rushing water often made me think there was an ox where there was none. I was listening at the different sounds intently, trying to discern the cause of each. I told my companions, if I found the oxen I would sing out. We had waded through brush, mud, bogs and everything else disagreeable, when I thought I heard one of the cattle. At this point the bank was about six feet high, and the willows and brush were very thick. I doubt if they can be found as thick at any other point along the river. Some of these had drooped over until their tops were kept constantly in motion by the agitated waters, which here had formed a very deep, ugly-looking place, as I afterwards saw, and had run in to a considerable distance under the bank.

When I cautiously advanced to the edge of the stream to ascertain the cause of the great splashing, the whole bank gave way, and in I went. I did not go to the bottom. I began to struggle for the bank as soon as I struck the water, and as soon as I could get my mouth open began to yell for the boys. The water was carrying me down all the time. I was badly frightened. I soon managed, however, to catch hold of a long root that was being dangled about through the water, and I hung on to this until the boys came with a rope and fished me out.

The cattle were finally found, and we tied them up to trees, and pulled for camp. I was too mad to talk to any one, and I do believe that at that time I would not have re-crossed the river for the whole train. The next morning we got the cattle back from where we had tied them, and spent the day in camp. But on the next day when the herder brought the cattle to camp, there were seven of them missing. We thought, perchance, they were in the bush, and had been overlooked; so we started out in various directions to find them. I struck for the high *buttes*, so that I could look back over the river. I had an idea that they had re-crossed and gone back. About noon I returned to camp, without any success.

I found a part of the other searchers in camp, but no cattle. They were having a big talk over something that William Stringan had seen. I made inquiries in regard to the matter, and in reply heard a rather curious story. It seemed, that, like the rest of us, Mr. Stringan had had poor success in finding cattle, but he had discovered a mysterious-looking track, which he had easily traced for some distance. The track of the right foot was in every particular like that of an ox's foot, with the foot stepping sideways, pointing out from the body, while that of the left foot was of a human barefoot. I listened very intently to his description of the track, and of how he had followed it, until it led to a certain thicket which he described, when he was afraid to proceed further, and had come to camp. My curiosity was now aroused. I must see that track, for I had never seen anything to compare with it. So, as soon as dinner was over, Hess, Stringan and myself started in search of the track, I wondering meanwhile what on earth it could be. After walking a considerable distance, we reached the place where Stringan had discovered the track, and, sure enough, there it was, just as he had described it. It could be seen plainly in the sandy soil; it led from the foot-hills at the base of the mountain toward the river. Hess and Stringan followed the track toward the river, while I took the back track, to see where the half cloven-footed "varmint" had come from. In the valley I could follow the track as fast as I could travel. On higher ground the track disappeared. In such places I would follow the general course I had been coming, and every time I found myself upon reaching the sand again entirely off the track. I thought this was curious; that a direct general course should be followed through the soft sand, but, as soon as the hard earth was reached, that then the course should turn in an entirely different direction. Before I had been fooled very many times, I made up my mind that this was a very cunning animal, and once or twice I imagined that there might be something or some body connected with the track, foreboding no good. I followed the track over hills and through hollows, and across gulches and gullies, for three miles or more, when I came to a place where it doubled on itself; then I had the two tracks to follow, one going and one coming. I followed these a short distance across the bench land, and into another deep gully, where I found a pony track, and near by I found where the pony had been picketed.

This was convincing proof to me, satisfactory enough of what was up; yet I thought it exceedingly strange that one person should come here in this way, and appear in such a peculiarly odd manner. The thought flashed through my mind that something unusual was going to happen, and it might be that there were more connected with this strange movement than one single individual. What could he want, who could he be, and why were his feet so disguised? It might be that he had confederates in league with him, and that they had run off a part of the cattle belonging to our train. Why had they not taken all? I could see no tracks of the cattle here; but they might have driven them in some other direction. A thousand questions suggested themselves to my mind. I finally came to the conclusion that there must be a band of Indians in the neighborhood, who had got part of our cattle, and were running them off. Of this, I would soon assure myself. I struck for camp after my horse. When I arrived at camp, it was already getting late in the afternoon, being after four o'clock, but the other boys had not returned.

My horse was picketed close to camp. It was the work of a few minutes only to throw on my saddle and make ready, and I was soon galloping out over the bench land. I had made up my mind to find where the cattle had been driven out, if they had been driven out at all. So I rode to the upper end of the valley, carefully noticing everything, as a man naturally would when looking for stock under such circumstances. I made a circuit of the whole upper end of the valley, and convinced myself that the cattle had not passed out on the Colorado side of the river. When I arrived in camp again it was dark. The company had all gathered in, but without finding the lost cattle. I was then convinced that the cattle had crossed the river.

So early the next morning, I saddled my horse and rode down to the river. Here I dismounted, and taking off my clothes, I tied them and my revolver in a bundle, and secured it to the barrel of my rifle. I then mounted my horse again, and started into the river. It was a frightful undertaking, for the river was high, and the current swift. At this time it was nearly one-half mile in width. Logs, brush, drift-wood and whole trees were sweeping along down the current, as if in a race. Our whole party was at the bank to see me across. It seemed to me at times as if I was riding on my last trip. But a horse is a noble swimmer, and mine faithfully carried me across one of the worst streams in North America. I immediately struck back on the road we had come. After going nearly a mile, I discovered the trail of the lost cattle, and, after riding fast, I caught up with them at the Rock Wells. They were all together. Here I met one of the Taylors from Utah. He was on his way to the Green brothers, at the old Mormon fort, near the junction of Green and Grand Rivers. We pushed the cattle back at a lively gait, and drove them across the river without much trouble. We stripped off our clothes and crossed the river the same way I had crossed in the morning. The next morning, another of the younger Taylor boys, who had been with the Green brothers, came into camp and reported the Greens killed, and their stock driven off.

There were two of these brothers; one named Cyrus, and the other W. T. Green. They had come to Utah a few years prior to this time. They had considerable money with them, which they invested in cattle and horses, until they had over two hundred head of cattle, and one hundred and forty head of horses. A greater portion of Utah is unsettled, and consequently the land is unclaimed, and belongs to Uncle Sam. So the boys drove their stock into the upper end of Castle Valley, or rather between Castle Valley and Fish Lake. Here they remained only a short time, as some other parties claimed a prior herd right, and notified them to that effect.

Now, these Green brothers, like hundreds of others who have come into the territory of the Saints, denounced them and their notions as wrong; and the general judgment of mankind likewise so denounces them. For the disciples of Brigham Young constantly proclaim their conscientiousness in accepting the dogma of polygamy, and one cannot oppose them in this particular without denying the validity of the authority they set up, both in and out of church. This is always the case with every doctrine that runs counter to the general human sense of right. The public judgment of what is proper, is that it must square with the generally accepted ideas of truth and right. What the Mormons call faith has been pronounced credulity.

ORSON PRATT, MORMON PROPHET.

What they dignify as a religion has been decided to be a superstition. Injustice has been done to all classes not believing in their wild and fanciful notions. Men have been compelled to either leave the Territory or to part with every earthly possession they had accumulated. And this Church works in co-operation together throughout the whole country. It has proved itself a power in the hands of dangerous men. Their leaders have honors paid them by all their followers, and the more virulence with which their character is attacked, the greater the esteem in which they are held among their own people. They have lived, however, to see the beginning of an exodus, which may yet involve consequences of political significance. Their career has been a marvelous one in its devotion to an absurd idea—marvelous in its extravagant notions, especially in reference to the doctrines of their religion. The men who founded these iniquitous institutions are passing away one by one. Those who are left pause in their busy work to do honor to their dead prophets. They seldom yield to any sense of justice. They scorn any policy based only on just principles. They follow their false premises to their logical conclusions. If they listen at all to reason or justice, they listen only to laugh or despise. The poorer classes make but little provision for their own support. They take a liberal view of the promises of their prophets, and obey their so-called divine injunction. If they fail to obey these, they call down upon themselves the guilt of unpardonable sin. They ponder and debate, in their weak way, the awful mysteries spoken by their prophets. How often in the course of their career must the doubt have come to them whether they were acting in the spirit of love and obedience, or in that of superstition and credulity. Unrestrained in their traffic, they almost control all that part of the country. A tremendous power is concentrated in the hands of the rulers of the

Mormon Church. They wield a power that any other people would hesitate to exercise. It is clear that it will not answer, even for those who hold the right of private judgment in matters of religion, to allow all to indulge in their vagaries. Wild and untutored notions will soon come to possess many, and the result will be that superstition will grow rife, and, in the name of faith, deeds will be done that will shock the common sense and the conscience of mankind. This, indeed, has

FORMER RESIDENCES OF BRIGHAM YOUNG.

been the case time and time again in Utah. The stranger and the Saint are frequently dickering together and oftentimes the pretended divine leads his newly formed acquaintance into a lengthy argument, merely for the sake of betrayal before the community. Oftentimes they run across one that comprehends well what these demonstrations mean, far better than if he had been told in so many words. These much-married saints generally appeal to their versions of the divine law. The saints, therefore, berate and oppose the Gentiles in their undertakings. They denounce the colonization of their Territory. There is, consequently, always a very bitter feeling existing between the two parties. Such was the state of affairs in the Territory when the Green boys drove their cattle over into the bottom lands of Grand River.

There had been a fort built there years previous to this time by the Mormons, who thought to colonize and settle up the valley. But to this the Indians were adverse. They attacked the Mormons in their stronghold, and routed them after a severe fight in which several from both parties were killed. The old fort had stood vacant until the Greens moved into it as a protection against the storms, and a place where they could store away such goods as they had with them. This is a beautiful little valley, with plenty of wood and water, and an abundant supply of grass, where stock by hundreds may graze. Game, of various kinds, is here found in vast quantities, and the waters afford abundance of fish. If this valley were not so far from civilization, it would be one of the most desirable places in all the country for a few families to settle in.

Here the Greens had been for over a year, witnessing the rapid increase and prosperity of their herd. Here they were massacred. The first that was known about the horrible butchering was when young Taylor brought back the report. He was not an eye-witness, but had gone to see Cyrus Green on some business.

He found their dog, but no person at the fort, and he went in search of the boys, and soon found every evidence of foul play. He stated that he could readily follow the trail by which the stock had been driven off, as numbers of them had been killed and left along the route. Some had been left crippled, but were not yet dead. He could find no trace of the boys, but from the looks of everything around he was sure they were dead, or had been hardly dealt with. Whoever had done the deed must have been in somewhat of a hurry, as nearly sixty head of the cattle were yet left on the range. Their dog was in the fort, but could not be persuaded or coaxed to leave. Everything about the place was just as the Greens had arranged it. Nothing had been meddled with. Even one of their coats still hung on the corner of the the fort, just as they had left it.

GEORGE A. SMITH, MORMON APOSTLE.

The news was carried to the settlements as soon as a horse could travel the distance. A large party was immediately organized, which made a forced march on horseback to the place. After considerable search, they found the body of the eldest brother, six or seven miles from the fort, lying near the trail in a a thicket of bushes, with a bullet hole in the back of his head. No trace of the younger brother was discovered. He had, doubtless, shared the same fate with his brother.

This, then, gave us some clue to the mysterious tracks and maneuvers around our own camp, about the same time. It was a warning to us to hasten on, or we might meet a fate similar to the Greens. We pulled out for Grand River, not wishing to encounter the danger of following up the trail of the murderers. We found travel between Green and Grand Rivers almost unendurable. There was neither feed, wood nor water, and these things are most essential, especially where the stock has to hunt for a living, and the teamsters do their own cooking. Without these, you will have to go to bed in a thirsty, fireless, supperless, ill-humored, cheerless condition, that will utterly take the romance out of your journey. It makes no difference what the weather is, a camp without a fire is lonely and desolate. The country was one continual plain of sand beds and knolls the whole distance. Sand is by all odds worse to travel through than mud. I resigned myself to my fate, and made the best of it. As some writer has said:

> "Let Fate do her worst, there are relics of joy,
> Bright dreams of the past earth cannot destroy."

No sign of a habitation is to be seen in this region.

We were now nearing Grand River, and, what a contrast is to be seen! And the nearer we approach, the more beautiful the place appears. As yet, Grand River, and the rare beauty and majesty of the scenery developed by the passage of the river through the great Rocky Mountain range of Colorado are but little known. The river is hemmed in on either side of the valley with mighty walls of rock, the lower parts of which are fringed with scattered, scrubby pine and cedar, which present a peculiar-looking appearance. But the grassy pastures of the river bottom lands are a thousand times better and prettier than the sterile plains we have been traveling over, which was certainly the most dreary and desolate-looking place I ever saw.

After our wearisome journey across burning sands and alkali bottoms, it was with a glorious feeling of pleasure that we set foot in this paradise of Colorado. Here are objects of interest to every lover of Nature's wonders, without number on every side. For who is so base as not to be moved by the beautiful handiwork of Nature. Here a sense of enchantment sends the blood coursing swiftly through the veins. Thousands of little birds are flitting about, amid the berry bushes, warbling their merry notes of praise to an ever-bountiful Providence. The river is thickly dotted with ducks and geese that go swimming over its surface. Deer and antelope are feeding and frisking about, unconscious of the danger that hovers over them with the approach of civilization. Thousands of bears inhabit these regions. Wild cats and wolves scream and howl continually. The higher gravel knolls of the valley, and those near the bench land are all burrowed out by badgers. Beaver and otter are numerous in the river, and the timber lands of the bottom bear evidence of their industrious gnawing, for they have most of the smaller trees either entirely cut off or badly scarred. Along the river banks the scene is a striking one. The cotton-woods with their brightly-glistening leaves of green, and the endless varieties of berries, peeping from out of the thickets that enclose us on every side make a robe of beauty for the hillsides. The swift, dashing water, rushing on in its mighty course, makes a noise that is audible for three miles. On either side of the cañon are numberless caverns, holes, cracks and crev-

"THE SWIFT DASHING WATER."

ices, which are safe and snug retreats for all such insects and animals as make these places their retreat. But what we appreciated just now the most was the berries. We all set to eating these, and as might have been expected, some ate so many that they made themselves sick.

Here, as in many other places in the West, ruins of ancient cities are found. When viewing these, one cannot help wondering what were the history and fortunes, the virtues and vices of the long since departed inhabitants of these places; those who at some remote time have here passed their day, and acted their brief part in the great drama of the life of the human race, whose unknown dust now mingles with the virgin soil. They have long since passed away; but the same hills, knolls and ridges still stand; the same river flows along through the same channel; the same skies look down upon this green valley, now uninhabited by white men. From the abundance of game that abounds here, and all the beautiful objects of Nature that break upon the view, we associate all that is poetic, romantic and heroic with the history of this bygone people, that once lived between these mighty hills and on the shores of this swift and beautiful river. All these lofty mountains, these beautiful streams of snow water, that have grown into mighty rivers; all those rough, craggy cliffs that continue to crumble, wash, and topple over, to form mighty slides of broken rock, these all remain as objects sacred to the memory of the past. Who is there that can tell of the deeds, mighty and valorous, that have been here performed? No one can do this. Nothing is left to record the history of this once powerful race, but desolated ruins and thousands of tons of broken earthenware. A mighty race has become extinct. No doubt, they loved their wild home, and were as happy and prosperous among themselves, at that remote day, as are the present inhabitants of the Mississippi Valley. For the love of country does not always keep pace with the country's growth, but often diminishes when not urgently aroused. For this reason, those who are constantly warring against other nations, keep alive a patriotic sentiment which links each individual more closely to home and friends, which they are ready to defend, even with their lives. The nature of man seems adapted to this. In all his wanderings, there is no place like home, no country like his own native land. It may be barren and rugged, swept by storms or earthquakes, or overshadowed by frozen hills, or poor in resources, where life is but one continued struggle for existence, with a sickly, sultry, or inhospitable climate, unpropitious seasons, and an unwilling soil. But it is his birthplace; it is where he roamed in his infantile rambles; it is his fatherland, and, sooner than he will see its name dishonored, or its soil invaded, he will shed his blood in its defense. And I have every reason to suppose that the inhabitants of wild, mountainous regions, and of sterile plains, manifest as strong a love of home and country, as any people in the world. With them, like ourselves, whatever deprives of liberty, trenches upon our power.

But here we are, where there are no other white people nearer than the settlements of Utah, two hundred and fifty miles behind. And we have been, since the 8th of March, coming this distance—and this is the 21st day of July. So that it will be seen that we have not made an average of two miles a day since we started. I have not seen a woman, either white or Indian, since

LONELY—THREE THOUSAND MILES FROM HOME.

I left the settlements, over four months ago. I have been once before, for a much longer period of time than this, without seeing women; but if the Lord spares me to outlive this miserable trip, never again will I spoil all peace, comfort and happiness, merely for the sake of gratifying an idle curiosity and small gain. I love scenery as well as any mortal on earth; but to gain a knowledge of this place is to sacrifice all earthly enjoyment, and to run a risk of falling a victim to the dusky warriors, who claim possession of an enormous tract of country of which this is a part. I find that the Indians are all dangerous, when permitted any liberty by the whites; consequently, they require to be kept within careful bounds. They will often abuse you, and that without provocation, other than trespassing by traveling across their country.

Yet variety and novelty are usually pleasing. Our natures demand something, once in awhile, to break the monotony of our every-day existence, for we find but little amusement in working hard every day, over the work-bench of life. Oftentimes we get disgusted with our daily routine of business; then Nature stretches out her ready hand and bids us come and behold her beauties, and forget our cares and anxieties as we feast upon her charms. I know that all men are eager to see new things, and are greedy of gain. The great gold excitement of California, in 1849, or, the White Pine excitement in Nevada, a little later, or, a little later still, the Black Hills' excitement, or, at the present writing, the Leadville excitement, are all good illustrations. People go wild to get there, and two-thirds that reach there go wild to get away.

CHAPTER XIX.

MORAL AND DESCRIPTIVE.

THE climate of Colorado has proved a great blessing to persons of weak constitutions. Many who have gone into the State confirmed invalids, have soon grown strong. The shattered system becomes restored again to early strength and vigor, and the pale and sallow cheek soon assumes a bright and healthy glow.

It is not that here there is as much or more to eat, than can be found in other places; but, then, even on such a trip as we are now making, we have good living for those roughing the wilds. We have plenty of flour, meat, both salt and fresh, all the fresh fish we want, and berries for the picking. These may not always be served in the most pretentious style, but then the reader understands that we have not all the modern conveniences at command. Remember, also, that neither among our cooks nor boarders are there any of the fair sex, and our white neighbors being a little remote, we seldom invite any of them to sit down with us.

We have no persons to dinner but those who are privileged, always welcomed, and generally wanted. We are here free from the necessity of paying visits. In these parts, the natives follow the usual custom of society and make the first call, but, unfortunately, this is generally done in a very rude and noisy manner, one not altogether sanctioned by the better usages of society.

But, then, what Lord Chesterfield says, is here to the purpose: "The nature of things," he remarks, "is always and everywhere the same; but the modes of them vary, more or less, in every country." It may be said that man derives knowledge from travel. I grant that he does; but that the knowledge obtained from travel over deserts of sand and alkali, yelling one's self hoarse, in driving stubborn cattle, is better than the knowledge that would naturally be gained from a residence in a polite, social community, is hardly reasonable to suppose. No rational-minded man loves entire solitude; neither do six or eight individuals enjoy staying out by themselves on these lonely plains, for a whole year at a time. Place a man in such solitude, and, although he may have all the books of the world at his command, in a few years time, the world will have marched on, and left him far in the rear.

"OH, SOLITUDE, WHERE ARE THY CHARMS."

I speak from two years' experience, when six of us had no companions, except ourselves, and the insects and brutes of the field. We had plenty to eat. We worked nearly every day on the Webster Mine, when it was first located, for nearly the whole two years. Some of the boys went to Salt Lake City after provisions; but I staid out the whole time, and kept up my part of the work. These were the longest two years of my life. I often look back to those days when I was wishing to be a rich man, so that I would not have to stay and toil my life away in solitude. But, as Mr. Haven remarks, "The man who has no higher principle than a regard for the opinions of others, is not likely to accomplish anything great or noble." He further says, that "the true theater for virtue is conscience. There is none greater. The praise of man confers no solid happiness, unless it is felt to be deserved; and if it be so, that very consciousness is sufficient."

This, therefore, is the best country in which to find men out, in regard to manliness and integrity, and also perseverance and energy. There is none better. We find this a splendid opportunity for the study of human nature, both of others and of ourselves. A man, here, soon shows just what he is. If he is disposed to evil, it is soon apparent. If he is a moral man, he shows it. If rough, noisy, and uncouth in manners, it is soon discovered. If industrious, he finds plenty to do, and does it. If lazy, he walks around camp, and watches his comrades carry the wood and water, build fires, and prepare something to eat. But "dead beats" are very common everywhere, and are easily recognized.

Of all the nuisances that the world is afflicted with,

the big, stout, lazy individual is the worst. He is worthless to himself, and a detriment and an aggravation to all those around him. There is no occasion for a man to be large and stout, unless it is that he may work. I esteem highly all that endeavor to do anything. Go to work with a will, and, if you do not succeed in doing much, do a little. Show a willingness to try, and I will insure you sympathizing friends, providing your pursuits are legitimate. If we get into adverse circumstances, we cannot do better than to study contentment. There is nothing to be gained by brooding and lamenting over the past, for time lost is gone forever. But with the full power of our strength and willingness of mind, we can use diligence and exercise patience, for these virtues offer a relief that the sluggard never gains. Let us try to elevate those around us. It is as easy to say a good word for a neighbor as to be eternally railing at and abusing him. An evil word does no good.

Give me the man that has a good word of cheer to all. How pleasantly time speeds along while in his company. Such an one does not live for himself alone, but for the good of the world. Such as these extend to their friends a cordial welcome. They have not learned to despise the world nor to hate the human race, and are never cut off from the society of their fellow-man. Aught of evil to mortal man, I cherish not; but fain would bless every living creature, and make happy all this wretched, suffering world. If we have anything to do, let us pluck up courage and do it, or we can rest assured that it will never be done. It costs labor on our part if we win anything, but when once won, it will appear to us the more glorious. Nor need any man fear the imputation of cowardice if he curbs his anger at direct abuse of himself. "A soft answer turneth away wrath." The approval of the company will always go with the man who keeps his temper, for not only does society feel that to vent wrath is a breach of its laws, but it knows that to conquer one's self is a far more difficult task than to overcome an enemy, and that, therefore, the man who keeps his temper is really strong, and truly courageous. Some people are foolish enough to think that everything depends on birth. What does it matter, for, if a man is fit for good society, it can make very little difference whether his father was a miner or chancellor, at least it should not with sensible people.

But wealth without breeding, generally draws the attention of others to the want of taste in its possessor, and gives envy an object to sneer at. I cannot think that rank is necessarily a recommendation to a man. For look around you. Not every officer of trust is by any means a gentleman.

Another feature of western life is the immense amount of tobacco used. I am a smoker myself, and in solitude with my pipe, I contemplate many things that will never be in print. The mind of the smoker is contemplative, rather than active. I know full well that I have now got my pen started on the subject, and will have to pen my way out. I will not take up the question in its medical aspects, and speak of the destroying qualities of the weed. I do believe, that used in moderation it diminishes the violence of the passions, more particularly, of the temper. But what is moderate and what is not, must be determined in each individual case. I believe that the use of tobacco induces a habit of calm reflectiveness. It is the solace of the weary laborer, the support of the ill-fed, the refresher of over-wrought brains, the soother of angered feelings, the boast of the exquisite, the pastime of the idle, the companion of the philosopher.

The ladies claim and protest that it is the dirtiest and most unsociable habit a man can indulge in. Some of the fair ones say they love the smell of tobacco, while others declare that they will never marry one who uses it, which by the way, they in the end generally do, however. Tobacco has won a fame over a wider feld, and among better men, than Noah's grape has ever done. I think that smoking has conduced to make the society of men, when freed from the wholesome restraints of female companions, less riotous, less quarrelsome, and less vicious than what it would be, were they to have nothing with which to drown dull care. In this way the idle man can pass hours away, which he would not have given to work, but, perhaps, to deviltry. With this solace he is no longer restless and impatient for excitement of some kind.

But it is no wonder that the ladies hate the habit. For the pipe is the worst rival a woman can have, and it is one whose eyes she cannot scratch out; one which improves with age as she herself declines; which is silent, yet a companion which costs little, and gives much pleasure. One can smoke, if he will, without making himself disgusting to his lady friends, or running them from their drawing-rooms. I do not think a gentleman would offer to smoke where the company was mixed, unless it were a cigar, and that with the consent of all present. But here in the West there are very few but what smoke, and many do worse, for they drink up all the money they make.

Again, one misses all entertainments of social life by being in such a place as we are now in. There are neither churches, Sunday-schools, theaters, balls, nor anything of that character, either good, bad, or indifferent. We are the sole inhabitants of the valley, at this present time. I, for one, am not at all satisfied here, nor would I be should Uncle Sam give me a clear title to this whole valley, if it were on the condition that I should spend the remainder of my days here. I do not want to be so rich, if it shall deprive me of all society in order to obtain such vast possessions. This valley will, of course, be settled up some day, but at the present time no white man lives near. The entire valley is in possession of the Ute Indians.

Take a person and put him in the most beautiful place on our continent, and doom to a solitary life, and you surround him with misery, to be continually tormented by a longing for companions. To live in such isolation is to sacrifice all self-esteem. Aristotle says, "Emulation is a good thing, and belongs to good men;

envy is a bad thing, and belongs to bad men, and what a man is emulous of he strives to attain, that he may

SCALP-DANCE OF THE UTE INDIANS.

really possess the desired object; the envious are satisfied if nobody has it."

Money making is the great consideration of all our scheming. Money enables persons to secure and pay for homes, which they cannot otherwise obtain. As a matter of course people generally congregate where the greatest inducements are held out. This has been well illustrated in the mining industries of the West. These began to develop with the discovery of the precious metals, and increased with a rapidity rarely witnessed in any country. These mining enterprises have proven highly remunerative in many instances, and through various channels of business, in addition to mining. All branches of industry, in fact, have profited enormously through mining. The farmer, the merchant, the machinist, the mechanic, and the laborer in every department, both East and West.

Mining is dependent largely upon the transportation of various kinds of stuff. With some of this our wagons are loaded at present, for the benefit of the miners at Ouray. Everything has moved so slowly, and gone so contrary to all expectations, that of patience and perseverance I have but little left. I thought when we left Manti that we would see Ouray inside of sixty days, at most. But now I have but little better idea of where Ouray is than one of the "Kanackers" of Central America. Some one has said that when a man is in the right path he must persevere. I am free to confess that I am thoroughly tired of persevering on this trip, and I feel that the sooner I can get rid of this outfit the better. I will sell out for half price. For I now feel that I have been duped, and that too, by those whom I thought were my friends. I know that many persons naturally look on the dark side of life, and borrow trouble, and become despondent. It may be that they cannot help doing so. But it is wrong. I think a person ought to set his stakes as to what he intends doing, and run for them, leaving despondent feelings far in the rear.

I, for one, will never again tie myself to the apron strings of relationship outside of the paternal roof. There is more to be lost than gained. I have been made despondent when I should have been elated, and that through no fault of my own. But then there is a little information to be gained every day, and we need never to be beaten twice the same way. I lacked caution when I ventured in this undertaking, or hardly this either, for if I had done as my best judgment dictated to me, when at Salt Lake City, I would have returned immediately to California. I do believe that if I would be governed more by the first impulses of my mind, that I would often work out consistent plans with greater ease than I do.

There is good in everything. It does not do for a complete stranger to put his hands in fighting posture, cock his eyes at you, and inform you by way of introduction, "Wall, I guess you're a tarnation logger-head, you aire," meaning to cast some reproach at another's personal appearance, and general mental capacities. You would see a hand gently moving towards the belt that always encircles the waist. It whould be a fine thing if these appendages had never been introduced.

Because the danger of being knocked down on the spot, and having his beauty spoiled, is likely to be a much greater inducement to proper behavior, than the pistol, to a man who can offend in this manner. Yet, there are times when the pistol has the effect of awing men into decent politeness.

Of course, to knock a man down is never good manners. But there is a way of doing it gracefully, and one thing should be observed. Whether you command your temper or not, never show it, except by the blow. Never assail an offender with words, for it has a tendency to make bad, worse. I would not speak as above, but the surrounding circumstances in the West are such, that every man you meet is weighted down with weapons of death and destruction. You very seldom see a man who does not have them, and then it is simply because he is not able to afford something of the sort. There are those here, who for a small gratuity, would decide for another whether their honor was hurt or not.

Hunting and shooting are the only amusements on Green River at the present time. In fact this, together with boating and hallooing at the cattle, are all the accomplishments we know; yet these are sufficient to drive away dull care, and to make time less tedious. I know there are a great many who hunt, who have accomplished but little when the day is over; yet I know of nothing that gives more pleasure to a skillful marksman than the chase. Here deer, elk, antelope, and wolves can be shot without traveling over miles of rugged country. Many parts of the West are very thinly settled, or are entirely uninhabited. In such places, game is more easily approached than it is in places where the hunter's or sportsman's fusilade is continually kept up, and where the baying of the dogs is heard on every side, as they go charging on in hot pursuit of the crippled or badly-frightened animals, and where, now and again, the huntsman's voice is heard breaking in, urging on his ever-faithful companions to the capture.

There are a great many things essentially necessary to be a good hunter. Skill is needed; as a man must be familiar with the habits of the game he is in pursuit of, in order to approach it. Pluck is needed, for it is wearisome work to carry a heavy rifle and trudge through the forests and over the desolate plains, all day long. Nothing escapes the eye of the old hunter. He quickly discovers the cause of the least rustle. He hears every sound. He is quickly aware of every danger. Years of careful hunting for game have made him familiar with all the various sounds; consequently, he will tell you on the instant what it is that makes a noise. And where a variety of sounds seem all mingled together, he quickly singles each one out, and traces it to its source.

There are various ways of hunting. In hunting deer, the hunter often goes early and reaches their resorts by break of day, as deer feed in the morning, early. When the sun is warm, they have to be routed from thickets or their sequestered haunts; starting early, then, gives the hunter many advantages that cannot be had later in the day. The hunter hides himself early, and watches for the feeding or traveling game. In a part of the country, where game is plenty, the hunter seldom misses his "luck" and fails to get something. If he is hunting sheep, he ascends to the highest, roughest, rockiest mountain fastnesses in the vicinity, as it is

HUNTING BUFFALO IN THE OLDEN TIME.

here where the mountain sheep love to gambol. Sheep are very different, by nature and disposition, from any other animal. Though they are large, they are innocent and inoffensive in every way. They are seldom seen in the low lands.

Deer, however, are found in every locality. They

frequent both high mountains and low valleys; but during the cold winter months, while the snow is deep, they become more numerous in the valleys and low bench lands. At such times they are more easily hunted, and their flesh is fatter and better flavored than at any other time of the year. In warm seasons they frequent the slopes of timbered mountains, high up, where the flies are not so bad. They are difficult to approach, and, once alarmed, they are gone like a shot. When a flock of them is started, in a thicket, they make the brush crack loud enough to be heard half a mile away. They are different from the antelope. The antelope is similar, in size and weight, to the white-tailed deer; their legs are longer, and they are very nimble. They are found, chiefly, where the country is rolling, and on the hills destitute of timber, where grass is found in abundance.

The country through here is different from any other portion of the West. Both sides are hemmed in with high mountain chains. The valley is thickly dotted over with sand *buttes* and destitute of water, for miles and miles. And yet, day after day, we seem to be constantly in sight of water; but each time we find that we have been deceived by mirages. This part of the country bears evidences of the presence of minerals, all the way from the Squash Mountains, or Three Peaks, clear through to Leadville. There is water coming from the cañons, on either side, but it all sinks ere it reaches the valley. In some of these places I saw as good indications of gold as there are anywhere in the gold diggings of the West. I have in some of these gulches, seen good pan prospects. Some were worth thirty-four cents. But the Indians are bad, and water is scarce. The supply of timber is limited to the short, scrubby pine and cedars. This is, moreover, three hundred miles from any settlements; so that it will be seen that a small band of men would run great risk in undertaking to stay in this section of the country.

These valleys constantly vary from one-half to three and five miles in width. This is a beautiful place, as far as looking at the grandeur of nature is concerned, but barrenness and destitution mark all its surroundings. Either range is covered, for the greater part of the year, with a varying thickness of snow. Here the ranges are white in June. I have been traveling through these valleys often with my companions, when we were all suffering from thirst, when, by looking in the distance, for half a mile or a mile, we could observe a large lake of water, and see men in boats and canoes paddling about in the water, everything looking as natural as if it were real. And the famished traveler makes for the lake to slake his thirst. He travels on and on and on, until, finally, the lake, boats and men begin to disappear, and, by and by, the thing is all gone. The traveler is by this time sick at heart, weary, and begins to despair.

One trip is generally enough to satisfy a wanderer that this is no place in which to linger. Contrast the barrenness of this country with the fertility of the valleys in the East, and mark well the difference, and there is no civilized man on the face of this christianized world that would envy the red man of the forest this country. He may like to hunt through the foothills for antelope, but the bottom lands contain no allurement for him. He soon grows foot-sore and weary, and it is with pleasure that he reaches a stream of cool water.

We are now approaching the Gunnison, a small river of snow water, which runs with a rapid current. When we first come in sight of the stream, we are still high up on the top of the mountain, where everything is barren and desolate. To come suddenly to the edge of this rugged precipice, and to get an unexpected glimpse across and up and down the deep valley at your feet, to see either bank carpeted with the richest of grass, and a luxuriant growth of joint rushes, and dotted here and there with clusters of cottonwood of magnificent growth, and to see game of all kinds in abundance, in every direction, is like taking a peep into the Indian's happy hunting grounds. The sudden contrast is so great as to make an entrance from the surrounding barren mountains into this rich valley like an entrance into a new world. This is certainly a most beautiful place, and I do not know where to find a nicer. This valley is quite small. I suppose that one thousand acres will include all the good land there is in it.

After crossing the Gunnison, we then travel along the Uncompahgre River. Here, again, we see some beautiful land. Along the river bank, however, is a wilderness of brush. It is only here and there that one can get through this, to the water's edge. We are now in sight of the stage road, that leads from Saguache to Ouray and San Miguel. And, oh, what a blessed sight it is to see the wagons coming toward you, from other directions. The stage road intersects our own road, six miles below Ouray village, which is an Indian town.

Reader, imagine yourself shut off for six months from all communication with the world, with no opportunity to hear a word from any of your friends at home, or to see a newspaper, from which to learn any events of the day, and then try to imagine how you would feel in meeting with friends again. I do think that twice as many events transpire during such a period of time as take place at any other time, when we see them and know them as they occur. Everything seems new, and one cannot help feeling that he has grown older rapidly, in a short time. There is a strange sensation, in such an experience, that cannot be pictured or told.

Ouray, the peace chief of the Ute Nation, lives here on the Uncompahgre River. He has a splendid location, in the heart of a beautiful valley. The old chief occupies a good house, which is as nicely finished as though built by a skilled mechanic. He owns one section of land, in his own name, which is somewhat improved, and enclosed with a strong fence. Quite a number of his tribe are always around him, but they seem more negligent in the matter of well-doing than Ouray himself. There are dogs here by hundreds, of all breeds, kinds and colors, and of every shade of disposition. They are all sizes and shapes—sleek ones and wooly ones, large ones and small ones. Some of them are good for hunting, and others for watching camp; some seem fitted only for barking, while there are others that will bite; all are lean and hungry-looking. When a white man enters the village, there is at once a regular pandemonium of yelping, growling, and barking. It is fearful to be beset with four or five hundred such snarling, ugly-looking curs as are found in an Indian village.

They have horses, cattle, sheep, and goats in large herds. These are seen in many parts of the valley, with Indian herders lying around watching them. They do no farming. I have often seen it stated that the Ute Indians are great farmers. Ten acres will cover all the little patches that are cultivated throughout the whole tribe. The hoe is the principal implement used in tilling these patches. They make no hay, since the country abounds in grass, winter and summer. Snow does not fall deep nor remain long. The valley is so situated that the sun shines into it lengthwise, and the climate is, in consequence, unusually warm, considering the fact that the valley is six thousand feet above sea level.

Ten miles farther up the river we came to the new Los Pinos Agency. Major Wheeler was at this time acting as distributing Agent for the Ute Indians.

Here the Indians would gather in for the supplies distributed by the agent and furnished by the United States government. There are only a few buildings here, erected by the Government, for the sole purpose of a distributing depot. They have an Agency Post-Office. Not that the Indians need such an institution, however, for none of them can read. They all talk broken Spanish and Indian quite glibly. Twenty-five miles on up the river we came to Ouray City. This is a bustling mining town of perhaps five hundred inhabitants, principally prospecting miners. Saloons are plenty, and there are more stores than are needed for the place, for they are all running behind. Not that there is not a demand for goods, but cash is scarce; cheek, and promises to pay, seem to be the chief currency of the place.

At this place we unloaded our wagons and sold out, taking almost anything we could get. We sold at ruinous prices. We got cash in part, and promises to pay for the rest, and experience has shown me that they will be promises to pay for a long time to come. And such is life!

CHAPTER XX.

SHALL THE YOUNG MAN GO WEST?

NOW I am once again in a mining community. Here, as in every mining region, we find that other branches of industry are very limited, and that everything depends upon the development of the mines. Quartz mining is always located in rocky regions, where fruits, vegetables, and grain cannot be cultivated. The consequence is that everything which miners consume, or need, must be shipped from other points. A prosperous mining town is always, therefore, a good market-place for vegetables and provisions of all kinds. They command a fair or high price, owing to the distance they are shipped, and the amount on the market.

American mining enterprises are generally carried on by corporations, which wield powers unknown in any other country. These, in their efforts to make dividends on fictitious capital, reduce the wages of their employes as low as practicable; and, except at competing points, burden production by heavy and discriminating rates for transportation. No such tremendous power was ever concentrated elsewhere in the hands of a few men, as is concentrated in the hands of the men who control these great corporations. A few men rule the whole mining business throughout the West. They put rates up or down at pleasure. They wield a power which absolute monarchs would hesitate to exercise.

They generally have no permanent investment of stock in any of their corporations. The business is usually built up by loans on the donated property, and the excess of stock, when disposed of, goes into the pockets of the ruling faction, who are stock-holders and directors. These men own (subject to the liens upon them) and absolutely control said incorporations, which have cost them comparatively nothing, and out of which they realize vast riches. They have the full control of the money and stock, and have no fear of competition. They generally control all the approaches to their magnificence.

Secure in their chartered rights, there can be no interference with their liberal privileges. Unrestrained in their traffic, they control the transportation of the productions, and in no small measure, the labor of a country vast enough and rich enough for an empire. Whenever two such contending parties begin to strive for supremacy, then good times come with a rush for the little folks on the outside. The indications of prosperity can then be seen in the crowded stores, in the busy workshops, in the hopeful and happy faces of miners, mechanics, and speculators; in every department of industry, in the active stock market, in the mining stock board, in the increased clearings. They can be seen in the buoyant spirits of men in every branch of trade, and in the increased confidence of those with money, and of hope among those without money. They open up fair fields, rich in the promises of a glorious harvest. There are new enterprises started, which were never thought of before; and these, when once started, are pushed on rapidly to completion. These are days of buying and selling—money is plenty, and business and speculation, in all directions, are brisk and lively. But it is soon apparent to all that the circulating capital is accumulating in the hands of the capitalist. Now, this is in accordance with the laws of trade, and must, inevitably, take place. The majority of the community are not hoarders of, or dealers in money, but spenders of money. Give them any quantity of it, and they will soon part with it for something more desirable. The consequence is, that it then finds its way into the hands of the people who make it their business to hoard it, or loan it at high rates; and no injustice has been done to any class. Yet corporations, as conducted, work injury to all classes. One word more, and then I will open up another subject.

If the naturalness of the laws of classification of business was fully understood, and, also, the fact that money is only really a commodity, subject to the same laws of exchange, supply and demand as other things, it would go far toward uprooting the pestilential economic heresies, which are such fruitful breeders of popular discontent. The tillers of the soil are the real sovereigns of labor, and of manly independence. A glance at the history of our own country, and at the present condition of industry in England and the continental nations, should be sufficient to make even the chronic grumbler reasonably contented. It is questionable whether there has ever been a time, since the discovery of America, when a large class of people were not complaining of hard times, and the scarcity of money. Some point to other days as "the good old times," when money was plenty and business lively. We can all have money if we earn and save it.

Having expressed myself as I have about the incorporated companies, and their control of the mining interests of the West, some might think I would guarantee fortunes to all who would come West. I cannot do that. You know some men will succeed in anything anywhere, while others will fail in everything everywhere. I desire to be no obstacle to hinder the success of the first, nor can I prevent the failure of the last, though I may aid in shaping the destiny of each. And, even should I do neither, I am not likely to learn of my instrumentality in the latter case, or to hear the last of it in the former. I will assume the pressure. It is my purpose and effort to make clear to the public a description of the West.

Now, mines can be bought here at prices ranging from a few hundred to a million or more dollars. Prospects are for sale for from a few hundreds up to many thousands of dollars, and mining claims from fifty dollars up to some hundreds. To obtain the immense sums asked for some of these mines, owners must show that their mines have yielded thousands of dollars' worth, or millions, as the case may be, of the precious metals. They may never yield as much again, however; for, though in sight, to an apparently vast extent, that extent and value can only be guessed. Still, men will pay millions for a mine that has been mined, who would not pay thousands for a prospect that has not been mined. Others will pay thousands for a prospect, who would not pay hundreds for a single claim, which sometimes sells for a few dollars, and proves of as much value as either of the others. Hence, all have a selling value fluctuating widely from day to day, being governed by influences peculiar to mining districts. There are numerous instances on record here, as elsewhere, where claims have been sold at large prices, that proved worthless when worked. We often see mines of this class that have been abandoned for years; and there are hundreds of others whose owners would be much better off if they would quit and let the claims go. Again, there are others that have cost their present owners very little, which have become of great value when developed. The sturdy prospector, when he finds himself the owner of a single undeveloped claim, though it be with rather unpromising surface indications, directs all his first efforts to testing its value, instead of wasting them in sinking a dozen more or less assessment shafts, on as many adjacent claims, which could afterwards be purchased at almost any offer.

HE PAID A BIG PRICE.

The success of judicious investments in partly developed claims is oftentimes well illustrated. There has been an expenditure of a vast amount of money and labor in some of these San Juan districts to establish confidence with capitalists in the wealth of some of these districts. One great feature in the establishing of a camp is to get men to believe there is no other camp comparatively its equal, and another is to have daily acquisitions of men who have faith in the theory, that underlying the entire district is a body of rich minerals practically inexhaustible, and who, having means to demonstrate the truth of the theory, will use money to do so. Always try to keep the outlook of a camp away in advance of what it really is. Keep mercantile interests well represented, if anything ahead of the mineral developments—the more rapid and the farther ahead, the better prospect for the excitement which must come to a camp before its merits are noticed. Wherever mineral is discovered, crowds soon become simply enormous. Hundreds of the new arrivals have not a cent in their pockets and no way of obtaining money. Hundreds of men line the streets every day, idle, because they cannot obtain work.

Here in south-western Colorado are numerous mining camps, and hundreds and thousands of people are continually on the move hither and thither, drifting toward the latest excitements. And the truth about the San Juan regions has not and cannot be told on paper, because as long as the excitements continue to start, the cry is, "Still they come!" Neither snow nor cold seem to offer any obstacle to the anxious crowd of crazy fortune-hunters, who are rushing to this country, supposed to be rich in carbonates and other ores. It is true that mines are in some cases paying. It is equally as true that not one in five hundred, who flock here to make their fortunes by digging for minerals, succeeds in making any more than a precarious living. The temptation held out by prospects of sudden wealth overcomes all obstacles, and thousands upon thousands of persons, who were making good wages at home, come here to find disappointment of the most bitter and perplexing kind. Unable to make discoveries that will warrant capitalists in investing their means, failing in their efforts to obtain employment at rates that promise immediate wealth, they become discouraged and dejected, and resort to the cup, and in a short time the story is told. This is by no means a fancy sketch, as any one not misled as to the circumstances can inform you.

In view of what I have seen in my long stay in the West, I think that any one who encourages immigration to mining regions incurs a grave responsibility. And, from what I have seen, it seems probable to my mind that, if the immigration still continues as it has for a few years past, the mountain ranges will soon be whitened with the bones of men who have died from hunger and cold; for it is impossible for the country to feed so many. You may take the richest mining country ever struck on the globe, and there is less than one in ten of the prospectors who ever discover any thing. But this dismal prospect does not alter the facts with regard to the mines. And these facts are readily ascertained by persons who are competent to weigh evidence, and have access to the proper sources of information. This San Juan country is very different from California or

Nevada. Here we do not find such pleasant regions; but we do find a barren wilderness, more than ten thousand feet above the sea, where the soil will not even grow potatoes; where snow falls every month in the year, and men were frozen to death in August, 1878.

Of Leadville, every one has heard. No discovery of mineral since the California gold excitement of '48 and '49 has attracted greater attention than the discov-

THESE DID NOT GROW IN A MINING REGION.

ery and development of the Leadville mines at the head waters of the Arkansas River. Where Leadville now stands was an old mining camp, which had been worked for gold from 1859 to 1867. The yield then was considerable. It is said that, in 1860, three million dollars were taken out. But the diggings were abandoned in 1867. In those days, it is said, the miners "daubed" their cabins with what was supposed to be mud, but which was really carbonate, worth three or four hundred dollars a ton.

Mr. W. H. Stevens, of Lake Superior mining fame, a resident of Detroit, was the first to undertake systematic mining operations for silver in Leadville. Old California and Nevada miners scoffed at the idea of finding anything of value in the carbonates. They were *soft*, not hard. They were "pancake" deposits, not veins. The oldest and wisest among them had never seen any metal extracted from such stuff. Still Stevens had his followers, however. Numbers of men swarmed upon the hills, and began to sink shafts. Some of them were speedily rewarded. Romantic stories are told of the vicissitudes of fortune which befell the early discoverers. How some of them would wander from store to store, vainly begging for a sack of flour to enable them to go on with their work, who, since, in some instances, have sold out for enormous sums, and now live in splendor. How some of them gave up in despair while others, on the verge of desperation, would strike the pick into the ground in their rage, and would uncover the wall of a fissure vein. Whatever of truth there may be in such tales, there is no doubt of the fact that some rich carbonates have been struck, varying in value from eight to ten hundred ounces per ton, and some large fortunes have been realized by the lucky discoverers. The carbonates have been found lying in nearly horizontal deposits, at depths of from thirty to one hundred and fifty feet below the surface. No blasting is required in the shafts, and the ore can be extracted for two dollars a ton.

Such astonishing bonanzas, of course, created an

excitement far and wide. A grand rush of men came centering from all quarters, twelve thousand arriving in the last three months of 1878. Huge machinery for smelting works and saw-mills was hauled over the mountains at an enormous expense. People came by the hundreds from Denver, walking painfully for one hundred and forty miles through the snow, by way of the cañon. In December of 1878 Leadville was full of men who had no homes, who, for want of better lodgings, slept in the sawdust on the bar-room floors. The most of these had a little money, perhaps enough to get them food without working. They spent their time in bar-rooms, gambling houses, dance houses, or on the sidewalk, discussing the last great strike. Half a bed in some miserable attic was worth two dollars a night. Mechanics' wages were from four to five dollars a day. Town-lots, that were worth fifty dollars in October, commanded three thousand four months after. This is astonishing. In 1876 this region was almost a wilderness; now a growing, bustling, roaring town of twelve thousand inhabitants forms the nucleus of a thriving settlement. These people have gathered here from all parts of the compass. Every State and Territory, and every "neck of the woods" are represented. The bulk of the population, however, poured in from western towns and cities, Chicago alone furnishing a large proportion. One paper said every road led to Leadville, and every road is lined with adventurers bound for Leadville.

On the occasion of a big mining excitement hundreds of people arrive during each twenty-four hours. People rush to the mines pell-mell, expecting to dig up great chunks of silver and to become rich in a day. A majority of them start with no more money than will pay their traveling expenses and a week's board, and are in a truly pitiable plight when, with no money and nothing to do, they discover that all those beautiful day-dreams of riches acquired suddenly, and without

AN OLD '49ER NOT YET RICH.

labor, are not to be realized. Even the western papers, which are interested in the settlement of the country, admit that the number of moneyless, idle men in the West is entirely too large. Many old miners who have been there since the discoveries were first made, and have been doing their level best to earn a livelihood, are still destitute. The mines are bonanzas, but men of capital usually harvest the profits. Brains and muscle, without money, amount to little in an excitement.

Here in the mountains poverty is of the most practical and unpoetic sort. It means association with reckless adventurers and desperadoes, and no probability of rising above that level. It means scarcely anything to eat; nothing but water to drink, and no railroad ticket for any other point. It means the severest hardships, which men are ever compelled to endure in this country. I have conversed freely with the best citizens of the West upon this question, and I have yet to find one whose sentiments are not fairly reflected by the foregoing statement. There is abundant room for men of moderate means or for capitalists. All over the mountains the mineral is deposited in strata as rich, no doubt, as any yet discovered, and only awaits capital to take it out. It is difficult to furnish employment to a hundred men when there is only sufficient to engage one-fifth or one-tenth of that number.

This is the status of the case in the West. The towns are filled with men, anxious to obtain employment, food and lodgings; but they can find neither. Food is plenty, but these persons have nothing with which to purchase it. The hammer of the mechanic can be heard in every city, in every quarter, and at nearly all hours of the day and night. But there is a limit to the employment of skilled labor. Large numbers of men are engaged in carrying on the different branches of industry. But there are three idle for every one at work.

When night comes on scores of them sleep wherever they can get an opportunity to lie down on the floor. I have seen them also under houses, barns, trees, and even out in the open air, unprotected from the weather, except by a thin woolen blanket. Lodging cannot be obtained without money, and people rush in here, without having the wherewithal necessary to furnish personal comforts. In some cases of extreme hunger, some live on "floaters;" that is, they gather the crumbs and crusts from waste baskets and swill tubs, and eat these. I have seen men, who could get nothing to eat, thus fishing in swill buckets for scraps, and eating things that have been thrown from the tables for the pigs and chickens.

DEAD BROKE.

I will gladly leave this subject, for I feel it none of the best to talk about. Although I have said nothing but what I can easily verify by witnesses, many of them men who will readily acknowledge that they were in the same boat, adrift without money, without friends, and without home, bread, or bed. One of the most painful sights in this world is to see poor, way-faring mortals, in their helpless poverty, thus compelled to throw themselves entirely upon the mercies of strangers. They are willing enough to work, but there is no work to do; consequently, they are left to beg and starve. But some may object, and say that no one ever yet starved in America. But I know that persons have starved, for I have seen it. I say this is a deplorable condition for men and women to come to.

Were it not for the hospitable people of San Francisco, one-tenth of the permanent population of that city would be dead in less than six months, and a large portion of the transient population would starve daily. And yet, San Francisco furnishes the cheapest living, and sets tables covered with the choicest fruits, and has the greatest number of wealthy men, according to the population *pro rata*, of any city in the United States. She has nicer churches, and more infidels; greater heaps of yellow gold, and yet more poverty; magnificent places of amusement, and yet more misery; a splendid climate, and yet more suicides; many most excellent citizens, and yet more leading lives of gambling, wickedness and sin, than any other city in America.

So in other places, also, the times are different from what they were a few years ago, when the country was new, and before the people had commenced to rush to the West without some ideas of their own before they started. Now it seems that as soon as a young man in the East gets money enough to carry him to the West, even though he sacrifice friends and a remunerative position, without any object whatever in view, only to get West, away he goes. When he gets here he finds all the mercantile houses well filled with clerks and salesmen. The schools are supplied with teachers. The mines have a surplus supply of miners, and, in fact, every branch of labor, science, or skill has already a surplus of "needies" to support.

To those with little means I would say: If you have been or are now contemplating going to the West, you will find it hard to get there, and much harder to get away. The best policy is to stay where you are doing well, and let "try to do better by going West" alone. To those who have plenty of money I have only to say: You know how you got it, and, if you would travel with it, you can behold untold grandeur in the works of Nature and of man by traveling in the West. You may behold its many rocky heights, some of them covered with perpetual snow. You may descend into valleys of continual spring where snow never falls. What a marked difference of atmospheric temperature one day's travel will make! You can go from the cold, chilly mountains, where ice and snow are thick and deep, to where it is Spring and the flowers are blooming in their many different colors of beauty. The change is so sudden that one almost imagines himself in a new world of glory, and such, indeed, it is to one who has been in the chilly hills for a year or so.

I am going to close this chapter, and soon my book. I am leaving out many things that are interesting; but I cannot undertake to write them all. I have sometimes thought as the puzzled Englishman did. I will copy his experience. It is a well-known fact that in high altitudes, owing to the rarified condition of the atmosphere, objects are visible at a great distance. At the city of Denver the Rocky Mountains, although some sixteen miles distant, seem to be very near by. An English gentleman, a tourist, came in on the Kansas Pacific train one morning, and stopped at the Inter-Ocean Hotel, in Denver. He soon made the acquaintance of two of the old citizens. The Englishman was captivated with the appearance of the mountains, and suggested to the two old citizens that, as the mountain range was such a very short distance from the city, they should all take a walk to it, and return in time for dinner. The two old citizens saw a chance for some fun, and immediately consented. The trio started, and walked toward the mountains for about two hours and a half; but the mountains seemed as far away as ever. The Englishman was a good walker, and kept a little in advance of his friends. Finally they saw him deliberately sit down as he came to a small, irrigating ditch, perhaps two feet wide, and begin taking off his boots and stockings. When they came up to where he was sitting, they asked him in some surprise what he was doing that for. The Englishman said he was going to wade the stream. Both the old citizens, looking at him in astonishment, asked him why he didn't step across it.

"Step across it," he replied, "step across it! Not I! What do I know about the distance in your confounded country? It may be three hundred feet across."

Now this is not given, of course, for a veritable fact; yet it has a meaning, showing how deceiving appearances are to one traveling across prairies, valleys, or plains among the mountains. The atmosphere is purer and lighter than at low altitudes. Consequently the eye can distinguish objects at a much greater distance than is realized. You see some point at a distance, and think you can reach that on horseback in two hours, when you might not arrive at it in a day's travel. In the mountains and cañons sounds rumble and re-echo with greater force than elsewhere. The roar of the thunder here is terrible. The lightning is sharper and more brilliant than in low altitudes. Waterspouts or "cloud-bursts" are numerous, often sweeping large gullies out before the roaring cataract. Trees, houses, earth, rock, everything standing in its course, will be swept on to destruction. Whole rivers of water seem to fall from the clouds at once. These are more numerous in the Fall than at any other season of the year. Sometimes they open up with a noise of thunder fearful to hear, that goes rolling and rumbling over the mountains to die in the distance. Oftentimes the winds sweep along at the same time with devastating effect.

CHAPTER XXI.

A SPANISH BULL-FIGHT.

AS I have before said, the Western people are great lovers of amusement. While I was at Ojo Calienta, in Mexico, there were advertisements posted, announcing that a bull-fight would take place on a certain day. I had never seen a fight between a man and a bull; so here was something new to me, and, as I had considerable curiosity to see how such a fight would be managed, I remained over until the following Thursday to see it. Ojo Calienta is a very pretty little place; but built after the fashion of all its sister towns. It is peopled with Spaniards and Mexicans. I did not see an American, while we remained in the town, other than the members of our own little party. There are about one thousand inhabitants.

The country people began to flock into town two days before the time set for the fight, and some of the comers were hardly of the first families of Mexico. The place was soon crowded with people from all parts of the country. Long before the time announced for the fight to begin, I made my way to the corral. I had waited to see the fight, and did not wish to be deprived of the opportunity. So I went early to get a favorable position. I found quite a number already assembled. I went forward, and secured a front seat; then I began a survey of all the arrangements for the entertainment. The fight was to take place in a corral that was enclosed with high adobe walls, so high that neither man nor beast could break out. On three sides of this corral a strong scaffolding has been raised to a level with the wall, gradually rising higher as it receded. On this, seats had been prepared for all those wishing to witness the sport.

From my seat I could see everything. I watched to see the character of the spectators as they gathered. I saw the old, white-haired Mexicans, with faces furrowed by deep-set wrinkles; so old and bent-up that they had to be assisted to their seats. The aged crone was there, browned and withered. Young women were there in large numbers, some of them with pure white complexions, and eyes as black as coals, and hair of the same color, long enough to reach the ground. The married man was there, with his arms full of children and bundles. The young man was there with his beloved maiden in her very ornamental dress. Many of the lady spectators were of pure Castilian blood, and good-looking enough to be the belles of any society or civilized community. With their long, black hair and their sparkling, black

MEXICAN OUTLAWS.

eyes; their clear, white complexion, and their gaudy dress, selected more on account of brilliancy of color than of any other quality, and with forms as symmetrical and graceful as can be found in any clime, I thought them as beautiful a group of the fair sex as I had ever seen anywhere. The young men, darker-colored than their sisters, were there with their broad-brimmed hats, from under which a pair of brilliant eyes shone out, apparently taking in all the surroundings at a glance. And, from their dark scowling at one another, I concluded I could easily guess their thoughts. Some of these fellows were well-dressed, while others wore only a hat, sandals and breech-cloth.

At length the Mexican, who was to be the principal actor in the scene, stepped into the corral. He was not a large man, but well-built and powerful. He was dressed suitably for the occasion, with a pair of light and close-fitting pants, the waist-band of which was encircled with a large, red morocco belt. On his feet he wore neat-fitting, light slippers, fastened with flashing buckles. A short staff, which he carried in his hand, and a knife in his belt were his only weapons for the deadly encounter, in which he was about to engage. The crowd had grown somewhat impatient with wait-

MEXICAN MAIDEN, LOWER CLASS.

ing for the entertainment to begin. I had been enjoying myself very much looking at the many fantastic and grotesque spectators gathered around me.

But, when the glaring, pawing bull was let in suddenly through a side door, an awful sensation shot through my whole frame. I could but feel a strong sense of fear and dread at the awful tragedy about to begin; and I think a sort of presentiment of something terrible thrilled the entire multitude. Every noise was hushed into perfect silence, more quickly than I can write this sentence. The animal was large, powerful, and active. As he stood there, pawing and snorting, his very hair seemed to stand out threateningly. He looked like a terrible opponent to meet in single combat. One of the guardsmen gave him a thrust with a sharp-pointed lance, and, simultaneously, others in attendance commenced to wave their red flags in front of him. The *matadore*, all this time, stood near the center of the arena, as firm and still as a post. I looked to see him falter, or show some sign of fear. I could not see the least change of color in his face, as he stood watching the beast, and expecting a rush at any moment.

I sat looking at the man, and then at the beast, wondering how the battle would begin. I had not long to wait, for the animal had now been tormented into such a state of fury, that his eyes looked almost green with rage. With a roar, that was terrible to all who heard it, he dashed suddenly at the *matadore*, with his head down, with the evident purpose of tossing him into eternity. I watched him rushing until I felt sure that his horns had reached their aim. But, no. The Mexican sprang to one side with the agility of a cat, dodging the horns of the angry beast, and, as the animal passed him, he punched him lightly with his staff, but still enough to enrage him all the more. The bull, finding himself baffled, turned, and, with more fury than ever, dashed at him again, only to be again evaded, and thrust harder than before by his adversary. Time after time the enraged beast would renew the encounter, but with no better success; and, every time the man would so nimbly spring out of the way, the audience would applaud and cheer loudly. The fight was kept up in this way until the animal was completely exhausted, and could not be brought to renew the combat. The man was then declared the winner, amid the loud applause of the multitude.

PUEBLO CACIQUE, NEW MEXICO.

Another fight was immediately announced to come off in one-half hour, between the same man and another bull. We all remained seated, watching some wrestling and jumping, which, by the way, was nothing extra. After about an hour's time another bull was let into the corral. This last was a much smaller animal than the first, but more ferocious, for he made direct for his antagonist. The *matadore* successfully employed the same tactics as in the first combat, until several rounds were fought, and we were all beginning to think that it would terminate like the first.

But this was not to be the case; for, all at once, the man either slipped, or made a miscalculation, and the bull caught him on his horns, and tossed him far over to one side, near the wall. The man fell with a heavy thud on the ground, badly hurt. The bull made at him again. Then ensued a scene far different from anything that had yet been seen that day. Women and children were screaming with terror. Several of the men, dreading accidents, began to shoot the bull. The spectators, rushing together in their

MEXICAN INDIANS.

terror, broke down some of the scaffolding, and several were hurt in that way. They succeeded in killing the bull, before he had killed the *matadore*. But the man was so severely hurt that he had to be carried from the field, and placed under the care of surgeons and nurses. There was such a crowd around him, that I did not get to see how badly he was injured. A general commotion followed the killing of the animal. Everything was in confusion; every one seemed to be trying to reach the ground first. As soon as the man was taken from the ground, the crowd scattered in different directions, toward their homes.

I was told that neither one of the fights was completed, as the man generally kills the bull by striking a knife deep into his neck. I do not know how that may be, but I do know that I will never be a witness to another bull-fight. It is a most horrible sight to look upon. But, then, this is no new thing among the Spanish people, for bull-fighting has been carried on as an amusement among them for ages. I would not go into a corral, and fight one bull, for all the money there is in the United States of America.

CHAPTER XXII.

THE INDIANS.

THE general character of the Indians is very similar throughout all the many different tribes. There is but very little difference in their habits and customs.

Their wigwams are built of small poles and skins, and most always in the form of a pyramidal tent. The top is open. A low door-way is cut or left in the tent, over which the skin of some animal is usually hung. The entrance is so low that one must stoop to enter. In the center of the hut, or wigwam, a small fire is built, and all the inmates gather close enough around it to almost smother it out. Nearly all the Indians are now in possession of some goods, obtained from the white people; hence, you will often see an iron pot, either on or close by the fire, containing meat, or other food. The wigwam is, of course, almost always full of smoke.

The floor is strewn with the skins of animals, on which they lounge. They sleep on these skins, lying in a circle around the fire. Each wigwam accommodates about seven or eight sleepers.

The Indians are natural hunters. Some of the tribes possess a great many excellent horses. They wander and hunt over a vast scope of country. The Indians have certain days of festivity and public rejoicing, when large crowds of them assemble together. They then have, as the principal part of the day's entertainment, horse-races, foot-races, and wrestling-matches. Shooting at a mark is another one of their pastimes, which is indulged in by the hour. They usually select

INDIAN WIGWAM.

as a target, some object on a steep hillside, and then watch, by the little puff of dust, to see where the ball strikes. Each shot, be it good or bad, produces the same effect upon the swarthy spectators.

The Indians are always ready to trade for horses or

guns. They never trade for anything they cannot move about with them. Often they will exchange a splendid horse, saddle and bridle for a gun, which, though it may be a good one, is worth not more than forty dollars, while the horse would, perhaps, command over one hundred dollars. They are all lovers of whisky, and when they can procure it in sufficient quantities, they use it to great excess. When drunk, they are very noisy, and some of them are dangerous.

Their modes of disposing of their dead differ in different tribes. The Sioux place their dead bodies in trees, or on a platform, supported by four stakes driven into the ground, whichever is the more convenient; for, on the plains, sometimes they may be hundreds of miles from timber. The Utes sometimes bury the body in the ground, and sometimes place it along the side of some ledge, where it is weighted down with rocks. If an Indian is afflicted with a malarial disease, he is generally left to get well as best he can. If he dies, his body is either left without any attention, or is burned. I was in Utah Territory when Black Hawk, one of the war chiefs of the Indians there, died from some disease he had contracted. His people burned his body, and one of his favorite horses with it.

At one time, near Manti, some of the Mormon boys were following a trail that led to the mountains above. At a certain place, where there were ledges and bowlders without number, they heard some strange noise proceeding from the rocks. Upon investigation they found an aged Indian woman, who, on account of sickness, had been unable to keep up with the train of her comrades. They had, therefore, taken and weighted her down with rocks, to suffer and starve to death; and, but for the timely assistance of the Mormon boys, who helped her down to an empty cabin, outside of town, where she was cared for, she soon would have been where no assistance could have reached her.

The Indians have doctors, or medicine men, among them. When one of the tribe is attacked with sickness his comrades gather around him in the evening.

BLACK HAWK.

Some of them will walk around his couch, and most dismally howl until tired out, when fresh ones take their places. Some will be dancing and singing with all their might. Others are out in the darkness shooting, and making all the noise in their power. In this way they keep up a dreadful racket during the whole night.

I have tried to gain admittance at such times, but always found sentinels surrounding the camp, who would allow no one to enter. They told me that this

UN INDIO BRAVO, TEXAS.

demonstration was made for the purpose of keeping off the evil spirits, that were supposed to hover around the couch of the sick one, ready to convey his spirit away. They think that, if they can keep up a sufficient noise and racket, they will be able to frighten the evil spirits away. The Indians are a very superstitious race of people. They believe in the future existence of mankind, but in this peculiar way. They think that, if an Indian is very courageous and brave, and obtains to that higher point of excellence in this life which, in their minds, constitutes him a "big brave," the good spirits will hover around his dying couch, and, at his last breath, will speed away, on swift wings, with his immortal spirit to a land that is beautiful beyond description; filled with sweet, fragrant flowers, and all kinds of game in never-ending abundance; where he may roam and hunt at will by the side of rivers of clear water, filled with the most beautiful fish. Such, they think, will be the future home of the good Indians. But, if an Indian is not good in their opinion, when he dies his soul is borne away on the wings of an evil spirit, to a land that is barren, wild, and desolate; where there is neither game nor fish. They seem, therefore, to have some sort of wisdom in these matters, even in their ignorance, that is far superior to some of the creeds and practices of their more-enlightened fellow men. I refer to Mormonism, Mohammedanism, and such like.

The Mormon obtains glory in a higher or lower degree, according as he increases his chances by marrying additional wives, each new wife lifting him a step higher toward perpetual happiness.

CHAPTER XXIII.

THE CUSTER MASSACRE.

[*From* WESTERN WILDS, *by permission.**]

ON a bright Sunday in June, 1876, while the nation was on the top wave of the Centennial enthusiasm and the opening of the Presidential campaign, the news went flashing over the wires that General George A. Custer and all his command lay dead in a Montana valley, the victims of a Sioux massacre. With him had died his two brothers, his brother-in-law and a nephew; and of all that entered that battle not one white man survived. For a brief space there was hope that it might be a false report, but soon followed official papers which confirmed every ghastly detail of the first dispatches. For a few days the public sorrow overcame all other considerations; then, by natural revulsion, sorrow gave place to indignation, and that in turn to a fierce demand for investigation and a victim. The public must have a victim when there has been a misfortune. Then ensued a performance which was no credit to us as a nation. His opponents attacked President Grant as the real cause of Custer's death; his friends foolishly defended the President by criticising

---

*To the kindness of Mr. J. H. Beadle, author, and Messrs. Jones Brothers & Co., of Cincinnati, publishers, of that very able work, WESTERN WILDS, I am indebted for this chapter on *The Custer Massacre*, and the following one on *Where Shall we Settle?* which I am sure my readers will find both very interesting and very valuable. THE AUTHOR.

Custer; the latter's friends in the army savagely attacked Major Reno and Captain Benteen as being the cause of the General's misfortunes, and thus the many-sided fight went on. Before stating any facts bearing on this issue, a brief sketch of General Custer's previous experience on the plains is in order.

George Armstrong Custer was born at New Rumley, Ohio, December 5, 1839, and was consequently but thirty-seven years old at the time of his death. At ten years of age he went to live with an older sister in Monroe, Michigan, and ever after considered that place his home. There, on the ninth of February, 1864, he married Elizabeth, only daughter of Judge Daniel S. Bacon. He entered West Point as a cadet in 1857, and graduated four years after — away down in the list. Worse still, he was court-martialed for some minor breach of etiquette, and, badly as officers were needed just then, had some trouble in getting located in the army. But we long ago learned that rank at West Point by no means settles the officer's later standing in the army. Soon after graduating he was made Second Lieutenant, and assigned to Company "G," Second United States Cavalry, and arrived just in time to take a little part in the Bull Run battle and stampede. A little later he served on the staff of General Phil. Kearney, and early in the summer of 1862 was made full captain and aid-de-camp of General McClellan. And this contributed not a little to some of his troubles in after years, as he was an enthusiastic "McClellan man," and by no means reticent in his views. Animosities were excited during that controversy which were not settled till long afterward.

Little by little Custer fought his way up, and the last year of the war the country was charmed and excited by the brilliant movements of Brigadier-General George A. Custer, of the United States Cavalry. After the war we almost lost sight of him. Except that President Johnson took him, along with a few others, as one of the attractions of that starring tour, "swinging 'round the circle," we hear no more of Custer till the army was reorganized in 1866, and he was once more a captain in the United States Cavalry, this time on the plains. But it was a different sort of army from that with which he had won his early honors. Language fails to portray the utter demoralization of our regular army from 1865 to 1869 or '70. All the really valuable survivors of the volunteer army had returned to civil life; only the malingerers, the bounty-jumpers, the draft-sneaks and worthless remained. These, with the scum of the cities and frontier settlements, constituted more than half the rank and file on the plains. The officers, too, had been somewhat affected by the great revolution. The old West Pointers were dead, or retired on half pay, or had grown to such rank in the volunteer army that they could not bear to drop back to their old position in the regular service. The officers consisted of new men from West Point; of men who had been appointed from civil life or from the volunteer army, in most instances to oblige some politician; and a few men like Custer, to whom military life

THE CUSTER MASSACRE.

was both a pleasure and a legitimate business. Desertion was so common among the private soldiers that it entailed no disgrace anywhere in the West. Hundreds enlisted simply to get transportation to the Rocky Mountains, and then deserted. When our wagon-train was on its way to Salt Lake in 1868, a deserter traveled with us two days, dressed in his military clothing, and without the slightest attempt at concealment. In this wretched state of the service in the West, Custer was promoted to the rank of Lieutenant-Colonel, and put in command of the Seventh United States Cavalry.

It was but nominally a cavalry regiment. The men were there, and the horses, with guns, equip-

"GO WEST."

ments, an organization and a name; but as a *cavalry* regiment he had to make it, and he did it so well that it soon became the reliable regiment of the frontier. The new Colonel's career, for some time to come, was among the hostile Indians of Western and South-western Kansas—then the worst section of the Far West for Indian troubles. The tourist who glides rapidly and with such keen enjoyment through this region, by way of the Kansas Pacific or Atchison, Topeka & Santa Fe Road, can scarcely conceive that but a few years have elapsed since it contained thousands of murderous savages; for it is a noteworthy fact that nothing so soon moderates the danger of Indian attacks as a railroad. It seems that, even if no fighting is done, the mere presence of the road, with daily passage of trains, either drives the Indians away or renders them harmless. But in the early days the routes to the Colorado mines were raided at regular intervals. One year there would be almost perfect peace; the next a bloody Indian war. It seems to have been the policy of the Indians to behave well long enough to throw emigrants off their guard; then to swoop down and murder and plunder with impunity. The region between the Smoky Hill and the Republican was particularly noted for bloody encounters. It was raided in turn by Sioux, Cheyennes and Arapahoes, and often by all three in concert. Every ravine and knoll on the route has its own local legend—the details, a blending of the ludicrous and horrible. Tradition relates that two bold settlers started for the mines in a time of profound peace, just after the Indians had concluded a most solemn treaty and shaken hands over their promise to live in eternal peace with the whites; the settlers, in Western mirthfulness, painting on their white wagon-cover the words, "Pike's Peak or Bust." A scouting party sent out from some post came upon them on the Upper Republican, just in time to see the savages vanishing in the distance. The oxen lay dead in the yoke. Beside the wagon were the corpses of the two settlers, transfixed with arrows. They had "busted."

In 1864 the savages broke out worse than ever, carrying off several women captive from the settlements in Kansas. In 1865 there was a precarious peace; but in 1866 and '67 the Indians raided every part of the stage road. Meanwhile the noted "Chivington massacre" had occurred, and General P. E. Connor had, by

"BUSTED."

extraordinary exertions, killed some Montana Indians; both events were seized upon by Eastern "humanitarians," and for a while they succeeded in completely paralyzing all portions of our army. And here it may be observed that our peculiar, tortuous, uneconomical and most unsatisfactory Indian policy, is the result of a certain conflict of forces highly liable to occur in a free republic. There is, first, a small but eminently respectable and powerful party, which is opposed to fighting the Indian at all, and think that he might be fed and soothed into keeping the peace; and that, at any rate, it would be cheaper to feed all the Indians to repletion than to fight them. And, as to this last point, they are emphatically correct. There is, next, a considerably larger number, mostly on the frontiers, who believe in a war of extermination, but they have little or no political influence. There are, also, the traders and agents, some honest and some otherwise, whose interests are involved; and the sensible middle class, who believe in keeping treaties with the Indians, and thrashing them if they break treaties. Of course, it sometimes happens that one of these parties is ahead, and then another. As a result, our policy is strangely crooked, inconsistent, and expensive. The Indian no sooner gets accustomed to one policy than another is adopted; he has scarcely learned to trust one officer till another is in his place, who takes a malicious pleasure, apparently, in undoing all that the former has done. This uncertainty entails frightful expense, both in treasure and life. But it is a difficulty inseparable, apparently, from our form of government.

It is unnecessary to trace the causes which led to Hancock's campaign against the Indians in 1867. It was a formidable affair on paper, but accomplished nothing. Our whole force consisted of eight troops of cavalry, seven companies of infantry, and one battery of artillery, the whole numbering 1,400 men. General Hancock, with seven companies of infantry, four of the Seventh Cavalry, and all the artillery, marched from Fort Riley to Fort Harper, and there was joined by two more troops of cavalry. Thence they marched southeast to Fort Larned, near the Arkansas. The hostile Indians, consisting of Cheyennes and Sioux, had appointed a council near by; but all sorts of difficulties seemed to arise to prevent their coming up to time. First, there was a heavy snow, although it was the second week in April; and the runners reported that the bands could not come. Then word came that they had started, but found it necessary to halt and kill some buffalo; and, again, that they had once come in sight, but were afraid on account of so many soldiers being present. Then General Hancock proceeded up the stream to hunt the Indian camp, and was met by an imposing band of warriors. Another parley ensued; midway between the hostile forces Generals Hancock, A. J. Smith and others met Roman Nose, Bull Bear, White Horse, Gray Beard and Medicine Wolf, on the part of the Cheyennes, and Pawnee Killer, Bad Wound, Tall-Bear-that-walks-under-Ground, Left Hand and Little Bull and Little Bear, on the part of the Sioux. There was no fighting; but after a few days more of excuses, the mounted Indians suddenly departed. Then it was discovered that the whole proceeding was but a well-played ruse to enable the Indians to get their women and children to a place of safety, and leave the warriors free for contingencies. The accomplished commanders of the American army had been tricked by a lot of dirty savages. Custer in the lead, pushed on with all possible speed after the Indians, but in vain. They had struck the stage stations on the Smoky Hill route, and murdered several persons; and the war was begun. It ended decidedly to the advantage of the Indians.

Custer's first experience in actual Indian-fighting was while escorting a wagon-train loaded with supplies from Fort Ellis. The Indians had selected for the fight a piece of ground well cut up with gullies—an

CUSTER'S FIRST INDIAN FIGHT.

admirable system of "covered ways"—by which they hoped to get close up to the wagons without being discovered, and then make a charge. But the watchful eye of a scout discovered their plan, and brought on the conflict on ground more favorable to the whites. The train was simultaneously attacked on all sides by six or seven hundred well-mounted Indians, outnumbering Custer's party twelve to one. The savages attacked in the manner known as "circling"—that is, riding round and round the whites, hanging on the opposite side of their horses so as to be shielded, and firing over the animal's back and under his breast. The scout, Comstock, had predicted a long and obstinate battle: "Six hundred red devils ain't a goin' to let fifty men stop them from getting the sugar and coffee that's in these wagons." And they did not yield the prize as long as there was hope. The soldiers were located around the wagons in skirmish order. The Indians encircled them in a much larger ring; but, though the firing continued for hours, only a few Indians were hit, so difficult was it to take aim at the swiftly-flying horse or rider. All this time the train moved slowly on over the comparatively level prairie, the teamsters shivering with terror, and scarcely needing the command to "keep closed up—one team's head right against the next wagon." This fight lasted three hours, and had the Indians maintained it much longer, the soldiers would have run out of ammunition. But the savage scouts, posted all around on the highest points, gave warning that something was wrong; and soon the whole band ceased firing and galloped off. Five of them had been killed and several wounded. The cause of their sudden retreat proved to be Colonel West's cavalry command, which soon arrived.

Custer's next anxiety was for Lieutenant Kidder and his party of eleven men, who were known to be moving across from the Republican to Fort Wallace, through a country now swarming with hostile Indians.

Soon after getting the supply train into camp, Comstock, the scout, was appealed to for his opinion as to Kidder's chances. It was far from encouraging. But Comstock's reply to the officers contains some hints worth recording. Said he: "Well, gentlemen, there's several things a man must know to give an opinion. No man need tell me any pints about Injuns. Ef I know anything, it's Injuns. I know jest how they'll do anything, and when they'll take to do it; but that don't settle the question. Ef I knowed this young lootenint, ef I knowed what sort of a man he is, I could tell you mighty nigh to a sartainty all you want to know; for, you see, Injun-huntin' and Injun-fightin' is a trade all by itself; and, like any other bizness, a man has to know what he's about, or ef he don't, he can't make a livin' at it. I have lots o' confi*dence* in the fightin' sense o' Red Beard, the Sioux chief, who is guidin' the lootenint, and ef that Injun can have his own way, there is a fair show for his guidin' 'em through all right; but, there lays the difficulty. Is this lootenint the kind of a man that is willin' to take advice, even if it does come from an Injun? My experience with you army folks has allays been that the youngsters among ye think they know the most; and this is 'specially true ef they've jist come from West Pint. Ef one o' 'em young fellers knowed half as much as they bleeve they do, you could'nt tell 'em nothin'. As to rale book larnin', why I spose they've got it all, but the fact of the matter is, they could'nt tell the difference 'twixt the trail of a war party and one made by a huntin' party to save their necks. Half uv 'em, when they first cum here, can't tell a squaw from a buck, because they both ride straddle; but they soon larn. But that's neither here nor thar. I'm told that this lootenint we're talkin' about is a new-comer, and that this is his first scout. Ef that be the case, it puts a mighty unsartain look on the whole thing; and, 'twixt you and me, gentle*men*, he'll be mighty lucky ef he gets through all right. To-morrow we'll strike the Wallace trail, and I can mighty soon tell whether he's gone that way."

Next day the relief party, led by Custer, came on Lieutenant Kidder's trail, and after a brief examination Comstock pronounced: "The trail shows

WESTERN SCOUT—WILD BILL.

that twelve American horses, shod all around, have passed at a walk; and when they went by this pint they war all right, because their horses are movin' along easy, and no pony tracks behind 'em, as would be ef the Injuns had an eye on 'em. It would be astonishin' for that lootenint and his layout to git into the fort without a skrimmage. He *may*, but ef he does, it'll be a scratch ef ever there was one; and I'll lose my confi*dence* in Injuns."

Custer ordered the command to hurry up, and, following the trail, they came, in a few hours, upon two dead horses with the cavalry brand, but stripped of all accoutrements. A little farther, and they saw that the American horses had been going at full speed, while all around Comstock pointed out the minute but abundant evidences that the Indians had fought them from all sides, the pony tracks being numerous. A little farther, and they entered the tall grass and thickets along Beaver Creek, and there saw several buzzards floating lazily in the air, while the trail was sprinkled with exploded cartridges and other debris. That told the tale. Nor were they long in finding the dead. The sight made the blood even of these brave men curdle. Lieutenant Kidder and his companions lay near together, stripped of every article of clothing, and so brutally hacked and mangled that all separate recognition was impossible. Every skull had been broken, every head scalped; the bodies were mutilated in an obscene and indescribable manner, and some lay amid ashes, indicating that they had been roasted to death. The scalp of Red Bead, the friendly Sioux, lay by his body, as it is contrary to their rules to carry away the scalp of one of their own tribe; nor is it permitted among most Indians to keep such a scalp or exhibit it. The exact manner of their death cannot be known, but all the surroundings showed that they had fought long and well. Custer's command buried them on the spot where found, whence the father of Lieutenant Kidder removed his remains the following winter.

Custer marched on to Fort Wallace with all possible speed, but troubles multiplied. The soldiers had begun to desert. Forty men took "French leave" in one night! The next day thirteen men deserted in broad day, in full view of the command, seven mounted and six on foot. After a desperate run the latter were captured, two slightly and one mortally wounded. It is to be noted that they were then in a region where the deserters apprehended no danger from Indians. Two men were killed by the Indians after all danger was thought to be past. From Fort Wallace the command marched eastward to Fort Hayes. The war was over and Custer applied for and obtained leave to visit, by rail, Fort Riley, where his family was then located; and for this, and other matters connected with that campaign, Custer was court-martialed! This proceeding appears to have been purely malicious, prompted by the dislike of some inferior officers over whom Custer had exercised pretty severe discipline. The charges were drawn by one whom he had severely reprimanded for drunkenness. He *had* left Fort Wallace without orders, because, under the circumstances, he thought proper to report to his commander in person. To this they added the fact that he went on to Riley to visit his family, and thus constructed a charge that he had abandoned his post for his private convenience! Mean as this attack was, it was successful. Custer was suspended from rank and pay for one year!

Meanwhile another summer campaign was undertaken against the hostile Indians, with equally barren results. General Sully marched, in 1868, against the combined Cheyennes, Kioways and Arapahoes, whom he struck near the present Camp Supply. If this was a "drawn battle," that is the best that can be said of it. Sully retired, badly crippled, and made no further attempts. At the same time General "Sandy" Forsythe, with a company of scouts and plainsmen enlisted for the purpose, was hunting for the hostile Sioux on the Northern affluents of the Republican. He found them. They also found him. Of his total force of fifty-one men, six were killed and twenty wounded; all their horses were captured, and the command was only saved from annihilation by the arrival of re-inforcements. The Noble Red Man evidently understood his business better than the Generals opposed to him. The people of Colorado grew sarcastic. Western people often do when mail and supplies are cut off for weeks at a time. It appeared that the mountain territories were in a fair way to be isolated from the rest of the country. California Joe, a scout who had been with several of the commanders, thus gave in his experience:

"I've been with 'em when they started out after the Injuns on wheels—in an ambulance—as if they war goin' to a town funeral in the States, and they stood about as much chance o' ketchin' the Injuns as a six-mule train would o' ketchin' a pack o' coyotes. That sort o' work is only fun for the Injuns; they don't want anything better. Ye ought to seen how they peppered it to us, and we doin' nothin' all the time. Some war afraid the mules war a goin' to stampede and run off with all our grub, but that war onpossible; for, besides the big loads of corn and bacon, thar war from eight to a dozen infantry men piled into every wagon. Ye'd ought to heard the quartermaster in charge o' the train tryin' to drive the men outen the wagons and git them into the fight. He was an Irishmen, and he sez to 'em: 'Git out of thim waggins. Yez 'ill have me tried for disobadience ov orders for marchin' tin men in a waggin whin I've orders but for eight.'"

But the rude common sense of General Sheridan, soon after his arrival on the plains, put an end to summer campaigning. He and Sherman united in asking for the restoration of Custer; and, on the 12th of November, 1868, that officer, at the head of his command again, started out on his famous Washita campaign. Soon after the departure from Fort Dodge, on the Arkansas, the command was overtaken by a violent snow-storm; but this the commander thought all the more favorable to his plans. General Sheridan could only point out to Custer the neighborhood of the hostiles' camp, and leave all details to his judgment. With four hundred wagons, and a guard of infantry for them, and the Seventh Cavalry in fighting order, he pressed rapidly southward to the edge of the Indian country, where a camp was established for the wagons, as a base of supplies, and the cavalry pressed on. California Joe and other scouts accompanied the expedition, besides a small detachment of Osage Indians, headed by

Little Beaver and Hard Rope, who did excellent service. After a terrible winter march, the command, eight hundred strong, arrived at the bluff of the Washita at midnight, and saw below them, in the moonlight, the hostile camp. It was evident, at a glance, that the Indians trusted implicitly in the old army habit of fighting them only in Summer. They had no scouts out, and were buried in repose. The command was divided into four nearly equal detachments; and, by making wide detours, the Indian camp was completely surrounded before daylight. The night was terribly cold, but no fire could be lighted, and the suffering was intense. As Custer stood upon the brow of the hill, and peered through the darkness into the camp, he distinctly heard the cry of an Indian baby, borne through the cold, still air, and reflected with pain that, under the circumstances, there was so much probability that the troopers' bullets would make no distinction of age or sex. Soon after daylight the attack was made. Although taken by surprise, the Indians fought desperately, but were utterly routed. It practically annihilated Black Kettle's band of Cheyennes. A hundred and three warriors were killed; fifty-three squaws and children captured, eight hundred and seventy-five ponies taken and a vast amount of other property. Of the force, two officers and nineteen men were killed, three officers and eleven men wounded. In the very hour of victory Custer discovered that this was but one of a long line of villages, extending down the Washita; but he had struck such terror that the others did not gather force sufficient to attack, and he returned to camp in safety.

And here it may be noted that, in plains' travel and fighting, there is no difficulty so great as dealing with the wounded. With all the appliances furnished our

RUDE SURGERY OF THE PLAINS.

army surgeons, there must still be many deficiencies; and, with the ordinary plainsman, a bad wound is either certain death or a long and terrible struggle, in which nothing saves the man but an iron constitution. In the old days a regular backwoods' science grew up among trappers and *voyageurs;* they treated gunshot wounds and broken bones, extracted bullets and arrows, or amputated shattered limbs in a way that would have amazed the faculty, but was singularly successful. The camp-saw and a well-sharpened bowie-knife were their surgical instruments; their cauteries, hot irons; and their tourniquets, a handkerchief twisted upon the limb with a stick run through the knot and turned to press upon the artery. Arrows were often drawn through the limb, the feathers having been cut off; and bullets flirted out of an incision quickly made with a sharp razor. In winter the wounded limb was almost frozen by snow or ice applied before the amputation; in summer there was nothing for it but to suffer it through. An old *voyageur,* with but one arm, gave me an account of his losing the other, which made my "each particular hair to stand on end." The arm was completely shattered below the elbow; it was amputation or death, and the party was a thousand miles from any surgeon. But with knife, saw, and red-hot iron the job was skillfully done; he survived such rude surgery without a shock to his fine constitution.

After a brief rest Custer was again sent to the Washita, where he alternately negotiated with and threatened the savages, until he had recovered some captives they held, and located the Indians near the forts. And here originated the difficulty between him and General W. B. Hazen, then in charge of the southern Indians—Custer maintaining that Satanta's and Lone Wolf's bands of Kioways had been in the fight against him, Hazen denying it. It was six years before the matter was settled, Hazen producing unquestionable evidence that he was right. We find evidences, from time to time, that Custer was somewhat hasty in his judgments, and very impulsive in giving utterance to them—in short, that he had some of the faults as well as all the virtues of a dashing, impetuous man.

For two years there was peace on the plains; but in the spring of 1873, the first Yellow Stone expedition went out. From Yankton the Seventh Cavalry, with Custer in command, marched all the way to Fort Rice, six hundred miles, Mrs. Custer and other ladies accompanying the column on horseback. There the ladies halted; but it was not until July that the entire expedition started—cavalry, infantry, artillery and scouts, numbering seventeen hundred men—all under command of Major-General D. S. Stanley. The main object was to explore the country, and open a way for the surveyors of the Northern Pacific Railroad. Custer, as usual, was put in the lead, and soon after reaching the Yellow Stone had several skirmishes with the Indians, who were desperately resolved against the passage of a railroad through the country. If they could only have looked forward over the next year of the financial world they might have been spared all anxiety on that point. During this march the sutler and veterinary surgeon of the Seventh Cavalry were murdered by a Sioux called Rain-in-the-Face; and out of that matter grew the latter's hostility to Custer, and perhaps the latter's tragic death three years after.

Early in 1874 began the memorable Black Hills expedition, an undertaking that began in the grossest injustice and ended in wholesale murder. From the first discovery in California, rumors had constantly prevailed of great gold placers in the Black Hills, but the region was a mystery. The Warren Expedition, in 1857, had gone around the whole district, but the Sioux emphatically prohibited them from entering it, stating that it was sacred ground. Other expeditions proved that the region was a great oval, about a hundred by sixty miles in extent, cut up by numerous low mountain ranges covered with timber; that it possessed, as do all such mountainous regions, a more rainy climate than the plains, and scores of little valleys of great fertility. It is obvious from the lay of the country, that the region cannot contain any great area of agricultural land, but quite probable that it abounds in good mountain pastures and timbered hills. The tenacity with which the Sioux clung to it only the more convinced the Westerners that it contained gold by millions, and many were the exciting stories told. The treaty of 1868 confirmed it to Red Cloud and other chiefs in person in Washington, and the Black Hills were declared inviolable—a section of the Indian reservation never to be trespassed upon by white men. The Custer expedition of 1874 was undertaken in direct violation of that treaty, and upon the half-avowed principle that treaties were not to be kept with Indians, if whites needed the country in question. Consistent with this ill-faith the expedition was made the occasion of ridiculous exaggeration, not to say downright falsehood. Correspondents were sent along with descriptive powers suited to an earthly Eden, and they described one; explorers went to find gold by millions, and they found it. The country needed a sensation, and the Government took the contract of supplying it. When the expedition had returned, and the brilliant correspondents had made their report, General Hazen undertook to moderate popular enthusiasm by portraying the high plains as they generally are; but the public rejected him, and found in his testimony only another evidence of his animosity to General Custer. The general result was, settlement of the Black Hills before the Indian title was extinguished and another expensive and fruitless Indian war.

The next year Rain-in-the-Face, a noted brave of the Uncpapa Sioux, was arrested for the murder of Dr. Honzinger and Mr. Baliran, of the Yellow Stone Expedition of 1873. He was brought before Custer, thoroughly examined, and sentenced to death, but managing to escape, joined the hostile band of Sitting Bull, and sent word that he was prepared to take revenge for his imprisonment. There is evidence, though not quite conclusive, that this Indian gave Custer the death-blow. Here it is necessary to point out an important distinction in the organization of different bands. The ordinary Indian government is patriarchal, and in many bands a majority of the families are in some way related to the chief; but, though the chieftainship is nominally hereditary, its continuance in any line finally depends on the prowess of the claimant. If he fails in any particular, another chief at once supplants him. Hence the absurdity of the plan generally adopted by our Government, of trying to choose chiefs for the Indians, or to recognize one rather than another. If the young men cannot have the leader they want, they generally join the "hostiles." These bands are made up on an entirely different plan—by convenience rather than relationship. Sitting Bull, Crazy Horse, or some other active fighter, gets a reputation as war chief, and all the discontented braves join him; as a rule there are few women in such a band, and the number of men is, therefore, apt to be underrated on distant view. Still more distinct is a third class, commonly known as "dog soldiers." These are outcasts or runaways from all the tribes, who get together in squads of from five to five hundred; sometimes they dissolve and melt into the original tribes; sometimes are merged into some one big tribe, or simply wear out. Their communication at first is entirely by the "sign language;" if together long enough, a new Indian dialect arises from the jargon of so many tongues. It has occasionally happened that a large band of "dog soldiers" would capture women enough for their wants, conquer a territory for themselves, and in time grow into an entirely new tribe. Thus the Comanches, Arapahoes and Apaches are said to have descended from the original Shoshonees; while the Navajoes resulted from the union of part of the old Aztecs with an offshoot of the Shoshonees—or of the original Athabascan stock, from which the latter sprang.

In 1876, Sitting Bull and Crazy Horse led the hostile Sioux, and to them rapidly gathered all the discontented young braves from the agencies. As near as can be determined, the latter chief began the season with eight hundred braves—the former with nearly twice as many. Their position was the best that military art could have selected. From it the affluents of the Yellow Stone ran northward; the lower affluents of the Missouri eastward; on the east and north it was doubly protected by the "bad lands;" northwest and west were rugged mountains, and southward the high plains stretched for many hundred miles. Around the extreme outer edge of the hostile country, from northwest and north to north-east and east, ran the Missouri; on that stream were located all the agencies, and from them, through "friendly" Indians, went a constant stream of supplies to the warriors. By careful examination of the books (after the damage had been done), it was proved that these bands received in five months fifty-six cases of arms, containing one thousand one hundred and twenty Winchester and Remington rifles, and four hundred and thirteen thousand rounds of patent ammunition, besides considerable quantities of loose powder, lead and primers. It takes many such lessons as this to convince the American people that this machine we call government is the most awkward, expensive and inefficient of all human inventions; and yet the lesson is not learned, for in spite of daily multiplying evidences of its inherent inefficiency, new parties start up every year, urging that government should run our schools and churches, our mills, mines and workshops, our social, moral and industrial institutions. Daily is the lesson thrust upon us, that whatever government does is done wrong; and daily we hear fresh demands that government should do things which it was never organized to do. The plain English of the foregoing figures is, that government first armed the savages with repeating rifles; then sent an inferior force to attack them on ground of their own choosing.

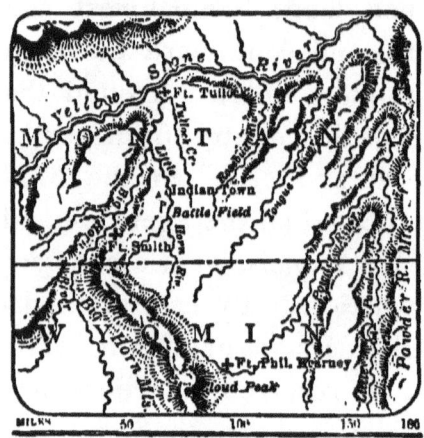

SCENE OF THE SIOUX WAR.

Three columns were to proceed from three points and converge on the hostile region: Gibbon eastward from Fort Ellis, Montana; Crook northward from Fort Fetterman; and Terry westward from Fort Abe Lincoln, just across the Missouri from Bismarck, Dakota. Of course they could not start at the same time. General Crook, with seven hundred men and forty days' supplies, started the 1st of March, and reached and destroyed the village of Crazy Horse, on Powder River, the 17th of March. But the Indians got away with most of their animals and supplies. The Gibbon column did not figure greatly till the junction with Terry on the Yellow Stone. Meanwhile the Terry column, in which General Custer was the leading spirit, was delayed in a score of ways. It *could* not start as early as that of Crook anyhow, as it was to move through a colder latitude, and, while waiting, Custer was summoned to Washington. The Belknap investigation was in progress, and Hon. Heister Clymer, Chairman of the House Committee, got it into his head that Custer could give important information. In vain did Custer dispatch that he really knew nothing about the case, and Terry urge that his call to Washington would delay and imperil the expedition. Clymer was all the more certain Custer had important information, and should be brought before the committee and rigidly interrogated. On the 6th of March, Custer telegraphed a request that he might be examined at Fort Lincoln. This Clymer flatly refused. Custer had to go to Washington, and there it was found that he really knew nothing about the case, and had only, as was natural to one of his impulsive nature, talked freely about what he had heard. But Heister Clymer had the satisfaction of compelling a General to come before his committee, and delaying Custer's march after Sitting Bull a whole month. Then President Grant took hold. The grim, impassive, hard-to-change General Grant took it into his head that Custer's talk about the case had been an intentional affront to him—*why*, no one ever knew. He refused to see Custer, though the latter repeatedly called at the White House, and once sent in a card, asking in plain terms for a reconciliation.

Custer then called at the office of General Sherman, only to learn that the latter was in New York, and might not return for some time; then, on the night of May 1, took the train for Chicago. Next day Sherman returned, and telegraphed to General Sheridan at Chicago, that Custer "was not justified in leaving here without seeing me (Sherman) or the President," and ordered that Custer remain at Saint Paul till further orders. *Somebody* was evidently playing sad havoc with Custer's character and plans. He had, *perhaps*, talked too much—that was his fault, if any thing—but it is impossible for the non-military mind to see any other harm he had done. He was in genuine distress. He telegraphed at length to General Sherman, and then to President Grant, and the final result was that, after a deal of red tape all around, he received permission to go with the expedition, in command of his regiment, the Seventh United States Cavalry. The Terry column consisted of the Seventh Cavalry entire, three companies of the Sixth and Seventeenth Infantry, with four Gatling guns and a small detachment of Indian scouts, about eight hundred men in all. Gibbon was coming in from the west with four hundred men, and Crook had made another start from the south with fifteen hundred men. Thus there were twenty-seven hundred armed men, distributed on the circumference of a circle about three hundred miles wide, to concentrate near the center where the hostiles were supposed to be.

Crook first found the enemy. On the 8th of June, his force had a skirmish with the Sioux, and repulsed them. A week later his Indian scouts reported that they had seen Gibbon's command on the other side of the hostile Sioux, on the Tongue River. On the 16th Crook pushed rapidly forward toward the hostiles. Next morning Sitting Bull attacked his camp in great force and with astonishing vigor. It was not exactly a surprise, but all must agree that Crook gained no advantage, and that Sitting Bull handled his forces admirably. Twice during the action he succeeded in getting his warriors into positions where they poured an enfilading fire into Crook's command. Meanwhile Generals Terry and Gibbon had communicated, and the latter had shown, by thorough scouting, that the hostiles were as yet all south of the Yellow Stone. A glance at the map will show that the Powder, Tongue, Rosebud, and Big Horn, run north into the Yellow Stone, and the Little Horn into the Big Horn; and that, after these various scouts, it was certain the hostiles were somewhere on those streams. Accordingly Terry commenced scouting for them in that direction. So far the general plan had worked well; its defect now appeared to be that Gibbon and Terry were separated from Crook by at least a hundred miles of mountainous country, and that in that region somewhere were the hostiles, in good position to move either way. The whole object of this plan was to prevent the Indians getting away without a fight, and as to that it was a perfect success. The contingency of the Indians being well prepared for a fight had apparently not been considered.

 Careful scouting narrowed the field, and finally it

was decided that the Indians were either at the head of the Rosebud or on the Little Horn, a ridge about fifteen miles wide separating the two streams. Terry and Gibbon, on the Yellow Stone, near the mouth of Tongue River, then held a council, and decided that Custer's column should be pushed forward to strike the first blow. Crook was too far south to be considered in this arrangement at all. The general plan is briefly stated in Terry's dispatch to General Sheridan, from the former's camp at the mouth of the Rosebud, just before the final movement, as follows:

> Traces of a large and recent camp of Indians have been discovered twenty or thirty miles up the Rosebud. Gibbon's column will move this morning on the north side of the Yellow Stone (see map), where it will be ferried across by the supply steamer, and whence it will proceed to the mouth of the Little Horn, and so on. Custer will go up the Rosebud to-morrow with his whole regiment, and thence to the head-waters of the Little Horn, thence down the Little Horn.

The object, of course, was for Custer to head off the escape of the Indians toward the east, while Gibbon would move up the Big Horn and intercept them in that direction. It has been absurdly said that Custer disobeyed or exceeded the general orders he received from Terry; but, in fact, those orders were so very "general," that, aside from the instructions as to route and sending scouts to seek Gibbon, they might have been condensed to "Go ahead, do your best; I trust all to you." Similar orders directed the march of Gibbon up the Big Horn. Should both columns march equally, all else being equal, it would result that they would come together on the Big Horn, some distance above (south) the junction of the Little Horn. There appears to have been no special order given as to rates of marching; and so far the witnesses do not agree very well as to what either commander was to do if he struck the Indians first. The reasonable supposition is, that it was understood beforehand that they were to fight on sight. It was hardly to be supposed that Sitting Bull would accommodate them by slowly retiring before either, until the other could come up in his rear. Custer's command received rations for fifteen days. Thus supplied, and thus directed with only general orders and plenary powers under them, Custer and his cavalry set out up the Rosebud on the afternoon of June 22, 1876, which is the last account we have from him in person. Thereafter his movements are known only by the report of Major Reno, who succeeded to the command of that section of the regiment which survived; the statements of various officers in the same command; the evidence of Curly, an Upsaroka scout, who alone survived the massacre, and some unsatisfactory accounts from the enemy. From all these sources, and a careful examination of the trails and battle-ground, the following facts are proved:

On the 22d, Custer marched his command about twelve miles up the Rosebud, and encamped. On the 23d, they continued up the Rosebud for about thirty-five miles, perhaps a little less. On the 24th, they advanced rapidly twenty-eight miles, and, finding a fresh Indian trail, halted for reports from scouts. By night they had received full reports, and, about 9.30 P. M.,

Custer called the officers together and informed them that the Indians were in the valley of the Little Horn, and that to surprise them they must cross over from one stream to the other in the night. Accordingly they moved off at 11 P. M.; but, about 2 A. M. of the 25th, the scouts gave notice that the command could not get across the divide before daylight; so halt was made, provisions prepared, and breakfast eaten. Right here, apparently, Custer's original plan failed. It would seem to have been his intention to repeat the Washita battle, and attack at sunrise. By 8 A. M., the command was nearing the Little Horn. Here the regiment was divided. Major Reno took command of companies M, A and G; Captain Benteen of H, D and K; Custer retained companies C, E, F, I and L, and Captain McDougall, with company B, was placed as rear-guard with the pack-train. As they moved down the creek toward the Little Horn, Custer was on the right bank, Major Reno on the left bank, and Captain Benteen some distance to the left of Reno, and entirely out of sight. As near as can be determined the command had marched some ninety miles since leaving Terry; but it is claimed by some that this last night and forenoon march was much longer than reported.

About noon they came in sight of the Indian camp, on the opposite side of the river, which at that point runs a little to west of north, with a considerable bend to the north-east. Enclosed within this bend, on the left (west) side of the stream, began the Indian camps, which continued thence a long way down the Little

Horn. As the command now enters the battle in three divisions, we must consider them separately. As

GETTING THE FIRST SHOT.

far as Custer's plan can be known, it was for Reno to cross, attack the upper end of the Indian camp, and drive them down stream, if possible; at any rate, to employ the warriors fully, while Custer himself, to be re-inforced by Benteen, should gallop around the bend of the Little Horn and down some distance, then cross, and attack from that side. It was evident that the time for a complete surprise was past. The last order Reno had from Custer was: "Move forward at as rapid a gait as you think prudent; charge afterwards, and the whole outfit will support you." Pursuant thereto, Reno with his command took a sharp trot for two miles down the stream to a convenient ford; then crossed, deployed with the Ree scouts on his left, and opened the battle, the Indians retiring before him about two and a half miles. And here comes in the first doubtful proceeding. Reno says: "I saw that I was being drawn into some trap. * * * I could not see Custer or any other support, and at the same time the ground seemed to grow Indians. They were running toward me in swarms, and from all directions." He retired a little to a piece of woods, dismounted, had his men fight on foot, and advanced again. He says that the odds were five to one, and he saw he must regain high ground or be surrounded. Accordingly he remounted his men, charged across the stream, some distance below where he had crossed before, and hurried to the top of the bluff, losing three officers and twenty-nine men killed and seven men wounded in this operation. In fact, nearly his entire loss occurred in this retreat, men and horses being shot from behind. It would *seem* to a civilian, who has, perhaps, no right to criticize an Indian fight, that it would have been far cheaper, and more nearly in accordance with his orders, to stick to the woods on the west side, and fight it out for a few hours. The surgeon present says there was *only one man wounded before Reno abandoned the timber*.

We turn now to Benteen. That officer, having been ordered to the extreme left while marching down the affluent toward the Little Horn, was necessarily several miles off when the rest of the command turned to the right and *down* the Little Horn. Finding no Indians, he re-crossed the affluent and marched down the trail left by Custer. About three miles, as he says, from where Reno first crossed, he met a sergeant carrying orders to Captain McDougall to hurry up the pack-train; a little further on he met Trumpeter Martin with an order from Custer, written by Adjutant McCook, and the last he ever penned, which read: "Benteen, come on; big village; be quick; bring packs." About a mile further on he came in sight of the Little Horn, and saw Reno retreating up the bluffs. He also saw "twelve or fifteen dismounted men fighting on the plain, the Indians there numbering about nine hundred!" About 2.30 P. M., he came up to where Reno had gathered his forces on the right bluff. The division of the regiment into three battalions was made at 10.30 A. M.; Benteen says that his scout and return to the main trail occupied about one hour and a half, bringing it to noon. How he consumed the time from then till 2.30 P. M., none of the reports inform us. The distance traversed could not have been over five miles, if we can trust any thing to the military map. It also appears from the report that Boston Custer, brother of the General, had time to come to the rear and pack-train, get a fresh horse, and go back to Custer, passing Benteen, and be killed in the final slaughter. The reports by various survivors seem to leave us in ignorance of much that we would like to know.

It was now near 3 P. M., and as senior major, Reno had in command his own and Benteen's battalions, and the company guarding the pack-train: Companies A, B, D, G, H, K, and M, numbering 380 men, commanded by Captains Benteen, Wier, French, and McDougall, and Lieutenants Godfrey, Mathey, Gibson, Edgerly, Wallace, Varnum and Hare. With them was Surgeon Porter. These officers are restrained, to a great extent, by military courtesy, but as far as their statements have been made public they indicate that there was no very determined effort made to aid Custer. Major Reno waited on the bluff awhile (length of time not settled yet), then moved slowly down the stream, and sent Captain Weir with his command to open communication with Custer. Weir soon returned with the information that the Indians were coming *en masse;* and, in a little while after, Reno's force was furiously attacked. We learn at this stage of the report that it was now 6 P. M. It seems impossible to stretch any action of which mention is made so as to cover the time between three and six. And yet it appears from an examination of the ground, that Custer could not, at three, have been more than three miles away. And, in the interim, the little squad of dismounted men whom Benteen saw across the river, had beaten off the Indians opposed to them and *succeeded in reaching Reno without loss!* But Reno's command was attacked, as aforesaid, about 6 P. M.; held its ground with the loss of eighteen killed and forty-six wounded, and had the enemy beaten off by 9 P. M. There is every evidence that Reno behaved with coolness and bravery, and Benteen with proper activity, during *this* battle; and still the report does not inform us as to the exercise of those qualities earlier in the afternoon.

And where all this time was Custer? The trail, the heaps of dead, and the few accounts from eye-witnesses tell a plain story. He came at high speed to a ford of the Little Horn, which would have brought him about the middle of the Indian camps. But in this short space of time the Indians had vanquished Reno, and their whole force was there to oppose him. He gave back from the ford, and the Indians followed in overwhelming numbers. They were now on the way he had come, and he continued his retreat along the bluffs down the river. He had in his command but four hundred and twenty men, and the Indians must have numbered nearly two thousand. Who can tell the agony of that terrible retreat and last desperate struggle? When the command had reached a point nearly a mile from the ford, Custer evidently saw that a sacrifice was necessary to save, if possible, a remnant of his command. To this end he chose his brother-in-law, Lieutenant James Calhoun; with him was Lieutenant Crittenden, their company having been selected to cover the retreat. They were found in line all dead together, the officers in their proper places in the rear, the company having died fighting to the last man.

A little further on another desperate stand was made. Then a mile from the scene of Calhoun's death, on the ridge parallel with the stream, Captain Keogh's company made a stand to cover the retreat. Keogh had evidently nerved himself for death. He was an old and able soldier. He was an officer in the Papal service when Garibaldi made war upon the Pope, and had served in the army of the Potomac during the war. Down went he and his company, slaughtered in position, every man maintaining his place and fighting desperately to the last.

Custer, with the remnant of his command had taken up his position on the next hill. Curly, the Upsaroka scout, tells us that he ran to Custer, when he saw that the command was doomed, and offered to show him a way of escape. General Custer dropped his head, as if in thought, for one moment, then suddenly jerking it up again he stamped his foot, and, waving Curly away with his sword, turned to rejoin his men. In that brief interval of thought he had decided to die with his men rather than attempt to escape. There had been a short lull in the fight, while the Sioux were maneuvering for a better position. The firing now re-commenced with more fury than ever. Curly dashed into a ravine, let down his hair so as to re-

FIGHTING HAND TO HAND.

semble a Sioux as much as possible, mounted a horse, and joined in the next charge; but watched his opportunity to put on a Sioux blanket, and in the heat of the battle slipped away.

Custer had now made his last stand. It was on the most commanding point of the ridge; and there, with Captain Yates, Colonel Cook, Captain Custer, Lieutenant Riley, and thirty-two men of Yates' command, he fought desperately to the last. One by one his companions fell around him. Nearer and nearer came the Sioux, like hounds baying a lion, dashing around and firing into the command on all sides. Finally, the whites made a sort of barricade of their dead horses, and again for a few minutes held the savages at bay. Then Rain-in-the-Face, bravest Indian in the Northwest, gathered his most trusty followers for a hand-to-hand charge. Custer fought like a tiger. With blood streaming from half a dozen gaping wounds, he killed or disabled three of the enemy with his saber, and when his last support was gone, as he lunged desperately at his nearest enemy, Rain-in-the-Face kept his oath and shot the heroic commander dead.

But the battle was not over. Captain Custer and Captain Smith tried to cut their way back to the river, and in the ravine leading that way twenty-six men were found dead. The heroic remnant made their last stand near the river, and there every man was found dead in position, every officer in his place, every wound in front. The awful tragedy ended with the day. General Custer lay dead on the hill. Beside him lay Colonel Tom Custer, who enlisted as a private at sixteen, was an officer at nineteen, and had been twice decorated for bravery in action. In the same slaughter died two more of the family. Boston Custer, forage-master of the Seventh Cavalry, had sought the open-air life of the plains to ward off a tendency to consumption, which early manifested itself. He avoided a lingering death by a heroic exit, fit subject for epic poem or thrilling romance. And there was young "Autie" Reed, a mere boy, named after General Custer himself, his nephew, son of the older sister, who had, in fact, reared the General. It was cruel that he, too, should die in this fearful massacre. Autie was just out of school, and was eager to go on the plains "with Uncle Autie." To please the lad Custer had him and a class-mate appointed herders, to drive the cattle accompanying the column. He had come with his uncle on this last scout, and here met with his death, equally brave with the bravest. Lieutenant James Calhoun, the remaining member of this relationship, had married Maggie E. Custer, the General's only sister, in 1872; and in every emergency showed himself worthy of adoption into this brave family. Cheered on by his voice, every man of his company died in place. With him was Lieutenant Crittenden of the Twelfth Infantry, a mere boy, just appointed, but cool as a veteran through all the terrible scene. A whole brotherhood of brave officers were cut off; for Custer had gathered around him a circle of choice spirits, who admired his dash, and emulated his bravery. There was the Adjutant, Col. Wm. W. Cook, a Canadian by birth, who had enlisted in the Twenty-fourth New York

Cavalry at the beginning of the war, and risen to be its Colonel. And Captain Yates, who enlisted as a private at sixteen and worked his way up. They used to call his company the "band-box troop," they were so neat in their dress and equipments; but every man of them died at his post. The last commander of all was Captain Algernon E. Smith, who won renown at the storming of Fort Fisher; was wounded, and for his bravery made brevet Major. But, perhaps, the saddest loss of all was that of Lieutenant William Van W. Riley. He was of heroic stock. His father, an officer in the navy, went down with his ship in the Indian Ocean a short time before William was born. He left his widowed mother for this expedition, and died in company with all the brave men who then made their last fight. The night fell upon all these brave officers and three hundred men, lying dead upon the field.

A full history of the battle is not yet known. This I say, despite the fact that military reports have been made by the commanders, and published by authority. But they leave much unknown. In a quiet way there has been much crimination and re-crimination; one party has accused Reno and Benteen of cowardice or disobedience; the other, including General Grant, has charged that Custer exceeded his orders and sacrificed his command. Without adopting the extreme view of either side, this would seem to a civilian about the correct state of the case: The regiment attacked a force of Indians outnumbering the soldiers two or three to one, and well armed, ready for fight, well posted, in broad day, when men and animals were fatigued, and so insured defeat; then, Reno and Benteen, seeing that retreat was a certainty, thought best to keep out of the fight, perhaps supposing that Custer would, in like manner, retreat after a brief skirmish. I cannot see that victory would have been possible in any event—no matter if the whole force had attacked at once, as originally intended.

This disaster, of course, spoiled the original plan. General Gibbon came up with re-inforcements, and the Indians moved. Successive minor battles and skirmishes followed, by which, though no one great victory was gained, the hostiles were slowly worn out and scattered. Many of the braves made their way back to the agencies, others retreated to less accessible positions in the mountains, and Sitting Bull, with a remnant, retreated into British America, whence, at this writing, negotiations are pending to have him removed. The war in that section is dying out, but a few words additional may be appropriate of the Indians in general. A glance at a map of Aboriginal America will show that very few of the Indian nations have retained their original locations; but it must not be judged therefrom that numerous tribes have become extinct. The Indian population of this country, at the landing of Columbus, has been greatly exaggerated. It is demonstrable that all that part of the United States east of the Mississippi never contained a half million of Indians; some authorities say a quarter of a million. It is apparent, at a glance, that a country like Ohio will sustain four hundred times as many people in the civilized as in the savage state. When men live upon game and the spontaneous products of the earth, it must be a fertile land indeed, which will sustain an average òf one person to the square mile. When we pass to the Indian of the plains the original population was sparser still. But there we find some of the races on the soil where first discovered. The Sioux have steadily contracted their eastern border, while maintaining their western border intact. But if, leaving history, we take tradition, we find that the Indian tribes have been engaged for centuries in a series of migrations, the northern ones, as a rule, slowly pushing southward. As all our mountain chains run north and south, it follows that the people of this country cannot grow into distinct races as in Europe, where different climates and soils are partitioned off by natural barriers. Hence the Indian, from Manitoba to the Gulf of Mexico is *one;* hence, too, half a million men of the West rose in arms to prevent the mouth of the Mississippi being "held by an alien government." Of the Indian migrations, the best authenticated are those of the Shoshonees and Sioux, which are referred to in the following legend, as related to the interpreter by Susuceicha, a Sioux chief:

"Ages past the Lacotas (or Dakotas, *i.e.*, Sioux) lived in a land far above the sun of winter.

"Here, then, the Shoshonee had all, but these basins were yet full of water, and the buffalo ranged even to Salt Land (Utah).

"Ages passed. The Shoshonees gave place to the Scarred Arms (Cheyennes). The Lacotas came toward the sun and fought long with the Scarred Arms. A great party came far into the inner plain (Laramie) and fell into a snare; all were killed by the Scarred Arms but six; these hid in a hole in the mountain.

"They built a fire and dressed their wounds; they hoped to stay many days till the Scarred Arms left the plain. But a form rose from the dark corner of the cave; it was a woman—old as the red mountain that was scarred by Waukan. Her hair was like wool; she was feeble and wrinkled. She spoke:

"'Children, you have been against the Scarred Arms. You alone live. I know it all. But your fire has waked me, and the full time of my dream has come. Listen:

"'Long ago the Shoshonees visited the Lacotas; the prairie took in the blood of many Lacota braves, and I was made captive. The Shoshonees brought me here, but I was not happy. I fled. I was weak. I took refuge in this cave.

"'But look! Where are the Shoshonees? The Lacotas will soon know them, and bring from their lodges many scalps and medicine dogs. They have fled before the Scarred Arms. One-half crossed the snow hills toward sunset; the other went toward the sun, and now hunt the buffalo east of the Ispanola's earth lodges. But my eyes were sealed for ages till my people should come. The Scarred Arms have long thought this land their own, but it is not. Waukantunga gives it to the Lacotas; they shall possess the land of their daughter's captivity. But why wait ye? Go, gather your warriors and attack the Scarred Arms. Fear not, their scalps are yours.'

"The warriors did return. They found the Scarred Arms at the foot of the mountain, and drove them to the South. Our grateful braves then sought the mountain to reverence the medicine woman, who told them so many good things. But woman and cave were gone. There was only a cleft in the mountain side from which came a cold stream of water. Then the Lacotas made peace with the Scarred Arms. Each year our warriors visit the Shoshonees for scalps and medicine dogs, and each of our braves, as he passes the old woman's spring, stops to quench his thirst and yield a tribute of veneration."

The Shoshonees not only have a legend answering to this, but name the various times when the Comanches, Arapahoes, and Apaches seceded from the main body. Thus, this great colony of the Athabascan race, slowly moving southward, has sent off branches right and left, from the Saskatchewan to the Rio Grande and Gulf of California.

It would surprise some people who have been indignant over the death of Custer and his companions to learn how small, comparatively, is the number of hostile Indians. A strip of five hundred miles wide, from the Missouri to the Pacific, is rarely visited by hostiles; and at no time, for the past ten years, have more than one-fifth of the race been in arms or even threatening. All the border States, except Texas, are free from hostiles. Of the nine Territories, only three have been seriously troubled since 1867, and the three Pacific States have had even a longer exemption. Within that time Indian hostilities have been confined to three districts. First, and greatest, is that strip of mountain, forest, and desert, including all Northern Wyoming, South-eastern and Eastern Montana, and a small portion of Western Dakota. Next are the highlands of Western Texas, raided by the Comanches and their allies; and, lastly, that part of New Mexico and Arizona dominated by the Apaches. To judge how contemptible a performance an Indian war is, how small the glory in proportion to the aggravation, be it noted that the whole Apache race numbers less than eight thousand, and cannot possibly mount two thousand warriors.

If it be decided that the three hundred thousand Indians in the United States (or rather the two hundred thousand wild ones) are to "die off," then by all means let a "feeding policy" be pursued; it is so much cheaper to kill them by kindness than by war. Since 1860 the average cost of killing Indians has been about five hundred thousand dollars each. One-tenth of that amount would stuff one to death. If, I say, the theory of final extermination be adopted, the most Christian and, by all odds, the cheapest plan would be this: Let central depots be established along the Pacific Railway and at other accessible points, and give general notice that every Indian who will come there and live shall have all the bread, meat, coffee, sugar, whisky and tobacco he can consume. The last man of them would be dead in ten years, and at a cost not exceeding twenty per cent. of the killing price. Since the Mormons began the feeding policy with their nearest Indian neighbors, the latter have died off much more rapidly than when at war. They can't stand petting any more than a rabbit.

CHAPTER XXVI.

WHERE SHALL WE SETTLE?

[*From* WESTERN WILDS, *by permission.*]

FIVE million Americans are asking this question. They will take Greeley's advice and go West; but are as yet undecided as to locality. Let us, therefore, briefly note the good and bad features of various sections. *Imprimis*, then, there is no paradise in the West; no region where one will not find serious drawbacks in climate, soil or society.

If you like a middle northern clime, there is no better place than southern Minnesota and the adjacent parts of Dakota. These have one great advantage over northern Iowa: the vacant land is still in the market at government prices; in Iowa it has been granted too extensively, and railroads and speculators own too much of it in large bodies. In the long run they lose money by holding it in this way; they would do well to sell and invest elsewhere; but they have not found that out yet. By and by the residents will learn how to make non-resident land pay all the taxes, as it now pays quite half, and then the speculators will sell cheap; but at present it would be advisable to locate where there is not so much non-resident land. The arguments now so common against these grants apply only to the border States; all the land given to the railroads west of longtitude 100, was not worth one day's debate in Congress. The income from it will never pay interest at a dollar an acre. The climate of Minnesota may be divided thus: summer, four months; winter, five months; spring and autumn, six weeks each. In fact, it is less than six weeks from the end of the snowy season to the coming of early fruits; but they call it spring the first of April, though the snow be six inches deep.

The quickness of vegetation is amazing. In August, along the Blue-Earth River, one can scarcely believe he is not in a tropical country; the heavy forests of lynn and walnut, the groves of sugar maple supporting a dense leafy mass, the dark green vistas and rich natural parks, with the rank grass on the prairies seem out of place so far north. By November this gives way to snow, which remains till April first or tenth. It then seems to disappear all at once. The black sandy soil dries out thoroughly in a week; but the air is still cool enough to justify an overcoat, and for a fortnight there are only brown plains and gray woods, with no hint of dawning life. A few days of warmth, and there is a swelling and fluttering perceptible on the bosom of Nature; then grass, bush, branch and vine spring quickly into living green, and in one month tropic luxuriance succeeds wintry death. But September clothes this region in its most attractive dress. The frost turns one thicket purple, another bright red or golden yellow, while the large timber is still green; through the glades blows the cool and stimulating air, and over all is the soft blue sky of the Garden State.

The advantages of this country are: abundant timber and running water, regular and exceedingly healthful climate, fertile soil, freedom from droughts and freshets, and land of excellent quality still to be had at

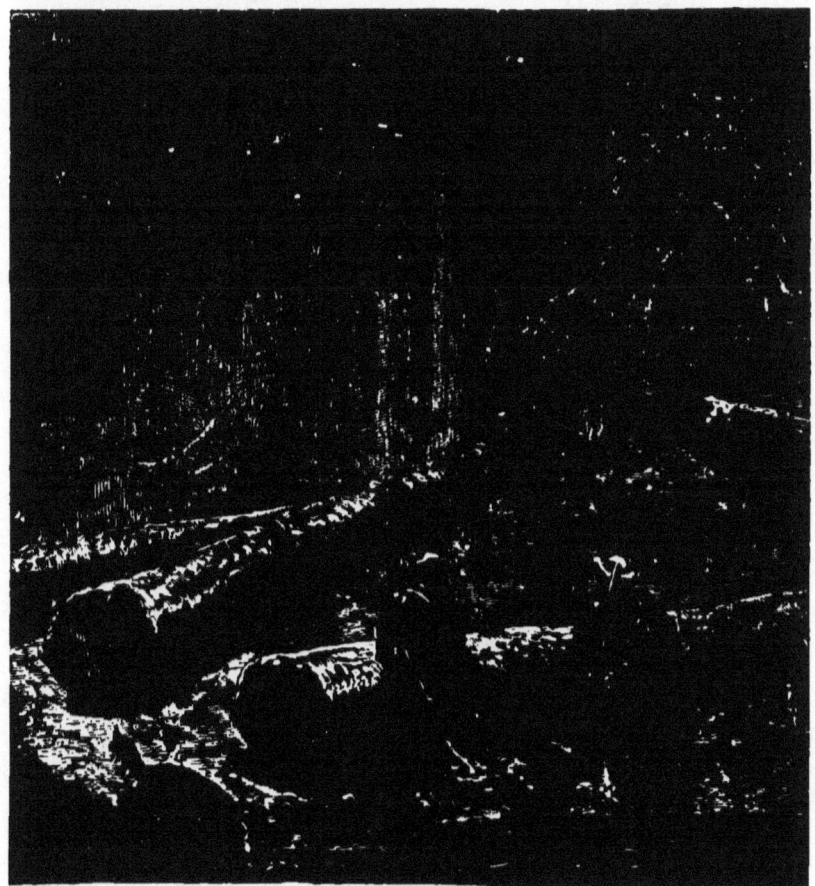

WINTER IN THE MINNESOTA PINERIES.

reasonable rates. Its disadvantages: a long cold winter and occasional liability to grasshoppers — the latter, however, very rare. The vegetable productions are remarkable, though report sometimes exaggerates. Tradition tells of one Minnesota Granger, who happened to be examining a cucumber just as the season of rapid growth set in. As he backed out to give it room, the growing vine followed him so rapidly that he took to his heels, but was soon overtaken. It grew all around him, tangled up his legs, and threw him down. Reaching in great haste for his knife to cut himself loose, he found that a cucumber had gone to seed in his breeches pocket.

The adjoining part of Dakota has similar climate and soil, but two disadvantages: there is less timber and more wind. But land is much cheaper. Hundreds of sections in every county can still be had at Government rates; and in the older settlements improved farms can even now be bought very cheap. Timber grows rapidly, and all the old settlers assure me they soon grow accustomed to the wind. I have noticed in all my western wanderings that the regions of abundant wind are those most free from malaria. The only exception, if it is one, is in the Indian Territory, where there is wind enough, and yet much complaint on the score of fever and ague. Despite my experience with the high winds of Dakota, I am inclined to set down as fabulous the statement sometimes made by the envious, that an old Dakotian cannot talk if the wind suddenly stops blowing. So used to it, you know.

Iowa I have already described at some length. I cannot get rid of the impression that the northern part of it is colder than the neighboring part of Minnesota.

There is less timber, and the wind has a fairer fling at a man. Artificial groves grow rapidly, and the soil is of great fertility. And, if you find there is too much non-resident land in your vicinity, you can help your good neighbors stick the taxes on it till the owner is willing to sell for whatever he can get. I have a friend who has paid $620 taxes in ten years on a quarter section of Iowa land, and is now ready to sell to some man who owns a gold mine or a spouting oil-well. We have all heard of the man who ate so much it made him poor to carry it. Similarly, some people own so much western land, that it will break them up to keep it. The settlers do not intend that non-residents shall get the benefit of their hard-pioneering— and who shall blame them?

Let us go a little further south. Northern Nebraska I know but little about, but in the southern part of that State is a region which seems to me peculiarly inviting to men from the Middle Northern States. "South Platte," as this division is called, contains at least twenty-five thousand square miles of fertile land, of which one-half or more is for sale quite cheap. The climate is perceptibly milder than that of "North Platte," and all the fruits and grains of the temperate zone are produced on a generous soil. Along the line of the Burlington and Missouri River Railroad, land is held at high rates; but in the rest of the country it can be bought at from five to eight dollars per acre. There is no government land in this section worth naming. The climate is about like that of central

Ohio, with dryer winters and more wind. This last you may retain as a general statement as to all the border States. Society is most excellent. The population is intelligent and progressive, and nowhere does a man find himself out of reach of the church and school-house. Going westward on any line one will find the winters growing dryer, also more "airish." So the doubting emigrant may ask himself "whether 'tis nobler in a man to suffer" cold healthful winds, to have dry roads and freedom from mud; or take refuge in the wooded regions of Indiana or Missouri, avoid the winds and suffer the other evils.

We now turn to a region more affected by men from the middle latitudes. In many weeks' travel between the Des Moines and Arkansas, one-fifth or more of those I met were from Ohio, and nearly all of them had sought this region since the war. Kansas, like Nebraska, is divided into northern and southern — this by the Kaw, that by the Platte. North-eastern Kansas is already an old country; Donivan County was pretty well settled twenty years ago. A hundred miles west of the Missouri land can still be had at reasonable rates, but I have never visited that section. When we come to southern Kansas an inviting field, indeed, is open to us. Good land is cheaper to-day than it was five years ago. This I happen to know from painful personal experience. But it don't follow that it will be cheaper still five years from now. Surely "the bottom" is reached by this time. In the second tier of counties, including Anderson, Allen, Neosho and Labette, the Leavenworth, Lawrence and Galveston Railroad Company have large tracts of good land for sale; and private owners a still larger amount.

This region boasts of many advantages: a mild climate, soil of rare fertility, timber sufficient for all ordinary purposes, rock in abundance, and easy communication with the rest of the world. Society is unsurpassed by that of any section, east or west. Churches and school-houses are within convenient reach of every section of land, and a man can not settle in so wild a spot that the mail will not bring him late papers at least twice a week. For seven years this region was blessed with good crops;

DROUGHTY KANSAS.

then came the "bad year" of 1874, when drought, chintz-bugs and grasshoppers in succession desolated the land. In Allen County large streams dried to beds of dust, the fish literally parching on the rocks; and pools and springs disappeared which the oldest inhabitants had considered perennial. In 1875 nature resumed her wonted courses; but the people had been too poor to sow wheat, and the country remained in a condition of general poverty. But such a crop otherwise I had never seen. There were miles on miles of cornfields, yielding from forty to eighty bushels per acre, and for sale at twenty cents per bushel; tens of thousands of tons of hay, worth two dollars per ton in the stack; potatoes by millions, and more feed than the stock could eat. And there was the trouble. The people had not a sufficiently diversified industry. They had relied almost entirely on the sale of grain, and this year there was no sale, and they remained poor despite their immense crops. I came down from the mountains on a visit just after the last grasshoppers had left, and a rural wag gave me this dialect picture of his experience with them:

"You see I bought early in '72—give two thousand two hundred dollars for two hundred and forty acres. Could a bought the same for half that two years after; can buy good land right alongside o' mine now for a V an acre. Been a deal o' cramp in real estate in this country. Well, nobody ever makes a crop the first year in a prairie country—think themselves in luck to get fences built and sod broke. I bought a hundred sheep—two blooded rams and the rest common ewes —and put all the rest of my money in improvements. Raised a little corn and oats in 1873, and put thirty acres of the new land, sod broke in 1872, into wheat and went to work with a hurrah in 1874 to make a God-awful crop. Everything come a booming, and I thought I had the world in a sling. Corn, oats, potatoes and wheat just got up and laughed; they grew so fine. Thought I never saw such a country for things to grow. Worked all the week, and used to set on the fence Sunday and calculate how rich I'd be. Went out one fine sunny morning about the first of June, and thought, by jiminy, the whole ground was a moving. Ten million hoppers to the square yard—all chawin' away as if the country belonged to 'em. Saturday morning they come into my farm from a ridge just south o' me—Sunday noon there wasn't a green thing where the corn, cane and potatoes had been. Job's luck wasn't a circumstance. My corn lot looked as if forty bands of wild Arabs had fell onto it. Not a smidgeon left—just bodaciously chawed up and spit out.

"Well, of course, I had the dumps. But I rallied. 'All right,' says I; 'got wheat and tobacco left anyhow.' Professor P—— said they wouldn't eat tobacco; but he's a fraud, sir—a barefaced fraud. The hoppers just went up on a ridge north of me and shed their second coats, and then come back on the tobacco. They eat every leaf clean to the ground, then dug up the roots and set on the fence and cussed every man that come along, for a chaw. About that time they got wings, and sudden as could be rose in the air and went off north a whirlin', like a shower o' white and yellow paper bits. 'All right,' says I; 'they've left my wheat anyhow.' Singular enough they didn't touch it; it was on t'other side the place, and out o' their track. Well, I rallied again, and counted on six hundred bushels o' wheat—and wheat's the money crop in this country. About June the middle, I noticed all at once that my wheat looked kind o' sick. Come to examine, sir, it was completely lined with a little, miserable, black and yellow, nasty-smelling bug. I took some to a man 'at had been here ten years. 'Neighbor,' says he, 'you're a goner; them's chintz-bugs, and every head o' that wheat that an't cut, 'll be et up in forty-eight hours.' Well, it was Sunday morning, and the wheat nothing like ripe; but it was a chance, and I got onto my reaper and banged down every hoot of it before Monday night. It cured in the sun and the bugs left it, and out o' the lot I got just a hundred and forty bushels o' shrunk-up stuff. It was a hundred and forty bushels more than any o' my neighbors got. You bet there was improved farms for sale in that neighborhood. My sheep had done well, and that was all I was ahead. Taking it by and large, the only sure crop is sheep."

He touched the right point in the last sentence; this is the country for stock-growing. Corn and hay can be produced so cheaply that the cost of bringing a full-grown ox into market is less than half what it would be in Ohio. The best of unimproved land, near the railroad, sometimes sells as high as twelve dollars per acre; from that it ranges down to four. In 1875 the surplus crop of the State was worth twelve million dollars. The report, for that year, showed that the corn raised in the State, if shelled and put in box-cars, would have loaded a train sixteen hundred miles long!

The Indian Territory is much talked of, but I would not advise any one to go there with a view to permanent settlement. Government cannot open the land to immigration without a shameful breach of good faith, and for one, as an humble citizen, I protest against it. There is such an abundance of good land elsewhere, that we can afford to leave this to the civilized Indians for the next fifty years. Then their progress will have been such that they will themselves throw it open and invite white settlers. Texas, just south of it, offers a far better field. Dallas is the center of a region two hundred miles square, which offers great inducements to Northern men. The winters are sharp enough to insure health and energy; and the summers are not, as far as I could observe, any hotter than in Minnesota. Land through all this section can be had at from four to eight dollars per acre. There are now Congressional lands in Texas; it is all State land. This comes of the State having been an independent republic when it came into the Union. It reserved the ownership of

TEXAS AND COAHUILA IN 1830.

all lands within its borders, though there are not wanting lawyers who assert that the general government might have rightfully taken those lands from the State, after the latter had seceded.

Look out for those beautifully colored maps which divide Texas into various agricultural sections, and locate the "wheat lands" away up on the heads of the Brazos, Colorado and Red River. One can put in his eye all the wheat they will raise up there without an expansive and expensive system of irrigation, and it will puzzle them to find water to irrigate with. If half that region is fit for grazing land, it is the best we can expect. Southern Texas is not very suitable for Northern men. Along the gulf are immense areas of fine sugar and cotton lands, but the climate is not favorable. Not that the heat is so great; but the summers are long, the autumns dry, and the winters first warm, moist and debilitating, and then very chilly. Central and northern Texas are free from these disadvantages. The immigrant from the North must learn a new system of agriculture, but that he can easily do.

Society? Well, I found it very agreeable. If there is any special hostility to Northern men, or Republicans, I never noticed it. The latter maintain their organization, sometimes elect their candidate, and always give him a hearty support, though the State has been Democratic since 1872. Texas may fairly claim to be one of the best governed States in the Union. Except on the south-western border the ratio of crimes is very small. In 1873 the law against carrying concealed weapons was strictly enforced in the railroad towns—a good deal more than can be said of any town on the Union or Kansas Pacific Railroads. It is in the "cow counties," in the extreme west and south-west, that some lawlessness still prevails. The law as to concealed weapons excepts those counties, it being considered a necessity that the *vacqueros* should go prepared for "enterprising Mexicans" and other cattle-thieves. If you like a wild country, that's the place for you, and if that is not wild enough, try the Comanche border. There the mountainous spurs put out toward the lower country, and cut it up into numerous little valleys. Down these spurs come the savages, often lying in ambush for days together in the scrubby timber, watching the ranches below. And all this time the settlers go about their usual work in assured safety, for there is not the slightest danger till after the "strike." One might walk within a rod of the hidden enemy and never be molested. The settlers see signs of Indians about, but feel no uneasiness; but once the raid is made, and the robbers on the run for cover, they kill all they encounter, and even slaughter stock they cannot take away. They can get five or ten miles more running out of a horse than can a white man; and five minutes after they leave him he is so near dead that he cannot be forced to walk. When hard pressed they draw a knife, hastily make a few incisions in the animal's hide, and rub in salt and powder. As the cow-boys express it, "it puts new life in a hoss."

But when long immunity has made the settlers careless, there sometimes occur tragedies which thrill the country with horror, and are told for years by the pioneers' hearth-stone, or around the camp-fire, where rude borderers teach their younger companions eternal hatred of all the Indian race. In the year 1850, a Mississippian, named Lockhardt, settled a little farther up the Colorado than was then usual with families, but still in a region thought to be safe from Comanche raids; and, in a few years, was surrounded with most of the comforts of his more eastern home. Wealth and good taste united to improve the wild beauty of nature; his house, elegant indeed for the border, was a temple of hospitality; his flocks and herds ranged over the arena of a dukedom; his colored servants scarce knew they had a master, so light was his patriarchal sway; and far and near the name of 'Squire Lockhardt was known as that of a natural nobleman and Texas gentleman. The friendly Indians that passed that way also partook of his hospitality, and he made the too common mistake of supposing that this would shield him against the incursions of their wilder congeners. But, of all his possessions, none was so widely celebrated as his daughter, Minnie. The rude *vacqueros* were charmed into unusual courtesy at sight of her; and, from far and near, young Texans of more pretentions sought her society. On the border, a young woman of beauty and accomplishments often acquires a wide-spread fame that would seem impossible to Eastern people; her graces are recounted in such fervid rhetoric, that the cold critic of an older community would think of her as a fabulous being. Even so the charms of Minnie Lockhardt were sung in a hundred camps, from the Trinity to the Colorado.

Many other settlers, generally single men, and skillful frontiersmen, had located between Lockhardt and the staked plain, and he had long ceased to think of an Indian raid as even remotely possible, when suddenly, as lightning from a clear sky, the Indian war of 1854 –'5 broke out; and, from the settlements on the upper Rio Grande, clear around to the Canadian, the border was in a blaze. The Utes and Apaches on the west pressed the Mexicans and whites, while the Comanches, from their fastnesses, carried destruction far down into Texas. The storm broke while Lockhardt was absent from home. Every settler near him was killed; his servants fled for their lives, and his daughter, then but twenty years of age, was carried into captivity. The frenzied father sent an appeal to his fellow-citizens, and it seemed that the whole Texan border was moved by one common impulse. Every young Texan who could supply himself with horse and gun was eager to assist in the rescue of Minnie Lockhardt; and, as soon as a force of two hundred had assembled, the father led them toward the high country, leaving word for the others to follow. Striking the trail of the Comanches, the Texans followed as fast as the strength of their horses would allow, their furious zeal continually aroused anew by the sights along the way, where worn-out captives had been ruthlessly murdered. Suddenly, at daylight, the pursuers came upon the murderers in one of those numerous cañons of upper Texas, where the savages had thought themselves safe.

Then ensued one of the most desperately contested battles of the Texan border. The Indian camp was set far back in a grove of scrubby timber, on all sides of which rose sandy hillocks and detached rocks, furnishing admirable lines of defense, as well as retreat. Again and again did the Texans, led by Lockhardt, penetrate almost to the camp, only to be driven back; and, on each advance, they distinctly heard the voice of Minnie calling on them for help, and dreaded lest their attack should be the signal for her death. But it appears the savages were bent on preserving their captive if possible. A double line of warriors surrounded the tent in which she was bound; and at last the wretched father, bleeding from a dozen wounds, was forced away by his men, who saw that the attack was hopeless. Having received re-inforcements, they renewed the fight the second day after, but the Indians had also collected their forces and taken a still stronger position; and to the father, lying helpless with his wounds, the men at last reported that the attack was hopeless, unless with a force large enough to surround the Comanche stronghold and reduce it by a regular siege.

Successive bands of Texans arrived, and in a few days the father again urged them to the attack; but the Indians had managed to retreat, carrying Miss Lockhardt with them. With the devilishness inherent in the Comanche nature, they were all the more determined to keep her when they saw the general

SKIRMISH WITH INDIANS.

anxiety of the whites for her recovery. But she proved a troublesome prize. The fact of her captivity nerved every Texan to desperate measures, and in a short time the Indians were attacked at all points, and forced back toward the Pecos. Then, as afterwards appeared, the band having possession of Miss Lockhardt sent her northward, and disposed of her to the Arapahoes. Convinced that she was the daughter of a great chief, by the exertions made to recapture her, this tribe opened negotiations with the commandants at Fort Union and Lancaster. But, before any thing could be accomplished, the Utes and Apaches were raiding the entire New Mexican border, and the captive girl in some way was transferred to the former tribe. Despite the awful hardships of a winter among the savages she survived, and in some way managed to make known her existence to the American commandant at Fort Massachusetts, New Mexico. About this time the Territorial Governor called out five hundred New Mexican volunteers, who were put under command of Colonel Ceran St. Vrain; and, joined by the First Regiment of United States Dragoons, under Colonel T. T. Fauntleroy, the whole force marched into the Indian country early in 1855. They defeated the Indians in one general battle and several minor skirmishes, but no trace of Miss Lockhardt could be found. The noted Kit Carson was then intrusted with the task of settling with the Utes and recovering all captives; but other means were at work.

Worn down by his wounds and mental suffering, Lockhardt returned home in despair; but another party of determined men set out to find the captive, **who** had, as it appears, been taken by the Arapahoes and Cheyennes from the Utes, with whom they were at war. Again and again were the whites almost suc-

FORT MASSACHUSETTS, NEW MEXICO, 1855.

cessful, and as often was the unfortunate girl hurried away to some more hidden fastness, almost before their eyes. The general Indian war ended, and a nominal peace was made; negotation was again attempted, but the third year of her captivity came, and still nothing was done. At length a company of the Texan Rangers, having penetrated almost to the heart of the Guadaloupe Range, came suddenly upon a village of Comanches, and, despite the hurried flight of the savages, who had their own women and children with them, the Rangers saw among them a captive white woman. They charged desperately upon the savages, who fled in all directions, but not till one of them had buried his knife in the body of the girl, who was still breathing when the Rangers came up. It was Minnie Lockhardt. She was just able to smile, as if to welcome the Rangers, then peacefully breathed her last. "And," said the weather-beaten frontiersman who gave me these facts, as he chocked down his emotions, "it was a God's blessin' she was dead, an' her father never seen her." For she had suffered the last terrible indignity savage malice could invent. As is common when a captive woman is not taken by one Indian, she became the common property of the band; and loathsome disease had worn her to a skeleton. Heartbroken and disfigured, death was to her an unmixed gain. Her afflicted father soon followed her to the grave. The Lockhardt place is now desolate; its dwellings burned, its tenants gone. But the chivalry and hospitality of the father are still the theme of local story, while the beauty and sorrowful fate of the daughter are still told around the camp-fires and hearth-stones of Texas and warm anew the hearts of its sons to undying vengeance against the Comanches.

Texas ends the list of the border States proper. Observe that in all these States, as one goes west, he rises slowly to a higher, dryer and more barren country, till at last, about longtitude 100 or 101, he enters on "the area of corrugation," as geologists call it, where barrenness is the rule; and this area includes all the western border of Dakota, Nebraska, Kansas, Oklahoma and Texas, of eastern Washington, Oregon and California, and all of Montana, Idaho, Wyoming, Utah, Colorado, New Mexico and Arizona. Let us skip this region of mountain and desert, and pass at once to the fertile section of the Pacific coast, lying west of the Sierra Nevadas.

California? Well, I should not be in a hurry to recommend it to any man of moderate means. The worst objection is the oppressive land monopoly. "A little ranche of twenty thousand acres" is a common expression. A dozen men each own a dukedom—all but the inhabitants. They will own them after awhile, unless this thing is remedied. The beginning of this system was in the Mexican grants. The old Spanish custom was to grant a county of land to an *impresario*, on condition that he should settle a certain number of families on it. The Mexicans continued the system with some modifications, and in due time the inferiors became *peons* to the lord. These titles were all confirmed by treaty when the United States took possession, and have been sustained by the Supreme Court.

Again, when the miners took the country they supposed the land to be worth but little except for grazing, and many of them took up claims and sold them for a trifle to speculators, and thus the best land in California is now held in immense tracts by an aristocracy. Of course these men are in favor of "Chinese cheap labor," and equally, of course, the poorer whites are unanimously opposed to it. Some have thought that, as our country grew older, all the lands would be held in the same way; but it is somewhat reassuring to note that there is less land monopoly in Massachusetts than in Ohio, and far less in Ohio than in California. In some of the oldest States the land is most equally distributed, thanks to our wise laws of descent and distribution of estates; and in the course of fifty or a hundred years the attrition of a free society will wear out this evil in California.

It is now very difficult for one to get a small piece of land in that State; and it would be better for intending emigrants to organize in some way, and buy out a grant, of which there are always a few for sale. There are a few places—very few I am afraid—where the best land is not in the hands of monopolists, and it is already noticeable that such communities improve faster than others. But for many years to come California will continue to be a land of the beggar and the prince.

In Oregon this evil is not so great, but still great enough. Land in the Willamette Valley is not much cheaper than in Ohio and Indiana, and I cannot think that enough is gained to make it worth while to go so far. I do not see how a man, wife and five children—average Western family—can get to Oregon comfortably for less than five or six hundred dollars, which amount would buy eighty acres of first-class land in Kansas or Nebraska, or a hundred acres in Texas; and, having got to Oregon, you must pay more for land than in the other States named, with a moral certainty that the country will develop more slowly. Oregon began to be settled by white men in 1830; before 1848 it contained about ten thousand Americans; its population now is about one hundred thousand. Kansas was thrown open to settlement only twenty-three years ago; it now contains a population of at least six hundred thousand. It strikes me that's the sort of a country to go

A CALIFORNIA BIG TREE.

to, if you want your future to hurry up. But, if you like a romantic border country—one that is likely to stay border for a long time—go to Oregon. Oregon climate? Well, some people like it. I don't. True, it is mild—and moist; but I am just Yankee enough to prefer the cold, dry winter to the warm, wet, muggy, and muddy. No five months' rain for me, if you please. I'd rather freeze than smother. In California it's different. There is no more rain there during the so-called "rainy season" than in Ohio, and half the time not as much. In fact, there never is too much rain in California, though there sometimes is too little. The summers in Oregon are delightful enough—more pleasant than in California; but, as at present advised, I would not recommend either State to the class of emigrants just now going West.

Let us now turn to the great interior, and see if we can pick out any oases inviting to settlement between longtitude 100 and the Sierra Nevadas. Nevada is not an agricultural State at all; and for aught we can now see, never will be. It contains ninety-eight thousand square miles, and less good land than three average counties in Ohio. It has population enough for one-third of a member of Congress; but our "paternal" government has granted the State one Representative and two Senators. Nobody need think of going there to engage in farming. In the far distant future, when land is in much greater demand than now, some way will perhaps be found to redeem those arid tracts. Trees will be planted wherever they will grow; the Australian eucalyptus may flourish even on the desert, and thus in a few centuries a moister atmosphere be created. But for the present the population must consist of capitalists and laboring miners, and their congeners. And here I might indulge in wearying words on the romance and hardship of a miner's life, had I not given him a chapter to himself. Strange it is that he should be the most imaginative of men with a life of such prosaic toil; but it is, doubtless, because his ways are in a path, as Job says, "which no fowl knoweth, and which the vulture's eye hath not seen: the lion's whelps have not trodden it, nor the fierce lion passed by it." (Job xxviii). And no finer, more poetical description of the silver miner's strange life underground was ever written than in that chapter, taking Louth's version: "He putteth forth his hand upon the rocks, he swings above the depths. He cutteth out watercourses through the rocks; and his eye searcheth for precious things. He makes a new way for the floods; he goes in the very stones of darkness in the shadow of death." The perils of the prospector above ground are equally great, but the life has its charms for all that.

In Utah are still a few unoccupied plateaus which could be redeemed by canals taken out from some large stream. Bear River Valley contains some sixty thousand acres of fertile land, which might be redeemed at moderate cost by a canal from Bear River. The climate is mild, not very hot in summer, and decidedly pleasant in winter. The Central Pacific runs through the valley, and the location is excellent for a thriving colony. On the Sevier is a smaller valley of the same character. East of the Wasatch Range are several beautiful valleys. That of Ashley's Fork contains land enough for three thousand farms, all of most excellent quality; and it can be had for the taking. Late in 1873 a dozen stock ranchers settled there, and have raised splendid crops every year since. Be it noted that in no part of the temperate zone is fruit a more certain crop than in Utah. Peaches never fail. The Ashley Valley slopes gently to the south-east; snow rarely lies on more than one night, and all the slopes are rich in bunch-grass. Game is abundant in the neighboring hills, and a good road can easily be constructed to the Union Pacific at Bridger Station. The valley of Brush Creek, east of Ashley, is about half as large and equally inviting. In these a colony of ten thousand Americans might make for themselves delightful homes.

Farther south are several fine valleys, none quite so large as the foregoing, but very fertile; and small settlements have been made in some of them. It is to be noted that these valleys which open eastward from the Wasatch are free from Mormon domination, and will remain so if settled by Gentile colonies. It has always seemed to me that life would be exceedingly pleasant in one of these alpine valleys. The elevation is about five thousand feet above sea-level; the winters are mild; the summer air dry and stimulating. There is game on the hills, and trout in the streams; land enough to produce grain for a sparse population, and almost unlimited grazing ground. But these districts will never sustain a large population. Between each settled valley and the next there will be a day's ride over barren mountain or grassy hill. All that part of Utah east of the Wasatch will never sustain a hundred thousand people.

Wyoming contains so little farming land that it is not worth while to discuss it; but it is rich in grazing tracts. Of the ninety-eight thousand square miles in this Territory, one-half is complete desert; the rest good grazing ground, with perhaps five hundred sections of farming land, though I never saw the latter and do not know where it is located. Of course no one pre-empts his grazing land; he merely takes up meadow land when he can get it convenient; and perhaps enough farming land for a garden, if there is so much in the neighborhood. One year with

NEVADA FALLS, YOSEMITE VALLEY.

another the herder puts up hay enough for three months' feeding. Sometimes none of it is used, and then it is on hand for the next winter. About half the time the common stock can go through the winter without hay, living on the bunch-grass; but blooded stock should be fed at least two months every winter. By the first of May stock can live well on the range. From that on the grass appears to get more nourishing every day till December. If the winter comes on with snow, grass remains good till the snow melts; but rain takes the sweetness out of it. It will then sustain life, but stock lose flesh rapidly while living on it. It requires a much larger area for the same number of stock than in a blue-grass country, as the grass makes but one growth per year, not renewing itself after being eaten off. From all these facts it will be apparent that Wyoming never can sustain a very large population.

New Mexico? Well, I must, as candidly as may be, admit that I was rather disgusted with it — that is, for any thing else than mountains and scenery. Bear in mind that the central portions of New Mexico are really older country than Ohio. Santa Fe was founded a hundred and fifty years before Cincinnati. All the good land in the valleys of the Rio Grande and its tributaries was long ago occupied, and the grazing lands of the central section are taken up. West of the Rio Grande the country is practically worthless to a man used to the system of living in Ohio. The Territory has all the faults of an old country, and few of its virtues. As a stock-rancher you have but two chances of success.

The one adopted by most live Americans is to go into partnership with one of the nobility. If you have business ability and a partner who can furnish the blue blood, respectability, local prestige and land, you may in time become a capitalist, and marry ten or twenty thousand sheep, with an incumbrance in the shape of a lady, whose priest will rule her, and her father insist on an ante-nuptial contract that the children shall be reared in the "Holy Catholic faith." The other plan is to go with money enough to buy a thousand sheep and a herd-right—that is to say, to be a capitalist yourself. But don't think of going to New Mexico to build up a fortune by hard work. The common fellows there can work for fifty cents a day, and live on jerked mutton and flour.

If you want to lead a wild harum-scarum sort of life for a while, free from social restraints, where chastity is not a requisite for good society, and morals in general are somewhat relaxed, New Mexico is a splendid place to sow your wild oats. As to the crop to be reaped, I refer you to a very ancient authority. But, if you think much of yourself, better set up your sheep ranche in Colorado or Wyoming, where there is not such an oppressive atmosphere of *genta fina*, and where the owner of two sheep is still one of the boys, and can dance with the daughter of the man who owns a thousand. In south-western Arizona a progressive community has been built up of late years, and though the fertile area is small, there is still room for thousands more. Colorado I have described at some length in a previous chapter. It is, in my opinion, the most enlightened and progressive of all the far western communities, though I doubt if it can ever have the population that Dakota will some day contain. Idaho I know very little about, and of Montana practically still less. But it is universally agreed that they are not agricultural Territories. There are valleys in both which contain considerable good land, and large grazing tracts; but mining will be the leading interest of both for some time. Taken as a whole, and allowing for every possible improvement in methods of farming and reclamation of desert lands, the whole vast interior, between longtitude 100 and the Sierra Nevadas, can never average one acre in ten fit for the farmer; and not more than half the rest is of any value for timber or grazing.

And can such a region ever be filled by prosperous States, which shall rival those of the Mississippi Valley? Never. All calculations as to the shifting of political power, made on the basis of new States, rich and populous, are sure to miscarry. That section has an area greater than that of all the States east of the Mississippi; but its population fifty years hence will not be greater than that of Massachusetts. Only in the Senate will the relative power of the East and West be changed in the future, and probably very little there. Colorado was only admitted after a ten years' struggle. Nevada ought to be set back to a territorial condition to-day, if there were any constitutional way of doing justice. The child is not born that will live to see her with population enough for one congressional district. Here is a liberal estimate of the maximum population these divisions are likely to have in the year 1900:

Colorado,	250,000
Wyoming,	100,000
Dakota,	300,000
Idaho,	100,000
Washington,	125,000
Utah,	250,000
New Mexico,	150,000
Montana,	100,000
Nevada,	75,000
Arizona,	50,000
Total,	1,500,000

Extraordinary discoveries may enable some one of the mining regions to get ahead of the others, but the grand total cannot be greater than here set down; and only the most favorable contingencies can make it so great. The influence which this may have upon our social and national life opens a wide field for discussion. The good land at the disposal of our Government is nearly exhausted. But a few more years and there will be no more virgin soil awaiting the immigrant. Then the half desert lands must be won with great toil, or we must turn back and fill up the corners which have been overrun in our rush for the best spots. Our surplus population will then have no rich heritage to look to, where a homestead can be had for the taking. The paternal farm in the East must be divided again and again, if all the boys are to have a share. What will be the effect on our discontented classes? Will it add a new strain to republican government, and will the troubles which menace the old world monarchies then come upon us and find us unprepared to treat them rightly? or is there yet room in the Eastern States for us to grow harmoniously for another century? These be momentous questions.

Certain theorists have further troubled themselves about the silver supply; and timid editors and politicians have suggested that, if more *bonanzas* are discovered, silver will soon be "cheap enough to manufacture into door-hinges." To such I guarantee comforting proofs. Let them invest heavily in undeveloped silver mines, and before they get their money back they will be convinced that silver is still a precious metal—hard to get at and correspondingly valuable when got. One Ohio editor says: "Suppose they should discover a mountain of silver!" Suppose they should discover a mountain of ice-cream in August! The one supposition is as reasonable as the other. In fact, the latter phenomenon would violate fewer of the laws of Nature than the former. Unchanging law decrees that, even in the richest mineral region, there must be many million times as much dead rock— "attle," "rubble," and "country-rock"—as silver-bearing rock. Let silver permanently cheapen but five per cent, and two-thirds of the mines in the world would cease to be profitable.

For another class there is comfort. Poet and romancer, as well as hunter and tourist, have lamented that in so short a time the wild West would be a thing of the past; that soon all would be tame, dull and common-place. Let them be reassured. The wild West will continue wild for centuries. There will be a million square miles of mountain, desert, rock and sand, of lonely gorge and hidden glen, of walled basin, wind-swept cañon and timbered hills, to invite the tourist, the sportsman and the lover of solitude. The mountain Territories will long remain the abode of romance; and "Western Wilds" will be celebrated in song and story, while generation succeeds generation of "the men who redeem them."

CHAPTER XXV.

CONCLUSION.

ON the 14th day of December, 1878, I left the old Los Pinos Agency for home. I came by way of Saguache to Del Norte on horseback. There I procured a ticket to Chicago for sixty-four dollars.

Then I was suddenly roused, as by an angel's touch, to the bright hopes of reaching home and meeting friends again after the lapse of fifteen years and nearly nine months. All my former years, all my former schoolmates and friendships returned to my memory, and it seemed as if I could not be conveyed fast enough to the home of my childhood. I sat for hours looking out of the car-windows at the vast fertile fields, covered at that time with a light snow. Everything seemed new and improved. Would my mother know me? was a question often in my mind. I wondered if she too had changed like everything else.

I arrived at home on the 23d day of December, 1878. I came in on the home-folks by surprise. What a gay and happy meeting it was. How glad every one was to see me, and how much more happy was I to see them. How pleasant to sit and talk over the events of the past! But, oh! what changes take place in fifteen long years! When I was a boy I thought I would never be a man. Now that I am a man time flies on fleeting wings. I find that many who were once my friends and companions have passed away. I am no longer permitted to hear that voice to which once I so loved to listen, which was so sweet to me with tender words. No more may I see those friendly smiles which once so thrilled me with pleasure. The beloved form has passed away, and now lies mouldering among the clods of the valley. The virtues of my departed friends all come flashing back upon my kindling thoughts.

I find my old Ohio friends, who are still living, better supplied with the luxuries and conveniences of life than are the people of the West, unless it be in California. Amid old friends and friendly comforts time speeds swiftly away.

The 6th day of June, 1879, found me at my father's house. I was preparing to go to Lewisburg, not thinking about this being the anniversary of my birthday.

My father rather surprised me by suddenly asking me to go over the place with him, to look at the corn, and to salt the stock. To this I readily consented, of course, and we were soon on our way. We left the house early and I thought we would soon return. But such I found was not my father's intention; for, after he had salted every animal on the place, then we must look at the corn; and after that we must cross clear over to the other side of the farm to see if the Colorado potato-bugs were eating up his peach-blows. I was, by this time, beginning to get tired, and I am inclined to believe that, had there been any thing more to see, I should have gone back to the house alone.

But when we did finally return to the house, I saw his object. He was keeping me out as long as possible to give friends and neighbors a chance to come in on me before I should get away from home for the day, as there was a surprise party arranged for my especial benefit. And I should be ungrateful, indeed, if on this occasion, when I enter upon my thirtieth year in the full enjoyment of health and surrounded by all these kind and loving friends, I did not recognize the Omnipotent hand that has brought me safely through all the trials and vicissitudes of my life up to the present, and has now crowned me with comfort and surrounded me with friends such as I never before enjoyed. Old and young, great and small—all are here. The presence of these friends and the happy surroundings of the day teach me that there is something infinitely better in this world and the world to come than money or position; and, by the help of the kind Providence that has brought me safely through so many dangers and trials, I will henceforth lead a new life, and a better one.

My faculties were not given me to be wasted in aimless inactivity, but to be kept from all that is corrupting; to be employed in all that is useful and ennobling. Henceforth let my opinions and judgment of things be formed by a supreme regard for the will of Him who has cared, and still cares for me. I desire to cherish every right principle, to seek every honorable and useful end; to do what is just and true, what is humane and benevolent; to set my affections only upon that which is most worthy to engage them, to love all that is good and to seek holiness and Heaven; to live for eternity, to be directed in all things by the word of God, and to be conformed to the example of Christ. Thus may I hope to rise into a new life of usefulness and of happiness, and to pass the remainder of my days in loving association with my fellow-men, and be beloved by them.

THE END.

www.ingramcontent.com/pod-product-compliance
Lightning Source LLC
Chambersburg PA
CBHW030345230426
43664CB00007BB/538